The Magic World Behind the Curtain

Artists and Issues in the Theatre

August W. Staub
General Editor

Vol. 5

PETER LANG
New York • Washington, D.C./Baltimore • San Francisco
Bern • Frankfurt am Main • Berlin • Vienna • Paris

Ed Menta

The Magic World Behind the Curtain

Andrei Serban in the American Theatre

PETER LANG
New York • Washington, D.C./Baltimore • San Francisco
Bern • Frankfurt am Main • Berlin • Vienna • Paris

Library of Congress Cataloging-in-Publication Data

Menta, Ed.
  The magic world behind the curtain: Andrei Serban in the American theatre / Ed Menta.
      p.   cm. — (Artists and issues in the theatre: vol. 5)
  Includes bibliographical references and index.
  1. Serban, Andrei, 1943–   —Criticism and interpretation. I. Title.
II. Series.
PN2287.S354M46   792'.0233'092—dc20   94-22375
ISBN 0-8204-2640-7
ISSN 1051-9718

Die Deutsche Bibliothek-CIP-Einheitsaufnahme

Menta, Ed:
The magic world behind the curtain: Andrei Serban in the American theatre / Ed Menta. - New York; Washington, D.C./Baltimore; San Francisco; Bern; Frankfurt am Main; Berlin; Vienna; Paris: Lang.
  (Artists and issues in the theatre; Vol. 5)
  ISBN 0-8204-2640-7
NE: GT

Cover design by George Lallas.

The paper in this book meets the guidelines for permanence and durability of the Committee on Production Guidelines for Book Longevity of the Council of Library Resources.

© 1995 Peter Lang Publishing, Inc., New York

All rights reserved.
Reprint or reproduction, even partially, in all forms such as microfilm, xerography, microfiche, microcard, and offset strictly prohibited.

Printed in the United States of America.

This work is dedicated to the loving memory of:

Pasquale Menta
Phyllis Pullano Menta
John Paul Menta

Acknowledgments

COMPLETING this study would have been impossible without the assistance and support of many people. First, I would like to thank Andrei Serban for his graciousness and his time. Robert Brustein, Artistic Director of the American Repertory Theatre, was very generous in allowing me to observe his company rehearse Serban's *Twelfth Night* for almost two weeks while also turning over to me the complete resources of that theatre's video library and print files. Ellen Stewart extended the same courtesy at The La MaMa Experimental Theatre Club in the early stages of my research as did the late Joseph Papp of The New York Shakespeare Festival. In addition, all of the above donated their precious time for my endless interview questions.

I would also like to thank all of the actors who shared their insight(s) on working with Serban over the years—Thomas Derrah, Jeremy Geidt, Rodney Hudson, Cherry Jones, Mark Linn-Baker, and Dan Nutu. I especially am indebted to the insight and generosity of Priscilla Smith.

Many designers have been particularly helpful as well—Howell Binkley, Derek McLane, Michael Yeargan, and Catherine Zuber. Other theatre artists and teachers who contributed were Bill Finlay, Rebecca Holderness, Mona Koppleman, Bonnie Raphael, Robert Scanlan, and the late Paul Walker, as well as the acting and directing students of Andrei Serban at Columbia University.

For their assistance in archival research I thank Katherine Ewald of The Guthrie Theatre, Pam Jordan of The Yale Drama School Library, Jonathan Marks of The American Conservatory Theatre, Serge Mogilat of The New York Shakespeare Festival, Ozzie Rodriguez of La MaMa E.T.C., Deb Styer of The Hammerstein Theatre Center at Columbia University, and Dorothy Swerdlove, Curator of The Billy Rose Theatre Collection and Betty Corwin, Director of the Film and Tape Department; both of the Lincoln Center Library of the Performing Arts.

All of the photographs in this study, with the exception of *Fragments of a Greek Trilogy*, are courtesy of Richard Feldman and George Joseph. For *The Trilogy* photos, I thank Priscilla Smith and Dan Nutu. The cover photo of the author was taken by David Curl.

I thank Dr. Georg Schuttler of Michigan State University for his judgment and dedication. Other colleagues and friends who gave their time, guidance, and encouragement are Dr. Rose Bank, Kent State University; Ms. Lee Costello of New York City; Dr. John Herr, The University of Connecticut; Dr. Christopher Innes, York University; Professor Brant Pope, The Asolo Conservatory of the Performing Arts; Dr. Farley Richmond, State University New York at Stony Brook; Dr. Daina Robins, Hope College; Mr. Robert Silverman of New York City, and Dr. Jeannie Marlin Woods, Winthrop University. Mr. Scott Friesner of Western Michigan University was a great help in the final stages of proofing.

Several departments at Kalamazoo College were quite generous in donating their services and resources. The Theatre Department allowed me to borrow a printer. Instructional Media Services assisted in the production of slides. The staff of the Computer Center, especially Ms. Liz Haskell, was also quite helpful in preparing this document, as was the staff of Upjohn Library in the early stages of research.

Selections from *The Director's Voice: Twenty-one Interviews*, copyright 1988 by Arthur Bartow. Used by permission of Theatre Communications Group. Selections from *"Andrei Serban Directs Chekhov," Theater*, 13.1: 56-66, copyright 1981 by Laurence Shyer. Used by permission of Yale School of Drama.

Finally, I must credit the love and enduring support of my wife, Tina, my son, Willie, and my daughter, Anna. Without them, this work would not be possible.

Contents

List of Illustrations		xi
Preface		xiii
Introduction	Early Directorial Development	1
1.	Serban and the Greeks	13
2.	Serban and Chekhov	45
3.	Serban and The New Fabulism	89
4.	Serban in Rehearsal	107
5.	In Place of a Conclusion: Serban in the 90s	147
Appendix	Production History	161
Bibliography		175
Index		197

List of Illustrations

Cover Photo. Thomas Derrah as King Deramo, with Bear puppet by Julie Taymor. From *The King Stag* at American Reperory Theatre, 1984. Photo by Richard Feldman.

Following Chapter Two, Page 77

1. Medea's triumph from *Medea* in *Fragments of a Greek Trilogy* at La MaMa E.T.C. Photo from the private collection of Priscilla Smith.

2. Electra and the snake from *Electra* in *Fragments of a Greek Trilogy* at La MaMa E.T.C. Photo by Dan Nutu.

3. The audience on stage from *Agamemnon* at New York Shakespeare Festival at Lincoln Center. Photo by George Joseph.

4. The murder of Agamemnon from *Agamemnon* at New York Shakespeare Festival at Lincoln Center. Photo by George Joseph.

5. Mme. Ranevskaya's exit from *The Cherry Orchard* at New York Shakespeare Festival at Lincoln Center. Photo by George Joseph.

6. The three sisters in the autumn leaves from *Three Sisters* at American Repertory Theatre. Photo by Richard Feldman.

7. Tartaglia Observes Angela. From *The King Stag* at American Reperory Theatre, 1984. Masks and Puppets by Julie Taymor. Photo by Richard Feldman.

8. The transformation scene from *The Serpent Woman* at American Repertory Theatre. Photo by Richard Feldman.

9. Viola's dilemma from *Twelfth Night* at American Repertory Theatre. Photo by Richard Feldman.

10. Andrei Serban directs *Twelfth Night* at American Repertory Theatre. Photo by Richard Feldman.

Preface

IN THE Spring of 1979, as part of my first year of training in the M.F.A. program in Directing at the University of Connecticut, I enrolled in a graduate seminar taught by Dr. John Herr of the Department of Dramatic Arts titled "Four Contemporary Directors." The directors we studied were Peter Schumann, Peter Stein, Richard Schechner, and Andrei Serban. The course began a lifelong interest for me in the scholarship and artistry of contemporary directing. While I gained a lasting admiration for the work of Schumann, Schechner, and Stein, it was the productions and methods of Andrei Serban that attracted me most. I realized that I had already seen two of his most recent productions the year before at The Yale Repertory Theatre in New Haven: Strindberg's *The Ghost Sonata* and *Sganarelle: An Evening of Molière Farces*. One of the course requirements was to choose one of the four directors for more intensive study, to see as many of his plays as we could, and also to personally interview someone who had worked with him in production. Over the course of the term, I saw Serban's only musical, *The Umbrellas of Cherbourg*, produced by The New York Shakespeare Festival at The Public Theater and a revival of *Fragments of a Greek Trilogy* at La Mama E.T.C. Each of these productions has remained very vivid to me over the years, particularly the latter which literally opened my eyes anew to the possibilities of live performance. I also interviewed Mark Linn-Baker, then a third year acting student at the Yale Drama School, who had acted for Serban in *The Molière Farces*. Little did I know I was conducting research for a project that would eventually expand into a dissertation at Michigan State University and finally, more than fifteen years later, culminate in a book. At the conclusion of the seminar, I wrote a brief paper on Serban's work and how it might help me as a director. Although that original document now seems to me hopelessly naive, it did begin a journey that is a testament to how the artistic efforts of some individuals can still inspire others.

This study examines Andrei Serban's theatre directing in the United States from his early work at the Cafe La MaMa in the 1970s to his last work at The American Repertory Theatre in 1989—a dark treatment of *Twelfth Night*. Drawing upon interviews with Serban, Joseph Papp, Ellen Stewart, Robert Brustein, and many actors, designers, and other theatre artists and practitioners; a firsthand viewing of many of the productions; hundreds of articles, reviews, and essays, and including a special chapter on observing *Twelfth Night* in rehearsal at A.R.T.; this investigation is the first attempt to document, on a large scale, the body of work and creative process of Andrei Serban in the American theatre.

Since coming to this country from Romania in 1969, Serban, a onetime assistant to Peter Brook, emerged in the 1970s as one of the most prominent and prolific directors in America. Specifically known for his provocative visual imagery, his apparently limitless imagination, and sometimes seemingly chaotic rehearsal methods, this study emphasizes his re-interpretation of classical works such as Greek tragedy, Chekhov, and Carlo Gozzi. Through his groundbreaking productions of both *Agamemnon* and three ancient Greek dramas, *Medea*, *The Trojan Women*, and *Electra*, which formed *Fragments of a Greek Trilogy*, Serban has expanded our perceptions of staging Greek tragedy. With his landmark production of *The Cherry Orchard* at Lincoln Center in 1977, and three other Chekhov dramas staged in New York and Boston in ensuing years, he's suggested Meyerhold rather than Stanislavsky as the inspirational model in directing a Chekhov play. With *The King Stag* and *The Serpent Woman* at A.R.T., his staging of Gozzi's tales for the theatre, Serban has helped to create a theatrical style some critics have called "The New Fabulism," a mixture of commedia dell'arte, traditional Asian theatre techniques, puppetry, masks, shadow play, children's theatre, and various other theatrical traditions.

In this exploration of his use of visual and aural imagery, his "confrontation" with text, and his work with actors and designers, Andrei Serban prominently stands as a prototype of the visionary director of the contemporary American theatre.

Ed Menta
Kalamazoo, Michigan
1994

Introduction

Early Directorial Development

PERHAPS foreshadowing the magic he would eventually create in the theatre, Andrei Serban was born in Bucharest, Romania, on Midsummer's Eve, June 21, 1943. The only child of a photographer and a schoolteacher, Serban later speculated that he inherited a strong visual sense from his father and an emotional sensitivity from his mother. He developed an interest in the theatre at an early age, recalling entertaining guests with puppet shows at age four[1] and organizing his childhood companions armed with sticks into dramatic battles at Bucharest's Park of the Icons.[2] More often, however, the young Serban played by himself. With few toys and little entertainment outside the home in the austere, Stalinist atmosphere of Romania in the 1950s, he often amused himself by reciting gibberish poems in front of the mirror and imagining he was Edmund Kean. At age thirteen, he directed his first play—a Romanian melodrama at his high school in which he also performed. Although he did not see a great many plays during his childhood, Serban recalled, "I knew I always wanted to be in the theatre. What fascinated me was the secret world behind the curtain and when the curtain went up, the secret would be revealed ... another world on the other side."[3] Even from such incidental information, one can see the beginnings of Andrei Serban's career in the theatre: his striking ability to create beautiful stage pictures; his interest in developing huge, outdoor, almost pageant-like pieces; his work in exploring different sounds to create new theatrical languages; and, above all, his lifelong childlike curiosity in the magic of the theatre process itself—all to create "the secret world on the other side of the curtain." All of these qualities can be found in his mature works—from *Fragments of A Greek Trilogy* at La MaMa E.T.C. during the early 1970s to *Twelfth Night* at The American Repertory Theatre in 1989.

Immediately after high school, he was one of the few accepted from among 1500 candidates at the Theatre and Film Institute at Bucharest.[4] Serban studied at the Institute for a total of seven years, three in the Acting Program and four in Directing. ("Time long enough to have done something serious—like studying medicine, my father would say!" Serban later joked.[5]) By the time he received his certificate in 1968, his productions had already won several awards at various student theatre festivals and he had directed professionally at Romania's leading theatre, the Lucia Sturdza Bulandra Theatre, under the artistic directorship of Livui Ciulei.

Why did Serban change his course of study from acting to directing after his first three years? He appreciated the discipline in the Stanislavsky-based program and the variety of courses in voice, movement, and scene study, but noted "I felt that my voice was not coming from my body, my head didn't agree with my emotions, and I could not put the fragments together."[6] Moreover, he wanted to express a relationship between actors and audience that he could only explore as a director. Serban felt much more relaxed and personally fulfilled as a director, but he never forgot his experience as an actor. He has never regretted starting over again at the Institute: "Any director should act in order to understand through experience how to help actors."[7]

Studying with Radu Penciulescu, the primary directing teacher at the Institute, was a liberating experience for Serban. He was inspired by Penciulescu's open-minded philosophy of allowing his directing students to find their own way amidst the techniques of Stanislavsky, Meyerhold, and Brecht. Penciulescu taught that none of these theatrical directions held any definitive truth. "I was continually encouraged by him to find my own voice," Serban reflected years later.[8]

Serban's early directing assignments at the Institute included *The Man Who Changed Into a Dog* by Osvaldo Dragun and Alfred Jarry's *Ubu Roi*. In 1965, his production of *The Chief of the Sector Souls* by Al. Mirodan won the prize for best show at the Student's World Theatre Festival in Zagreb in former Yugoslavia. The following year, Serban directed another Romanian play, *I Am Not the Eiffel Tower*, an allegory of contemporary politics, by Ecaterina Oproiu. Described on its program as "a pseudo-comedy with serious senses," the play told the story of He, a young architecture student on his way to Bucharest, who meets Her, the doctor of a rural medical district, in the middle of a field. It was the first dramatic effort for theatre and cinema critic Oproiu, later to become Cultural Minister, who categorized her play as "... the permanent interdependence between fiction and reality allowing the achievement of the senses followed by the author with a character of generality. The leading idea of the play is the belief in the power of love ..."[9]

Almost twenty-five years later, Romanian actor Dan Nutu, who played a small role in *I Am Not the Eiffel Tower*, described this play and Serban's other early projects as "silly jokes, now looking backwards. At that particular time ... it was avant-garde. It gave Andrei the opportunity of freedom to play with the text ... and bring in his own ideas."[10] Nevertheless, the production again won first prize at the festival in Zagreb and was seen by the visiting Ellen Stewart of the Cafe La MaMa. Although she admired the production and its young director very much, they did not meet.[11]

Serban thrived on the opportunity to travel to the various student theatre festivals around Eastern Europe and see different productions. One in particular would become a very strong influence.[12] In 1967 in Wroclaw, he met Polish director Jerzy Grotowski for the first time. Grotowski's international reputation had just been established the year before with his production of *The Constant Prince* at the *Théâtre des Nations* in Paris. Overall, Serban's study at the Institute provided a solid foundation in dramatic literature and the fundamentals of theatre production as he embarked upon his professional career. At age 23, he had already been studying and practicing theatre for seven years. When he later came to the United States during the Off-Off-Broadway movement of the 1960s and early 1970s, he would particularly appreciate this discipline.

It was at The Bulandra Theatre that Serban came under the influence of not only Livui Ciulei but other Romanian directors such as Lucian Pintilie and David Esrig. Working with Ciulei was perhaps the first major turning point in Serban's directing career. For both his provocative writing and his professional position, the Bulandra's Artistic Director was a mentor for most of the young directors in Romania. In 1967, Ciulei invited the 24 year-old Serban to direct *Julius Caesar* with Ciulei designing. Serban chose to stage the play in Japanese Kabuki style, which, according to Serban, contradicted the official Romanian hard line of social realism for the arts: "Of course, it was a scandal."[13]

It is necessary to understand certain artistic and social trends in Romania in order to view Serban's early work in context. Since 1948, when the Communist Party, with the aid of the Russian military, took power in Romania, the dominant post-war theatrical trend throughout the nation, as well as in most Eastern Europe, was Soviet Socialist realism. "The Romanian theatre was marked by a sort of state conformism and bland bourgeois taste. It had very little significance. There was no experimentation," Lucian Pintilie explained.[14] Due to their cultural and political isolation, Romanian artists were quite eager to learn of trends in the United States and Europe. Perhaps it is because that most of the books available to Romanian theatre artists were on visual design and because Ciulei had been trained as an architect that a strong visual orientation has been a lasting legacy amongst most of the Romanian directors, including Serban.[15] At the same time, even in the post-Stalinist era, due to political pressure for artistic orthodoxy, and hungering to join their European counterparts in breaking cultural and artistic traditions, according to *American Theatre* magazine contributor Mike Steele,

> Romanian theatre artists became expert at walking tightropes ... Since modern Romanian plays were scrutinized carefully by the authorities, many directors looked to time-worn and far less suspicious classics. They became masters at reading texts closely, finding contemporary resonances in them and bringing out those resonances through re-interpretation, layers of allusions and skillful use of visual metaphor.[16]

Former Romanian critic and current dramaturg at The Guthrie, Michael Lupu adds:

> In the post-Stalinist era, Romania looked on art, especially theatre, as a major tool for education and propaganda. They gave it great importance and great financial support. Consequently, it was a place where talented people could drift to. In it you could make statements not only about literature but about the state of the world ... This helped sharpen

directors' abilities to discover and explore texts, not to accept ready-made traditional ideas.[17]

The above remarks, when applied to Serban's career, certainly reflect tendencies in his later work such as his famous *Cherry Orchard* at Lincoln Center in 1977 where he was accused by some American critics of distorting Chekhov's text with his strikingly visual and farcical production. They also obviously point to his fondness for re-interpreting classical texts from the Greeks to Shakespeare.

Even at the Institute, Serban had always wanted to create theatre that was original. He wanted his productions to be different from any others he'd seen. Perhaps instinctively this had led him to read about Kabuki, which was almost totally unknown at that time in the Romanian Theatre. Now at the Bulandra Theatre, at age 24 in his first professional directing assignment and working with many of the established "stars" of Romania, Serban enjoyed playing his role of "enfant terrible." He used the classical Japanese theatre more as an inspiration rather than following its strict form. Also heavily influenced by his reading of Meyerhold's stylized productions, Serban created a ritualized and very theatrical *Julius Caesar* which literally shocked audiences and critics who were accustomed to more traditional realism. He and Ciulei devised a playing area consisting of a sand pit banked on two sides by audience bleachers, like a basketball court. The Roman senators were placed in the bleachers within the house. The Soothsayer appeared on a ramp above the audience like a Noh dancer on the hanamichi. Much of the movement was in slow motion. Caesar was murdered in a five minute ritual which started at the top of the bleachers and slowly worked all the way down into the sand pit as he was passed from hand to hand and stabbed over and over again. Finally, he was covered with blood and sand by Brutus in a near naked wrestling match that evoked both terror and love. This sensational image eventually became much imitated in the Romanian theatre perhaps because of its political connotations to Dictator Nicolae Ceausescu's recent rise to power. In the battle scene of Act Five, the toga clad actors stirred up so much sand that much of it went flying into the eyes of the opening night audience, including the wife of a prominent Romanian theatre critic who lost her hat in the process. "I became an instant celebrity," mused Serban.[18] Needless to say, the production also added to the notoriety of the young director's growing reputation for controversy. Fifteen years later, as Artistic Director of The Guthrie Theatre in Minneapolis, Livui Ciulei would once again invite Serban to direct at his theatre—this time *The Marriage of Figaro* by Beaumarchais.

Despite the negative reviews of *Julius Caesar* in the Romanian press, the production was extremely popular with students and others in the Romanian counterculture and Serban continued to direct—the anonymous Elizabethan tragedy, *Arden of Faversham*, Brecht's *The Good Woman of Setzuan*, (which won a prize for the best performance of 1969), and Goldsmith's *She Stoops to Conquer*, thus further adding to his characterization as an unconventional young director who "tackled works of diverse types."[19] Almost thirty years later, Serban remains particularly proud of his production of the Brecht play in Piatra Neamtz, a small town outside of Bucharest. In this first of the three times he would direct *Good Woman*, Serban fashioned the production as a direct political response to the recent events in Prague. "The situation in Czechoslovakia had filled us with violent rage and caused us to treat Brecht not in a cold or distant way, but with a sense of heated passion," he noted.[20] The overt political nature of the production would prove to be unusual for Serban, indeed his later treatments of the same play would be lighthearted and fanciful by comparison. (See Chapter Three.)

In the meantime, a series of fortuitous circumstances evolved that enabled Serban to leave Romania in 1969. In 1968, while in Prague, American avant-garde producer Ellen Stewart had been asked by a Romanian journalist what she knew of the Romanian theatre. She replied she'd seen a student production in Zagreb a couple of years ago that was incredible but she couldn't remember the director's name. She had wanted to ask him to work at La MaMa.[21] When the article appeared, Serban didn't even read it but was called and congratulated by friends who assumed he was going to the States. Serban dismissed the article as "polite diplomacy."

Yet a week later, he did receive an official invitation from Ellen Stewart. Serban didn't have a passport at the time, but a grant from the Ford Foundation simplified that process. In 1969, with "only three shirts and two pairs of pants," Serban arrived in the United States. He intended to stay for only three months. Instead, it was the beginning of a long career in the American theatre.

Arden of Faversham & *Ubu Roi*—La MaMa E.T.C., 1970

As a grant recipient, Serban was required to tour the major theatres of the United States: "The Tyrone Guthrie in Minneapolis, the A.C.T., the Alley—all the big theatre centers in the States in eight days. I learned about architecture and theatre, and how lifeless and unnecessary the relationship could become if builders get stuck in a cold space concept."[22] But it was at the Cafe La MaMa in New York City that Serban spent most of his time.

It is difficult to separate the story of Andrei Serban's early career in the United States from the story of Ellen Stewart. Serban's encounter with Stewart constituted another major turning point in his professional career. Not only is Ellen Stewart, a.k.a. La MaMa herself, responsible for Serban's initial efforts in the American theatre, she, along with Joe Cinno, is responsible for the climate of Off-Off-Broadway itself. It would be almost impossible to list all of the major theatre artists who received their start at her Cafe La MaMa in the East Village. Just a few of the playwrights include Sam Shepard, Paul Foster, Ed Bullins, Harvey Fierstein, Leonard Melfi, and Lanford Wilson; some of the actors are Kevin Conway, F. Murray Abraham, Bette Midler, and Billy Crystal; while the directors number Marshall Mason, Tom O'Horgan, Robert Wilson, Wilford Leach and Serban. In addition, such composers as Liz Swados and Philip Glass, performance artists such as Ping Chong, theatre collectives such as The Mabou Mines, and musicals such as John-Michael Tebelak's *Godspell* and Megan Terry's *Viet Rock* all originated at La MaMa. Moreover, it was La MaMa's commitment to experimental theatre on an international scale that supported touring abroad of its various troupes and visits of many guest artists from all over the world. In short, the La MaMa Experimental Theatre Club, (La MaMa E.T.C.), its official title derived in 1964 to ease licensing problems, was an international hotbed of experimental theatre in 1969. Many theatre artists and critics maintain it has remained so.

Into this atmosphere stepped Andrei Serban. Although he later admitted that he "went along with it," Serban told Richard Eder of *The New York Times* that he was initially appalled by the "looseness" of the American experimental theatre:

> Coming here in the '60s and seeing the whole looseness of the avant-garde, where the idea was to be free in this very sentimental way, smoke drugs, let the hair grow—it seemed cheap to me. There's something in me more connected to discipline and intensity than to this freedom and looseness.[23]

Nevertheless, Serban did admire the discipline of Merce Cunningham's work in modern dance and Joseph Chaikin's Open Theatre. It is possible that he was influenced by Cunningham's abstract and non-psychological approach to performance, but there is no question that he was taken with Chaikin's idea of the "presence" of the actor and his investigation of the immediacy of the actor/audience relationship. He was soaking up as much of the Off-Off-Broadway and East Village theatre scene as he could. Ellen Stewart recalled that she insisted that Serban participate in movement classes at La MaMa and "he didn't like that. He was uptight. I saw him one day in one of the theatre exercises, wearing a coat and tie and walking up and down the back of an actress on the floor—and furious he had to do this. I got him to take off the coat and tie."[24]

In 1970, Serban began working on the two plays that would constitute his American debut: *Ubu Roi* and *Arden of Faversham*. He thought he would simply repeat his European stagings and return to Romania. Instead, after several days of struggling to remember his original blocking and haltingly communicating with his actors (by his own admission, his English was very poor at the time and he conversed with the actors with a few words of English, many in French, and mostly through exercises) he realized that he had to throw away his old ideas and start anew: "I didn't want to repeat my Romanian success. But to start from zero is impossible. My source was Artaud. By doing *Arden*, I tried to understand in practice his idea of cruelty."[25]

The result was indeed an Artaud-inspired 50 minute version of *Arden of Faversham* that was reduced to a few words, lots of sounds, and many startling images. In one scene, the only light on stage was the actors holding flashlights underneath their eyes; in another, two lovers spoke according to the rhythm of a metronome. Belts cracked on the wooden floor, actors stood in red and green spotlights, and the climax of the play was a castration ritual in which Arden's body was wrapped naked in a plastic tarpaulin while his wife sawed off his genitals, and using eggs for the severed organs, smeared them on his face. During this scene, members of the audience would inevitably gasp and some would even leave the theatre.

Preceded by a circus-like staging of fragments of *Ubu*, with the stage strewn with garbage, litter, and a commode, and the actors often moving like Gordon Craig marionettes, the double-bill received very favorable reviews from Clive Barnes of *The New York Times* and Henry Hewes of *The Saturday Review*. It was *Arden* that drew most of the attention and Barnes in particular was effusive in his praise, preferring it to a more conventional production of the Elizabethan tragedy directed by Joan Littlewood in London: "Why this young Romanian, Andrei Sherban (sic) should come to the U.S. and offer this remarkably sophisticated and explosive double bill I cannot imagine. Romania must be trying to tell us something."[26] For the next ten years, Serban would be referred to in print as "the brilliant young Romanian director." The company of actors, which included Lou Zeldis, Michelle Collison, William Duff-Griffin, Patrick Burke, and Billy Crystal, later of *Saturday Night Live* fame, was also highly praised and sent off to Europe for a La MaMa tour of the productions. The plays were also seen by British director Peter Brook, another turning point in Serban's early career.

Orghast—CIRT, 1971

By 1970, Brook was known as the most important theatre director in the West. His reputation rested largely on such visually stunning productions as *King Lear*, with Paul Scofield, (1964), *A Midsummer Night's Dream*, designed by Sally Jacobs, (1967), and Peter Weiss' *Marat/Sade*, starring the then relatively unknown Glenda Jackson. Serban himself had seen Brook's *Lear* when it toured Bucharest in 1964 and had broken through a police line around the theatre in order to see the production. In all of these productions, and many others, Brook had made brilliant use of various theatre techniques from Artaud to Brecht to the circus. He was also heavily influenced by Grotowski. Yet a continual quest for discovery, for questioning, and for investigation into the very meaning that the theatre holds in contemporary life had led him largely to abandon the commercial theatre to develop his research center in Paris—the International Centre for Theatre Research (CIRT) in 1970.

Brook invited Serban and two of the *Arden* actors—Lou Zeldis and Michelle Collison—to join him at the Centre in Paris. In 1977, Serban told Richard Eder:

> Brook never told me what I was supposed to be doing ... By chance, I learned my title was assistant director. Well, I assisted, but in the French sense of the word—*assister:* to be present. I "assisted" everywhere and didn't do anything. At least that's what I thought. I realized later that I had been active by my living through it, by my dislocation.[27]

But in 1994, Serban offered this insight on why Brook invited him to CIRT: "Brook didn't want me to assist him. He was interested in a subtle form of collaboration where roles are not easily defined. I guess he was creating conditions in the theatre as a way of life. At every moment there was something that could be seen and a new direction possible."[28]

Serban spent a year with Brook, arriving in Paris in the Fall of 1970 and observing the company's workshop production of *Orghast*, produced in the summer of 1971 in the ruins of Persepolis in Shiraz, Iran, with a group of theatre artists from twelve different countries. *Orghast* was not only the title of the experimental piece that was the result of the Centre's first year, it was also the term applied to the new language itself, devised for the piece by British poet Ted Hughes.

Brook's reasons for organizing the Centre and his stated goals for their first year of research are important, not only for their results in *Orghast*, but for their marked effect on Serban, and particularly his work on *Fragments of a Greek Trilogy*, versions of Euripides' *Medea* and *The Trojan Women* and Sophocles' *Electra*, the productions that would eventually establish his international reputation.

Years later, Brook described the primary objective of the Centre: "The theme of the first year's work of the International Centre of Theatre Research was to be a study of structures of sounds. Our aim was to discover more fully what constitutes living expression."[29] Part of the reason for investigating a non-verbal language of sound was the notion of finding a common language in this truly international and multicultural company. Serban later told Arthur Bartow that the company explored sound exercises for a whole year, passing sounds in circles, repeating sounds, rhythms, exploring physical and emotional sensitivity to sounds and developing a "perception of inner listening, a perception of the meaning of what is hidden which its sound cannot really explain."[30] Serban also noticed that Brook would drop a particular exercise just as soon as it appeared that the actors were beginning to get comfortable and were in danger of developing mannerisms as actors.[31]

After observing the actors improvise on random syllables and then on a bit of text by Aeschylus, Ted Hughes eventually invented a phonetic language for the piece which would revolve around the central themes of the Prometheus myth using Avesta, a Persian ritual language created exclusively for prayer, and fragments of the text of Aeschylus' *The Persians*. In an article for *The New York Times*, drama critic and author Margaret Croyden described *Orghast* as

> having no linear plot and few discernible characters. It is an evocative dramatic poem written entirely with a poet's tools: metaphor, image, and symbol ... Using a language with no recognizable words, Hughes and Brook force the spectator to listen to the work as they listen to music, and to watch the action as if it were a religious experience.[32]

Croyden also noted the breathtaking outdoor setting for the action—the moonlit ruins of Persepolis, rich in ancient myth and ritual, and that the performance was given at midnight and again at 4 a.m. The effect of half-naked bodies carrying torches, racing along the mountaintops and raging at each other in an unknown language in the moonlit ruins was for some spectators riveting, for others confusing.

The above really could be a description of the reaction to Serban's *Trilogy* in 1974, particularly in regard to the experience of listening to language as if it were music and watching the event as if it were a religious experience. Moreover, the sheer visceral excitement of the outdoor settings seemed to prefigure the La MaMa tours of the *Trilogy* and *As You Like It* in the mid-1970s.

Ultimately, Serban felt *Orghast* missed its final destination, i.e., a transmission of a universal language of the heart, because of its cold, intellectual quality, but he acknowledged it to be a remarkable failure and that "it fed me for the next five years."[33] Serban has always publicly acknowledged Brook's influence on his life and career:

> It literally changed the direction of my life. Never before had I questioned why I was in the theatre. I was just doing it because I felt like doing it, like most people in the theatre ... Working with Brook helped me not necessarily to find the answers or solutions, but to ask the questions—Why am I in the theatre? What is available to the theatre? What is possible for me?[34]

Like the public relations tag of "brilliant young Romanian director," the "disciple of Peter Brook" label followed Serban for a long time in the press. Nonetheless, Serban feels grateful for what he calls Brook's inspiration for:

> my curiosity for theatrical journeys, for taking complicated side paths before returning to the main road and then testing what has been found. He helped me to open my eyes in the right direction, to search for what is not easily visible rather than accepting ready-made answers.[35]

Serban's initial "theatrical journey" began when he returned to La MaMa in the Fall of 1971. He wanted to continue this type of investigation and realized that it was impossible to do so if he returned to Romania. At age 28, Serban became an artistic exile from his homeland, eventually acquiring American citizenship. As it turned out, this coincided with an increase in censorship of the Romanian Communist regime. Dictator Ceausescu admired the Cultural Revolution in China and tried to emulate it in Romania, so Serban never regretted his decision.[36] As for Serban's theatrical journey, it could best be summed up by Brook's notes on the original production of *Orghast*:

> What is the relation between verbal and non-verbal theatre? What happens when gesture and sound turn into word? What is the exact place of the word in theatrical expression? As vibration? Concept? Music? Is any evidence buried in the sound structure of certain ancient languages?[37]

These were the questions that guided Serban's research and experimentation in his investigation of Greek tragedy.

Notes

1. Jan Hodenfield, "Romania's Gift to the Theater Raises His Repertory Sights," *The New York Post* 31 January 1976: 8.
2. "Serban, Andrei," *Current Biography* 1978: 377.
3. Andrei Serban, personal interview, 2 February, 1994.
4. "Unlike here, one cannot wake up one morning and say it's up to me, I'm going to be an actor." Serban, Hodenfield 8.
5. Serban, letter to author, 7 June 1994.
6. Serban, 7 June 1994.
7. Serban, 7 June 1994.
8. Serban, 2 February, 1994.
9. Theatre Program, *I Am Not the Eiffel Tower*, The Bucharest Drama Student's Group, Romania 1966.
10. Dan Nutu, personal interview, 12 December 1989.
11. Serban attempted to see the La MaMa troupe's production at the same festival, but was unable to obtain tickets. Robb Baker, "Andrei Serban: The Intelligence of Emotion," *The Soho Weekly News* 17 October 1974: 18.
12. Julius Tyszka, *Widowiska Nowojorskie* (Poznan, Poland: Ars Nova) 61–71.
13. Hodenfield 8.
14. Mike Steele, "The Romanian Connection," *American Theatre* August 1985: 7.
15. Steele 7.

16. Steele 8.
17. Steele 8.
18. Serban, 2 February, 1994.
19. Theatre Program, *I Am Not the Eiffel Tower*.
20. Serban, 2 February 1994.
21. Serban insists that members of the La Mama company (though not Ellen Stewart) saw his production of *I Am Not the Eiffel Tower* in 1966. Ellen Stewart later told him that they accidentally brushed shoulders while in line at a cafeteria that year although they did not meet. In 1968, after she'd heard so much about his productions, she picked him out of a crowd of hundreds of people at a Romanian airport based on the "vibrations" she'd received from him earlier. It was during this trip to Romania that she saw *The Good Woman of Setzuan*. Andrei Serban, personal interview, 2 February, 1994.
22. Serban, 7 June 1994.
23. Richard Eder, "Andrei Serban's Theatre of Terror and Beauty," *The New York Times Magazine* 13 February 1977: 45.
24. Eder 45.
25. Serban, 7 June 1994.
26. Clive Barnes, "Double Bill at La MaMa," rev. of *Arden of Faversham* and *Ubu Roi*, *The New York Times* 17 February 1970: 33.
27. Eder 46.
28. Serban, 7 June 1994.
29. Peter Brook, *The Shifting Point* (New York: Harper and Row, 1987) 108.
30. Arthur Bartow, *The Director's Voice: Twenty-one Interviews* (New York: Theatre Communications Group, 1988) 293.
31. Eder 46.
32. Margaret Croyden, "Peter Brook Learns to Speak Orghast," *The New York Times* 3 October 1971: Sec. 2, 3.
33. Eder 50.
34. Bartow 292.
35. Bartow 296.
36. Serban qtd. in Margaret Croyden, "A Director Revolts," *TheaterWeek*, 21 February, 1994: 22.
37. Brook 110.

1

Serban and the Greeks

SERBAN'S productions of *Fragments of a Greek Trilogy* and *Agamemnon* in the 1970s represented a departure in the production of Greek tragedy in the United States. Although there had been attempts in various productions to emphasize the ritual quality of Greek theatre, such as *The Trojan Incident*, a dance piece based on *The Trojan Women* and produced by The Federal Theatre Project in 1939, and *Dionysus in '69*, based on *The Bacchae* and produced by The Performance Group in 1968–69, none embraced this ritualistic quality as wholeheartedly as Serban's. Making full use of what he'd experienced with Brook's *Orghast*, *The Trilogy* eventually became a landmark production of the American avant-garde theatre, so much so that it was revived in 1987 as part of the 25th anniversary festival at La MaMa. *The Trilogy* was such a critical and popular success that some critics have viewed the production as a highwater mark in Serban's professional career. Reaction to *Agamemnon* suffered because of it. In truth, no one could live up to the accolade of critical notices that summarily declared Serban the "boy genius" avant-garde director of the 1970s.

Beyond the implications for Serban's career, however, *The Trilogy* in particular provoked several key questions in the staging of Greek tragedy in this country. First and foremost, is it possible to "unlock the power" of these ancient texts in a fashion that is both vital and viable for audiences of today? Is it possible for the performers and audiences to experience the original language of the text "in their blood," so to speak, without the benefit of a pedestrian English translation? Finally, could one use the ancient tragedies to create a theatre experience of emotion, not intellect?

If some of the above questions are reminiscent of the ideas of Antonin Artaud, perhaps it is because *The Trilogy* may represent one of the most successful of all of the Artaudian based experiments of the American avant-garde. One really does recall *The Trilogy* in a series of strong visual and aural images of torches, smoke, chanting, music, and actors mingling with audience in the unconventional space of the La MaMa Annex. Moreover, the audience and performers were united and transformed in a very mysterious and experiential way that defied most analysis. In Artaud's terms, Serban's *Trilogy* explored "the poetry beneath the text ... the actual poetry-through-theatre which underlies the Myths told by the great tragedians ... a theatre in which violent physical images crush and hypnotize the sensibility of the spectator ... a theatre which abandoning psychology ... induces trance."[1] In reviewing the revival in 1987, Michael Feingold wrote that "You are transfigured, purged by pity and terror, and renewed, which is what the Greeks invented theatre for in the first place."[2]

Finally, Serban's *Trilogy* and *Agamemnon* helped to establish new standards of aesthetic criteria in producing Greek plays. With the collaboration of composer Liz Swados, Serban's productions restored the crucial role of music in the staging of Greek tragedy. *The Trilogy*, in particular, with its long period of training and rehearsal, invited future performers of Greek tragedy to match its company's discipline, rigorous physical and vocal technique, and an acting style seeped in a collective mythical consciousness as opposed to a Method-based psychological realism.

Fragments of a Greek Trilogy—La MaMa E.T.C., 1972–1987

When Serban returned to New York in the Fall of 1971, his direction was clear. He wanted to continue Brook's investigations in his own way. Again, Brook's notes on the original production of *Orghast*:

> What is the relation between verbal and non-verbal theatre? What happens when gesture and sound turn into word? What is the exact place of the word in theatrical expression? As vibration? Concept? Music? Is any evidence buried in the sound structure of certain ancient languages?[3]

These very questions were reprinted on the first program of *Medea* and later the complete *Trilogy*.

With these questions buzzing in his ear, Serban chose to explore *Medea* in both the Greek by Euripides and the Latin by Seneca, after rejecting such possibilities as *Measure for Measure*, a play he'd worked on in Helsinki, and Seneca's *Hercules*, which he considered staging in Latin. He ultimately rejected the Senecan play as he felt it might be misconstrued as a political piece in light of American involvement in Vietnam. According to Romanian dramaturg and friend, Ana Maria Narti, before he left for the States, Brook advised him "to stage an old tragedy in an old language." Serban himself said he chose *Medea* because it is "a play I do not understand ..."[4] (I'm indebted to Narti's unpublished thesis "*Medea*: Andrei Serban's Work on the Tragic Acting" for much of the following discussion of the rehearsal process of *Medea*.)

In helping Serban to assemble the company, Ellen Stewart introduced him to two artists who would have a tremendous effect on his future work: composer Elizabeth Swados and actress Priscilla Smith.

Swados, originally from Buffalo, was still a student at Bennington College when she met Serban. (She later submitted her work on *Medea* as credit towards her degree in absentia.) Serban felt he didn't need to audition her to compose for *Medea* despite Swados' request, but instead hired her upon meeting her in the La MaMa lobby, perhaps borrowing a method from La MaMa herself, because "there was something about her." Swados not only eventually composed all of the music for *Medea* and the rest of *The Trilogy*, but went on to work with Serban in *The Good Woman of Setzuan, As You Like It, The Cherry Orchard, Agamemnon, The Ghost Sonata*, portions of *Sganarelle: An Evening of Molière*

Farces, and *The Seagull*. To this day, Ellen Stewart feels that Swados did not receive the credit she deserved for her role in helping to create *The Trilogy*. Serban himself has stated that "it's very hard to tell after a certain point who directs and who composes."[5] On the other hand, Serban acknowledged that the day he met Swados "was another great change in my life. All my work since has been influenced by her very unique talent, her explorations of the possibilities of sound"[6] and "she is to me, after Kurt Weill, the one who understands the most how music should apply to theater. She scored almost every moment of those three plays." (*The Trilogy*)[7]

Priscilla Smith, an original member of Richard Schechner's The Performance Group, would create the characterizations of Medea, Andromache, and Electra in *The Trilogy*. Describing herself as a soft-spoken person with a small voice, she went on to win several Obies for her work with Serban, largely due to her tour-de-force performance of sound—a mixture of violent screams, ominous, guttural invocations, and soul-shattering wails that has remained a landmark in modern American performance. Smith became the prototypic Serban performer—she played leading roles not only in *The Trilogy*, but also in *The Good Woman of Setzuan, As You Like It, The Cherry Orchard, Agamemnon, The Ghost Sonata*, and *The King Stag*. Years later, Serban said of her work on *The Trilogy*:

> She had a great sense of devotion to the project. She just threw herself completely into the work. She had the courage to inhabit the work and to leave all destructive distractions aside. That's a rare quality not many people have. (Her greatest contribution) was the discovery that she was vocally capable of making sounds that she had never produced before.[8]

Indeed, Smith would later describe her commitment and vocal and pyscho-physical discoveries as "the Evel Knievel approach to acting", meaning that at the time she had no idea that the work she was doing would not hurt her voice. Instead, she recklessly threw herself into the work with almost a sense of daredevil abandon.[9]

Medea was a piece that would be built over a period of four months of rigorous training and rehearsal with the actors. The design was a fluid process that developed in tandem with the growth of the play. Serban himself helped costumer Sandra Muir design the "neutral, yet functional costumes", as Serban described the solid colored tunics that the performers wore. In regards to the "set", from the beginning, Serban chose to stage *Medea* in a long and narrow rehearsal room in the basement of La MaMa. Here in this windowless catacombs, deep beneath the "real" stage of La MaMa, and far removed from the street noise of New York City, Jason and Medea would confront each other. Eventually, the performance was staged to begin with the audience gathering in the stage above and then descending the basement stairs together, lighted by members of the chorus holding flickering candles. In a long cinderblock corridor, the Nurse, children, and chorus delivered the "prologue" of the play. Soon the audience was led into the dark, narrow room, sitting on either side of the space on benches against the long walls while Medea stood at one end, chained to the wall. Other than a few hand props, there was no real "scenery" for *Medea*. The mostly candlelit production was augmented by lighting designer Laura Rambaldi.

The intense four month training and rehearsal period began with vocal exercises similar to those Serban had learned from Brook. The company was committed to experiencing the sound of the ancient texts in their bodies—to have a visceral and physical, rather than an intellectual understanding of the words. This objective turned out to be a literal truth in the sense that Serban would pick and choose sections from the ancient Greek and Latin texts as they were read aloud in the original language by various translators. The actors would then memorize these sections phonetically—painstakingly writing out their lines sound by sound. Much of the time, they had no understanding of the literal meaning of the line—they were communicating only through the sounds. The actors also experimented with exploring every syllable of the sections of text that were chosen—intoning the vowels in a yoga-like chant, using only the consonant sounds in the line, then gradually putting a whole line of text back together.

In the early part of the rehearsal period, the company also explored many types of sound production exercises. For example, one day the actors sat listening to a pot of boiling water for almost an hour, then tried to reproduce the sound as closely as possible. Many times, sounds were passed in a circle, with the actors again either reproducing each other's sound as closely as possible, or gradually expanding into "conversations" of abstract sound. On another occasion, the company passed sounds in a circle while at the beach, gradually widening the circle to determine the maximum distance for listening, concentration, and correct reproduction. Sometimes they would just face the wall and hurl their sounds against it—figuratively attempting to batter down the cement wall with a torrent of sounds. Again, the primary objective of such exploratory work was for the actors to *inhabit their bodies with sound.* They explored many different areas of physical resonators in the body—not just the usual chest, face, and head.

These exercises had another objective as well—the company was becoming highly trained. They learned through experience what muscles were used to whisper, to scream, and all of the variations in between. Priscilla Smith, in particular, became adept at speaking and chanting on an indrawn breath, the opposite of the normal speaking process of expired air. The actors were training their vocal instruments to handle the intricacies of the demanding texts. They also developed more raw power in their voices. This would be particularly useful when they would tour *Medea* to all of the outdoor locations of the European theatre festivals in the summer of 1972, including the ancient ruins of Baalbeck in Lebanon where the performers would actually have to project their voices across hundreds of yards of desert sand and air.

The training was also very physical. Hours were spent in simply learning to walk gracefully with deep concentration back and forth across the room. This walk was taught by an accomplished Japanese Noh actor, Katsurhiro Oida, who had worked with Brook at the Centre for International Theatre Research, and was known to the La MaMa actors as Yoshi (hence they always referred to it as the "Yoshi walk").

Although the actors did not perform *Medea* in a true Japanese Noh style, Serban was attempting to expose the actors to many different physical disciplines including Noh, Kabuki, and the Indian Kathakali, in order for them to develop a new consciousness of integrating voice and body in a fashion that is more spiritual than the Western tradition of actor training. Serban also introduced the company to the work of Zeami, the 14th century critic of the Noh theatre and often incorporated Zeami's use of poetic images when speaking to the company: "Your acting is supposed to become like the sea, like the clouds that rush in the sky, like a tree in the wind."[10]

Another very physical acting exercise was the exercise with the sticks which Serban learned from Brook, who had originally developed it from the Chinese circus for work on his production of *A Midsummer Night's Dream*.[11] There were many variations in this exercise, but the basic idea was for the actor to use a long stick or pole in an acrobatic, rigorous, yet beautiful way, almost as an extension of an arm, rotating it, balancing it, performing movements in unison with other actors in a light and airy fashion that did not represent anything specific in terms of meaning beyond its aesthetic effect. Despite all of the time that Serban spent choreographing these "stick motions" for the chorus, he removed them from the production only days before it opened. (Over twenty years later, Serban continued to use the stick exercises for his student actors at Columbia University.)

Gradually, the company began to do more specific work on the ancient texts. As Serban chose the passages that he wanted the actors to learn, Liz Swados would set them to music, helping the actors find a specific rhythm for each section of text. The musical scoring of *Medea*, like the acting and design aspects, was a process of constant flux and discovery and re-discovery. For example, during the rehearsal period, Swados wrote two complete scores that were eventually abandoned—an opera and a musical. The opera was used by Serban and the actors only as a starting point—a way into the mythic proportions of the Medea story. The musical *Medea* came a bit later in the rehearsal period. It had the flavor of a children's performance and was based on seven key themes in the story—for each of which Swados wrote a song. The themes were journey, crime, exile, witchcraft, jealousy, marriage, and lullaby.[12] Like the opera, this too provided the actors an opportunity to enter the mythic world of a play so different from their own, but it too was only a stepping-stone, a part of the process, not an end result in itself. According to Ana Maria Narti, both the opera and the musical were ultimately dropped because "they offered too easy solutions and thus determined the actors to stay within a circle of known experience."[13]

The eventual musical score of *Medea* combined a number of different instruments and influences. Swados used African drums, Filipino percussion instruments, many different types of bells, and even the amplification of cogged wheels and an abstract, metallic sculpture. Although Swados' music would remain "incidental" in this first of *The Trilogy* pieces, already her eclectic and multicultural approach was apparent. She was an extremely active voice in coaching the actors in dealing with the rhythm of the text and also in writing music based upon the improvisations, some of which she designed, for a particular company of actors. As he did with the actors, Serban often communicated his ideas of the music to her in terms of mythic images such as "It must sound like the sound of fire at dawn" or "like the sound of someone telling an incredibly ancient secret."

The original company consisted of Priscilla Smith as Medea, Jamil Zakkai as Jason, and Natalie Gray as the Nurse. The Chorus consisted of Stuart Baker-Bergen, Patrick Burke, Nancy Gabor, David Rosenblum, and was lead by Valois Mickens. Baker-Bergen and Burke doubled in the roles of Aegeus and the Messenger respectively. In addition, Nancy Heikin was brought into the rehearsal period late to play the role of Creusa, Jason's new wife, a role that does not exist in Euripides' original text, while Diane Lane and Dennis Leiberson played the children. As often happens in workshop situations, no one knew at the outset who would be playing specific roles. As rehearsals continued, it became clear to Priscilla Smith that she and Natalie Gray were the prime candidates for the role of Medea and even when it was decided that Smith would play the role, she and Gray had already developed an intimate, even somewhat competitive psychological relationship which carried over into Gray's portrayal of the Nurse and even Serban's staging of these scenes. Smith recalled:

> Andrei cultivated and orchestrated a polarity between Medea and the Nurse. You might say that the character of Medea was split down the middle and consisted, in performance, of the increasing tension and confrontation between the furious maternal instinct and the equally furious impulse towards a destructive act which liberates a primitive, but powerful, autonomy. This polarity, and that between Jason and Medea, were conduits through which an enormous amount of energy was exchanged.[14]

This polarity was further underscored visually by Serban's casting as Gray was a black actress and Smith white. Only five of the actors, Smith, Gray, Baker-Bergen, Burke, and Mickens would remain in the company two and one-half years later when the first complete version of *The Trilogy* would be unveiled, only a few of them would make all of the overseas tours throughout the 1970s and only two, Smith and Mickens, then known only as Valois, would appear in the 1987 revival, almost 16 years later.

About half-way through the rehearsal period, one of the actors, Stuart Baker-Bergen, brought in an Elizabethan translation of *Medea*. Perhaps feeling that the audience might not be able to understand the production, Serban decided to incorporate the English translation into the production and began to conduct similar sound exercises in English as they had done with the ancient Greek and Latin. Soon afterwards, however, Serban reversed himself, feeling that there was just not enough time to fully explore this language as well, or perhaps regaining the courage of his original vision. In any case, no English was spoken in the final version of *Medea*.

On the whole, Serban's approach to the acting was disciplined, demanding, and committed to the idea of communicating a mythic essence of character without relying on the personal approach of the Americanized version of the Stanislavsky system—The Method. Instead of searching for psychological motivations in the text or themselves,—e.g., why *does* Medea murder her children? What sort of marriage had she and Jason had ? etc.,—Serban urged his actors to view the ancient text as a musician would a score: "instead of thinking, like Stanislavsky, what feeling must I have to raise my left hand, I raise the hand and this creates or reveals the feeling."[15] Priscilla Smith exemplified this approach later in *Electra*. In the scene of mourning over the ashes of her brother Orestis whom she presumes dead, instead of personalizing or imagining her own pain at the death of a loved one, she used the sound of water dripping in order to communicate the rhythm of raindrops in the syllables of the passage. "The process was not an intellectual one ... Once I became committed to realizing the sensation of water dripping and I kept listening, the pitches and sounds began to come out in a very unexpected way. They came from a place other than the mind ..."[16]

In the final days of rehearsal, as would become indicative of his personal directing style, Serban made many changes in the staging. As we have seen, the stick explorations were cut. So was a small altar upon which Medea created her spell and a ladder which she mounted triumphantly at the end of the play. More than just removing props, however, by eliminating gestures, movements, and even light cues, Serban pared the piece down to the very simplest actions that were absolutely necessary. The mood of the play became more static and grave. In distilling the months of work of the company, the language remained at the forefront of the theatre experience. The play *became,* in the minds of many, the long confrontation between Jason and Medea which was solely the two actors spitting the ancient sounds at each other—*sans* movement, *sans* props.

As noted, *Medea* opened with the audience descending the basement steps at La MaMa, already hearing the frenzied whispers of the Nurse, children, and Chorus. After a brief scene, performers and audience together walked down the long corridor to an adjoining room where Medea was already chained to the wall, shouting and growling her text. The 45 audience members were seated along the long walls of the narrow room with members of the Chorus interspersed throughout. At both ends of the room stood short platforms, one for Medea and one for Jason and Creusa. Jason and Medea faced each other at opposite ends of the room in silence. Then began their long verbal duel of accusation, building slowly in intensity, tempo, and volume—crescendoing in a torrent of emotional screams as the text switched from Latin to Greek—from the rich vowels of Seneca to the "wild, uncontrolled", alliterative consonants of Euripides.[17] In the climax of this fifteen minute stychomythia, Medea hissed like a snake. The effect was a distilled passion of primal sound. Next, Jason's new wife, Creusa, slowly crossed the length of the entire space to Medea. After a moment of silent confrontation, she suddenly snatched Medea's crown from her head, utterly humiliating the former queen.

Medea's revenge began in the center of the room. Medea knelt before the wedding presents, touching them only with the flame of her candle, placing the curse that would kill her children and Creusa. The company called this scene "the magic scene." This section was acted only in candlelight; the electrical stage lights were turned off. Here, Smith utilized the "intoning" or speaking/chanting on the indrawn breath as the children slowly filed offstage to their death and the Chorus around her whispered its warnings. Borrowing from Seneca's version in which the children are murdered on stage, the children were slowly and meticulously lowered through a hole in the burlap-covered ceiling below to the dumbfounded Jason, standing inert on the stage floor. This was followed by Serban's version of Medea's triumphant chariot escape: first Medea's wild laughter from above, then Medea re-appearing upside down through the same hole, her head directly above Jason's as she softly chanted a song of triumph. (See Figure #1)

At the end of the play, Jason and Medea had traded places, Jason lamenting over his children on Medea's original platform while Medea silently appeared on Jason's, adorned in a huge Kathakali ceremonial hat which Priscilla Smith had first seen in Ellen Stewart's apartment. All exited behind the door of one of the platforms, the last being the Nurse who cast a long, final glance at the audience. With no formal curtain call, the audience usually reacted with a long silence, despite occasional desperate attempts at applause, sitting immobile for some minutes, then gradually moving about after this period of meditation, and only speaking in hushed tones and whispers as they left the theatre.

The critical reaction to *Medea* was overwhelmingly positive. The major New York critics raved, especially Clive Barnes of *The New York Times* who called it "superb ... remarkable ... a potent theatrical event" offering "deep insights into the nature of the dramatic experience"[18] while Henry Hewes of *Saturday Review* described it as "a 55 minute experiment ... constitutes the most dedicated and pure piece of theatre we have seen in some time."[19]

Looking back, *Medea* was similar to the work in *Orghast* but with a well-known and cohesive plot and characters. The gestalt effect of ancient language, superbly concentrated and committed acting, and a simple *mise-en-scène* achieved what Serban had once termed "the intelligence of emotion." He won a Drama Desk award for his direction.

Medea went on a European and Middle Eastern tour in the summer of 1972, but not before Serban directed a student production of *Romeo and Juliet* at Nassau Community College.[20] Serban had previously directed *She Stoops to Conquer* at NCC, the invitation coming from La MaMa member (and later artistic director) Wesley J. Jensby, who was then chair of the Theatre Program at the Long Island school. *Romeo and Juliet*, again with music by Liz Swados, featured much of the verse sung rather than spoken and many portions of the play staged on circular catwalks above the stage floor. The project is significant only in that it represented a deepening of his collaboration with Swados.

In 1973, Serban was invited by famed French director Jean-Louis Barrault to create a new piece for the upcoming Theatre Festival in Bordeaux, France. Continuing his investigation of Greek tragedy, ancient languages, sounds, and ritual staging, Serban directed a version of Sophocles' *Electra*. According to Priscilla Smith, Serban originally wanted to do Artaud's version of *The Cenci* but was unhappy with the French actors who auditioned. This time, as Swados was away with Brook's company, the music was composed by Catherine Mueller. Swados later re-did the score for the New York production. *Electra* was not seen in the U.S. until 1974 when Serban added *The Trojan Women* to complete *The Trilogy*, but it was well-received by the French in Bordeaux and in Paris, despite the fact that Serban insisted on bringing in the La MaMa company of actors including Priscilla Smith, Patrick Burke, Valois Mickens, William Duff-Griffin, (who had joined the company for the European tour of *Medea* in 1972) and others from *Medea* while the French were relegated to chorus roles.

France was by no means the extent of his travel in 1973. Earlier in the year, Serban traveled to remote villages in Bali and Japan for three months. Like Brook, Artaud, and many other theatre artists of the 20th century, Serban was drawn to non-Western cultural rituals in his investigation of what constitutes the theatre form. One could view this tendency in many contemporary theatre artists as a throwback to the 19th century Romanticist vision of so-called "primitive cultures"; yet one could also defend it as a genuinely curious desire to evolve a theatre that cuts across barriers to communicate in a truly global fashion.

Perhaps out of deference to those who found *Medea* difficult to follow, Serban began *Electra* with the major characters identifying themselves, solemnly repeating their names: Electra (played by Priscilla Smith), Clytemnestra (Natalie Gray), Aegisthus (William Duff-Griffin), and Orestis (Patrick Burke and William Duff-Griffin alternating). Once again, the audience was seated on either side of a long space. Much of the action took place on an octagonal platform in the center. At one end stood some stairs leading to another platform, this one covered with foliage. The arrangement of the space allowed a more formal and patterned sense of movements to develop. Essentially, the blocking consisted of a series of long horizontal crosses from platform to platform. This was a very different feeling than the internal rage of the very static *Medea*.

Electra used a blanket to lament her father, walking very slowly toward the center platform with it draped over her arms. A chorus of four women surrounded the platform, supporting Electra's slowly building statement of revenge. Crisotemis (Valois Mickens) entered, carrying a huge snake which she gave to Electra who ascended the stairs with it. (See Figure #2) Now the stage was set for Electra's confrontation with Clytemnestra. Again, as in *Medea*, these two adversarial characters faced each other across the entire length of the space, spitting their words out at each other. When the Tutor (Peter John De Vries) entered, holding a blanket to represent Orestis' cloak and announced that his pupil is dead (the first spoken, as opposed to sung text, since the introduction) Electra began a long wail of lament while Clytemnestra rejoiced. As soon as Clytemnestra left, Orestis appeared up high on the platform while Pilades (Charles Hayward) brought Electra an urn of ashes where she performed a breathtaking lament.

The recognition scene between brother and sister was staged as a true miracle by Serban. (He sub-titled the piece "A Miracle Play.") The Chorus very softly and slowly began to strike a melody on hand bells as the Orestis moved slowly down the steps to his lamenting sister. As the bells increased tempo, the two slowly embraced on the platform while the faithful Pilades stood nearby holding a torch. Electra and Orestis moved up the stairs, both chanting where they were met by a masked apparition of Agamemnon, also ringing a bell.

Aegisthus appeared with the snake wrapped around his chest. When he was killed, he placed the snake on a long stick and removed his shirt while the Chorus surrounded him on the center platform and blocked the view by spreading their garments when the death blow was delivered. He was then dragged off the platform upside down. The Chorus screamed a cry of triumph through long, tube like horns which they'd also used at the beginning of the play. Electra then returned with a dove. She and Orestis were crowned with garland and went up the stairs into the palace together as the entire cast surrounded them with ringing handbells. (In New York, Ellen Stewart would join in with her own handbell, the one she'd been using for years to welcome audiences to La MaMa.)

Despite the inclusion of Aegisthus' death on stage, the mood of *Electra* remained lyrical and joyous. Again, the *mise-en-scène* remained fairly simple and without spectacular effects (save the snake!) but what differed from *Medea* in addition to a more formal structure was *Electra's* prevalent atmosphere of hope, recognition, and justice. It contained the simple faith of a fairy tale and indeed Serban had used extensive improvisations based on Cinderella during the company's French residence. There was a sense of stillness and quiet to this piece that was found nowhere else in *The Trilogy*. Whenever all three plays were performed in New York, Serban usually chose to perform *Electra* last.

Back in the United States, Serban and Swados did a guest workshop at the Carnegie-Mellon Institute in Pittsburgh, creating a new musical work called *Crow*. Then, in 1974, they traveled to Brazil to the Sao Paulo Festival where they were joined by Priscilla Smith and a Brazilian cast to begin work on *The*

Trojan Women. Serban recalled: "What we did was very close to the traditional South American sensitivity, to their understanding of ceremony very close to their own origins." Unfortunately, the piece was not completed in Brazil, apparently due to political problems:"... there were people who said 'Why do you work in Greek, not Portuguese?' So we could not finish. It was sad. Because the actors really wanted to do the work. There was an extremely interesting energy at work."[21]

When they returned to La MaMa, *The Trojan Women* was rehearsed with the rest of the company where a compressed hour version of all three plays featuring only six actors was opened in June, 1974, under the title *Fragments of a Greek Trilogy* and sub-titled "A Work-in-Progress." Although Serban later said that "we did that simply as a demonstration, to get a grant," the reviews were laudatory. Mel Gussow wrote in *The New York Times:* "The plays become primitive rituals. It is as if they are happening for the first time, and the audience is witness. This is an uncommon evening of primal theatre"[22] while Robb Baker of *The Soho Weekly News* thought it the most extraordinary theatre he'd ever seen: "You *feel* the meaning of the Greek text; you don't *hear* lines."[23]

With the funding secured, Serban now went to work expanding *The Trilogy* (working mostly on *The Trojan Women*) and re-staging the entire event for the official opening of the new La MaMa Annex—an enormous space; actually a reconverted television studio with 30 foot high ceilings, a proscenium stage at one end, and two tiered wooden galleries at the sides that could be used for audience or performing space. The design was similar to many experimental and environmental theatre spaces of the late 1960s and early 70s, perhaps best exemplified by Jerry Rojo's design for The Performing Garage which housed Richard Schechner's The Performance Group.

What Serban was able to incorporate from the Brazilian experience into the eventual finished piece of *The Trojan Women* was the incredible sense of energy of a disorganized city, of political turmoil in the streets. This is what the audience would feel as they watched the piece. *The Trojan Women* evolved into the most visually spectacular of the three plays, although it was sub-titled "An Epic Opera." By now, Swados had studied with Brook and had traveled and researched the music of many different cultures all over the world. The score for *The Trojan Women* included not only Ancient Greek, but fragments of Mayan, Aztec, Nahuatl, and Inahien. The instrumentation of the musical score had expanded to include trombone and flute as well as percussion.

Like *Medea*, *The Trojan Women* began with the actors leading the audience from the lobby into the theatre. Unlike *Medea* and *Electra*, however, audience and actors shared the space in a much more environmental fashion. As the program note stated, "the audience is invited to follow the action of the play by moving together from one area to another where the action takes place, and by taking a seat when the actors so indicate."[24] This was made possible, of course, by the vastness of the Annex itself. Serban and designer Jun Maeda's only additions to the natural configuration of the Annex as described above was a space for the musicians on the floor to the left of the proscenium stage and a steel ramp leading to a high platform above the entrance way. As the audience moved into the theatre, they were greeted by pounding drums, smoke, screaming, and torches. On the platform, Cassandra (Valois Mickens) danced bare-breasted with a torch in each hand. All of the other women were huddled together on one of the galleries while the men stood below them, encircling the captive women with their spears.

The audience stood scattered around the space and traveled about to watch the first three sections of the play—the suffering, humiliation, and destruction of Cassandra, Andromaca, and Helen. First, Cassandra moved down off her platform, still singing her prophecies and performing her torch dance, accompanied only by drums. She reached a paroxysm and collapsed. She was comforted by one of the women, then a soldier slipped a rope around her neck and violently dragged her up to one of the galleries. She and the soldier pulled back and forth in this "rope dance" before Cassandra collapsed again. Then slowly, she was led up the stairs, lamenting a single melody with no other accompaniment, lighted by a single spotlight.

On another part of the high gallery, Andromaca, (Priscilla Smith) bathed her child-king, Astianax, (Diane Lane) the last King of Troy. The women all lined up on the stairs, their arms held high, their hands crossed. The soldiers placed the child-king in a cage. Andromaca very slowly rinsed her hands off three times in a basin of water. Then, once again using the harmonics of the indrawn breath, Smith very gradually built the intensity of this long lamenting section, anointing the child with water. Lane stayed absolutely motionless. The lament climaxed with a soft piercing scream as Andromaca raised the basin over her head and poured the water out over Astianax's outstretched hands. She clutched the child to her breast just before the cage was hauled away by the soldiers. Screaming defiantly, Andromaca was dragged away behind her in a smaller cage. Then followed one of the most startling moments in all of *The Trilogy*. Smith crawled out of the cage, up the platform, stood on the very edge with arms extended, then with a stabbing motion, leapt off the high platform into the darkness below where she was caught by a group of musicians and actors.

Of the three women, Helen's punishment (Joana Peled) was the cruelest. A wooden caged cart hurdled through the space—spectators literally ducking and running out of its path to keep from being trampled. Inside was Helen who was taunted by both the soldiers and the women, because of her role in the cause of the war. They stripped her naked, including removing her wig to expose a shaved head, smeared her with mud and straw, and watched jeeringly as an actor in an enormous bear costume entered the cage and symbolically raped her. This "rape dance" was concluded when the bear held her high above his head. Finally, she was carried off to the highest point of the platform where, in a crucifix image, she was strapped to a pole through her arms while another woman spat in her face.

At this point, the mood and action of *The Trojan Women* changed. The audience was moved to the seats on the sides. What followed were more lyrical and symbolic scenes of the community's suffering. Three child messengers holding lighted candles sang an acappella refrain as the audience re-positioned themselves. A single flute announced the beginning of the weaver-woman suicide scene. Here a woman carried her loom up the ramp, slowly stabbed herself, and very, very slowly slid down the ramp. The blue light on a shimmering sheet of mylar reflected a strange, but beautiful image of drowning. This quiet mood was broken by a scream—the spirit of Achilles' Hunger appeared on the platform. All of the women then began to frantically climb up the ramp, only to be beaten down by the whips of the men at the top. Once they were all turned back, the soldiers rounded up the women in a circle, who huddled together whispering while they were bound together with rope. They were led off to the end of the space, onto the stage where an image of a boat was constructed with the men on either side of the seated mass of huddled women. The soldiers held up the frames of the ribs of the boat on either side of the women while directly behind them hung a tattered flag. They swayed gently back and forth as the women sang "Dios Limna" over and over, very slowly getting softer and softer and the lights ever so gradually dimmed. Finally, they swayed a good half-minute in complete silence and the lights faded to complete black, with only the torches of the soldiers flickering in the darkness.

On Friday, October 18, 1974, an unusual opening night for a New York theatre because of the print deadlines and complications for reviews in the Sunday newspapers, *The Trilogy* and the new theatre had its grand opening with all three plays. The total running time was five hours. (Most of the time, the plays would run in repertory, two at a time.) The critical and popular reaction was immediate and sensational. It is not an exaggeration to say that *The Trilogy* took the New York theatrical community by storm. As astonishing as it may seem, *every* single review by both major and minor newspapers, the weeklies, and the television and radio, was positive—and most were wildly enthusiastic. In *The New York Times*, Clive Barnes called it an event that

> sent shivers down the back of my typewriter ... The immediacy of Mr. Serban's theater far transcends the narrative notion of knowing what happens in any literary sense. Mr. Serban makes you feel such basic emotions as love, suffering, anguish, disgust, and fear, at a level not so far removed from reality. Of course, they are in essence totally removed—no theatrical experience can duplicate, for example, the raw thrust of real pain—but that particular removal has the tincture of poetic honesty to it. Mr. Serban's theater helps you to know what to think.[25]

Douglas Watt of *The Daily News* said it was a "fascinating occasion"[26] while Stanley Kaufmann of *The New Republic* described it as a "brilliant revolt against the drudgery and trudgery of the merely conventional, a refreshment of the theatre's bloodstream at the source."[27] Other headlines included "A Night at Blockbuster's Anonymous," "Awe-Inspiring Event," and "*Greek Trilogy* is Magnificent Theatre," while in *The Nation*, Harold Clurman wrote an extensive analysis surmising that *The Trilogy* was

> The only effective and nearly complete application of Artaud's inspiration I have thus far seen ... I have a high regard for Serban's achievement. He is one of the most dedicated and gifted directors anywhere, and his trilogy may well prove a seminal work. Among other things that must be praised is the training of his company—nearly all American—which in turn displays an entire devotion to the arduous tasks set for them.[28]

The astounding success of *The Trilogy* insured its continued stage life for the next five years. The La MaMa company immediately made plans for a *Trilogy* European and Middle Eastern tour that summer. The tour was repeated in 1976 and throughout the 1970s. In the decade, *The Trilogy* toured over 40 festivals in 15 different countries, including such triumphs at the Vienna Festival; Baalbeck, Lebanon; Venice; Paris; the Bitef Festival in Belgrade; the Shiraz Festival of the Arts in Iran, former site of Brook's *Orghast*, where *The Trilogy* started at the gates of Persepolis and proceeded through the ruins of the ancient city; and, finally, Athens itself, the location which Priscilla Smith still feels was the emotional and artistic zenith of the long arc of the life of *The Trilogy* in performance:

> It felt like a plug being put into a socket. Despite the fact that the structure of the plays had been stripped down to the bare essence or altered (in the case of *The Trojan Women*) and that we were speaking (approximately) an ancient language incomprehensible to the Greeks as well as ourselves, one could sense immediately that it had "come home." I attribute this to Andrei's ability to "grow" this material from its own conceptual nuclei rather than simply interpreting it.[29]

The Trilogy won the Grand Prize at the Bitef Festival and, back in New York, Obie awards for Serban and Smith. It was also revived in New York in 1975, 1976, and 1979 to renewed acclaim.

The performance changed in each space. In the ancient ruins in Baalbeck, Serban re-staged *Medea* to use the entire space of the ruins and the temple. Medea and Jason faced each other from a distance of approximately 150 feet. Medea performed her chariot departure on a cornice over thirty feet in the air. Other events also marked the long life of the touring years. In Baalbeck, the actors in the company went on strike, refusing to perform for over an hour, until the Lebanese armed soldiers vacated the premises. The soldiers had beaten a member of the company when he tried to enter without his security card. Serban had also been hit when he tried to interfere. There were similar political disturbances in Greece. And yet, somehow, the company always did manage to perform and always to tremendous audience response.

Artistically, the biggest issue on the tours became maintaining the quality of performance for so many months at a time, especially with so many changes in the cast. What had been intended as a research experiment in sound and discovering the raw power of the ancient texts was now a highly successful commercial production for La MaMa. When the company had begun rehearsal for *Medea* at La MaMa in the Fall of 1971, no one had dreamed that they would still be performing it in Jerusalem in 1979.

And certainly no one had foreseen that *The Trilogy* would be performed 16 years after the first production of *Medea*, but that is precisely what happened in 1987. Ellen Stewart asked Serban to re-stage the show to help celebrate the 25th anniversary of La MaMa. By now, Serban was an international superstar director, known for his innovative (some would say outrageous) interpretations of operas and the classics, such as his productions of *The Cherry Orchard* at Lincoln Center and *The Marriage of Figaro* at The Guthrie. Perhaps somewhat reluctantly, Serban agreed to revive *The Trilogy* once more. Out of possibly more than a little deference and respect for Ellen Stewart, some of the original artists were rounded up—including Liz Swados (her first project with Serban since he'd been replaced by Joe Papp on her musical version of *Alice in Wonderland* in 1980), Priscilla Smith, Valois Mickens, and a few others, but mostly new actors were hired to complete the company. Later, Serban offered these thoughts on the revival:

> By doing them again in 1987, I tried to find out if what Peter Brook said in *The Empty Space* was true, that "No production of a play can stay alive unchanged longer than five years." *The Greek Trilogy* was fourteen years old! With films, the older they get, the more valuable, just like wine. Theatre is made for this moment, for right now. It works only in the present. That's why, for me, what is called the definitive production of a play is nonsense, because it's definitive only so long as the fashion lasts ... The plays go on but the format of the plays and the whole involvement of the audience change. The audience in *The Trojan Women* moved along with the actors and participated standing most of the time. It was a device very much in use in the 1960s and 70s which is almost gone now. So I was interested to see if this format, which I considered old-fashioned avant-garde, was just an experiment of the time or if it had something of value that could surpass stylishness.[30]

In a New York season that included the musicals *Starlight Express* and *Les Miserables*, and Neil Simon's *Broadway Bound*, reactions to *The Trilogy* revival seemed to very much bear out that it had that "something of value." In *The New York Times*, Mel Gussow wrote that it made "other current theatre seem insignificant in comparison."[31] Michael Feingold echoed this sentiment in *The Village Voice*, noting that *The Trilogy* "makes everything around it now look puny."[32] Perhaps Sylviane Gold of *The Wall Street Journal* spoke for an entire generation of theatergoers who had seen *The Trilogy* the first time around in the early 70s: "What this revival proves is that those of us who were entranced back in the 70s were not just young and foolish. We were right."[33] It is perhaps ironic that it took a revival of virtually his first large scale American theatre production to earn Serban a rave review in New York City after several negative reviews of his productions in the 1980s.[34] By 1987, Serban was no longer regarded by the theatre press as the fair haired boy genius director and his productions of *Uncle Vanya* at La MaMa in 1983 and *The Marriage of Figaro* at Circle-in-the Square in 1985 had been severely criticized. Again, to some critics, *The Trilogy* continues to be the standard against which all of his productions are measured.

Ecstatic critical and popular reactions not withstanding, elements of *The Trilogy* had undoubtedly changed. Some original members of the company looked askance at the newer members inviting their agents and prospective casting directors to performances, in short, in treating it as any other showcase production. This sort of professional "careerism" was not at the forefront of the La MaMa company in the early 70s. Too, some wondered about the comparative lack of training for the new actors considering the original *Medea* had rehearsed for four months and the lack of day-to-day presence of Serban and Swados during the revival's rehearsal period. Finally, a summer European tour of the revival ended in a rather chaotic foray of disorganization, lacking the charm and spontaneity of the tours of the 70s. For some, the magic had gone out of *The Trilogy*. And yet, when Serban was asked to take over the Romanian National Theatre after the revolution of Christmas, 1989, the production he chose to inaugurate the theatre was *Fragments of a Greek Trilogy*. And some of the actors who had confided their disappointment in the 1987 revival traveled to Bucharest to help him teach it to the Romanian actors where it was presented to enormous popular and critical reaction in the Fall of 1990, almost twenty years after the initial rehearsals for *Medea*.

What ultimately is the significance of *Fragments of a Greek Trilogy* in Serban's work with Greek material?

The significance lies in primarily two areas: in the context of the American avant-garde theatre and in the context of Artaud's theories.

Because *The Trilogy* actually spanned a total of fifteen years in its performance life from the initial production of *Medea* in 1972 to the 25th anniversary revival of all three plays in 1987, it contained a barometer of the pressure of contemporary events on performance style. In its planning, construction, and public and critical reception, *The Trilogy* reflects a cultural context of an expatriate Romanian producing ancient Greek tragedy in the United

States of the early 1970s. Indeed the very nature of the American avant-garde theatre of the 1960s and the popularity of Artaud's theories in such work as Allan Kaprow's Happenings, The Living Theatre of Julian Beck and Judith Malina, Joe Chaikin's Open Theatre, and Richard Schechner's Performance Group, reflected a diverse theatrical response to the growing alienation of Americans living in a society increasingly aware of its corruption, consumerism, and social inequity. In the decade's explosion of racial violence, assassination, sexual revolution and eventual failure of moral values as symbolized by the Vietnam war, it was perhaps only natural that theatre experimentalists were united in their creation of a theatre not based on the playwright's words and an exploration of a more confrontational relationship between audience and spectator. Serban was not an American, however, and neither was his primary immediate influence, Peter Brook. Therefore, *The Trilogy,* like *Orghast* before it which had been conducted in an international setting with performers from many different cultures, continued these explorations of the American avant-garde in a less overtly political fashion. Obviously part of the trend of "new theatre" that Americans saw in New York throughout the decade, it also differed from the work of The Living Theatre and The Performance Group. Although there were no direct or obvious references to Vietnam or the United States in *The Trilogy*, in *The Trojan Women* in particular, audiences intuitively recognized the atmosphere of a society torn apart by war and political upheaval in the streets. As we have seen, these images came from Serban's experience in Brazil in 1974, but they also subliminally reflected New York City of the Vietnam era.

Serban had clearly tapped into the American avant-garde theatre community's need for a primarily non-verbal event. Given the context of the various theatre experiments of the 1960s of such American groups listed above and such European experimentalists as Jerzy Grotowski's Polish Lab Theatre and, of course, Brook, Serban's *Trilogy* seemed to be the logical end of such attempts to re-examine (and perhaps reduce) the role of language in the theatre. What better way to do this than to explore and discover the visceral meanings of the very sounds of the words themselves? And yet, in doing this, *The Trilogy* re-cast the role of language in the theatre event to its primary importance. It was merely a different point of view in considering the role of language—one that went beyond the intellect. Serban explains:

> The ancient Greek language is perhaps the most generous material for actors that has ever been written. At that time, poets felt the need to invent a poetic language to try to accomplish an enormous task to send messages, through words, great distances, in a space open not only to the assembly of Athenian citizens, but also to the sea, the air, and the stars ... The reason we used ancient Greek was to really examine what is hidden in those sounds—in those particular sounds. What is there is the potential for a special energy to be acted, to be rediscovered again

after being buried for 2000 years at the bottom of the sea, and which will enable us to look at the tragedy in a different way.[35]

Critics and audiences alike saw in *The Trilogy* a work of high visceral excitement that did not rely on the intellectual understanding of language. *The Trilogy* also involved the audience member in more than what many considered to be the usual passive experience in the proscenium theatre; and yet, without an offensive sensibility or a direct polemical point of view. Many reviews in 1974 and in the coming years during the various revivals of *The Trilogy* stressed that in *The Trojan Women*, when actors and audience mingled, Serban's actors did not treat the audience with hostility as members of The Living Theatre sometimes did.[36] *The Trilogy* was also accessible to a wider audience than much of the work of the previous experimentalists. (Only *Medea* had been restricted to a small audience in its original production.) Serban himself noted "No experimental work is healthy unless it opens up at some point to a large public."[37]

Finally, *The Trilogy* helped to raise the standards of acting in the American avant-garde theatre. In the views of many, the La MaMa company was highly physically and vocally trained, committed, and disciplined in comparison to what was perceived as sloppy and emotionally indulgent performances of some other experimental companies. What Serban's company did have in common with other groups was a spirit dedicated to exploring an acting style that went beyond the traditional boundaries of the realism of American method acting. Again, Serban explains:

> A contemporary actor must have the curiosity to meet this language on its own terms, which is a different method of approach than studying something like *The Crucible* or *The Glass Menagerie*, where everything is small realism or detailed psychology. He must approach this unknown language with his intuition. The actor has to forget about mind analysis, and even the logical understanding of language, and has to jump into a territory of the unknown with his imagination.[38]

The intensive training and dedication of the La MaMa troupe combined with Serban's relentless desire to push each actor to her/his absolute limits in search of a more poetic way of working and Serban's own seductive power of charm as a director certainly resulted in the actors "jumping into the territory of the unknown," Priscilla Smith being the most obvious example. Like his work with Swados, Serban often coached her with metaphors such as in the early work on *Medea* when he demanded that she increase the volume of her shouts because he did not yet believe that they would awaken an entire city. Smith later gathered her thoughts regarding the training and the demands on her voice throughout the long tours:

In New York I thought it was impossible to cover the space of the acting room and of the corridor. I really did not believe it possible. Then I discovered that I could shout without any difficulty over the whole first part. When I saw the acting hall in Amsterdam, a space three times bigger than La MaMa, I thought I would lose my voice after the first performance. To my great surprise, my voice became only stronger ... In Baalbeck, I looked at the temple and I froze. But my awe soon disappeared. From the very first attempts I felt the surprising acoustics of the temple at work and everything became easy. Now I am wondering whether it would not be possible to develop the voice further.[39]

Harold Clurman was right in suggesting that *The Trilogy*, intended or not, was a cohesive culmination of Artaud's disparate theories. Indeed, Peter Brook, in his seminal book *The Empty Space*, and in his production of *Marat/Sade*, had paid homage to Artaud. It seemed to be the theatrical "Age of Artaud." As we have seen, there also seemed to be a counterculture feel to *The Trilogy*, given its linkage to the perceived notion of the Artaudian theatre of screams, images, sounds, violence, sexuality, audience participation, the audience member in the center of the theatre space with the event happening all around her/him, (as happened with *The Trojan Women*), and the context of the recent political, social, and cultural upheaval of the 1960s. Underlying all of this was perhaps a basic Romantic mistrust of the written word, of literary values. Again, this is ironic because *The Trilogy*, in some ways, was actually highly textual, as the starting point for the project had been the ancient texts themselves.

However, one must probe the meaning of *The Trilogy* in the context of Artaud's legacy beyond the surface connections. First, in regard to the acting, Priscilla Smith confessed that there were times in playing Medea that she felt exactly like Artaud's actor "signalling through the flames." She felt as if she were on fire.[40] Like the members of Grotowski's Polish Lab Theatre and like Brook's description in *The Empty Space*, the La MaMa actors seemed to make "holy" gifts of themselves to the audience in performance. Their almost ascetic sense of discipline and rigorous physical and vocal technique seemed to recall Artaud's demand for the actor to return to his original function as shaman in a spiritual ceremony. Artaud wrote:

> The gifted actor finds by instinct how to tap and radiate certain powers; but he would be astonished indeed if it were revealed to him that these powers, which have their material trajectory by and *in the organs*, actually exist, for he has never realized they could actually exist.[41]

Certainly, Priscilla Smith had learned to "tap and radiate these certain powers."

Secondly, the unique connections that *The Trilogy* made with audience members surely recalls Artaud's wishes for the spectator's sensibility to be hypnotized by violent physical images and "a whirlwind of higher voices."[42] The shocking violence of *The Trojan Women*, the raw, concentrated power of *Medea*, and the miraculous joy and discovery in *Electra*, all mesmerized audiences. They seemed to be images of terror and beauty that were unlocked in a deep part of a collective consciousness that spoke to audience members in an ancient language across the currents of more than two thousand years. Too, in addition to the audience's capacity to receive these ancient texts and be affected by them, there was a sense of participation in the event itself, of simply being present in an event which had expended so much energy, and of having assisted and helped make the specialness of that event by one's presence. Priscilla Smith recalled that an audience member would cease to clap during curtain call, if she smiled directly at that person. "It was almost as if they became aware of the fact that a circle had existed, that they had assisted, that a movement of energy had been there between them and me."[43] Ellen Stewart summed up her feelings on this issue: "That's what I think theatre is—for me—when an audience, for that short time, breathes and lives the same moment—and for those moments every person is one person."[44]

Finally, *The Trilogy* epitomized Artaud's wishes for a theatre language of sound, music, gesture, dance, and violent spectacle—a theatre of *ceremony*, not psychology; a theatre which created poetry through the abstraction of life, rather than seeking to imitate it. Serban's decision to explore the sounds of the ancient languages is evidence of this poetic abstraction. Serban echoed Artaud's call for the written poetry to be read once and then destroyed in "No More Masterpieces" when he wrote:

> The word is written to be experienced at the moment it is spoken, in an immediate relationship with sound, with an infinite possibility to create moods and situations as music does. It exists on its own. It comes from somewhere—and it goes away. We sense its vibration. We hold on to it. We can try to make it vibrate inside us.[45]

Agamemnon—New York Shakespeare Festival, 1977

By 1977, Serban was considered to be one of the leading innovative theatre directors in the world. His reputation had been built largely on *Fragments of A Greek Trilogy* but he'd also directed *The Good Woman of Setzuan* and *As You Like It* for the La MaMa company which had been reformed into The Great Jones Repertory Project. He'd also "come uptown" in the New York theatre community in a big way by directing a wild and controversial *Cherry Orchard* for Joe Papp's New York Shakespeare Festival then in residence at Lincoln Center. Serban's startlingly visual production in the vast expanse of the Vivian Beaumont Theatre caused a sensation (discussed fully in the next chapter). It now seems clear that, after some years of mixed success at Lincoln Center, Serban was an important aspect of Papp's direction for the company to produce classical plays by young revisionist or metaphorical directors such as Richard Foreman's *The Threepenny Opera* in 1976. After *The Cherry Orchard* opened in February of 1977, Serban immediately went to work on *Agamemnon*, also produced by The New York Shakespeare Festival at Lincoln Center.

By 1977, too, the popularity and excitement of the avant-garde theatre of the 1960s had changed. The Open Theatre and The Performance Group had disbanded and The Living Theatre was performing mostly in Europe. Jerzy Grotowski had eschewed formal theatrical performance altogether for investigation of actor/audience paratheatricals. Peter Brook had made several trips to Africa and Asia in conducting research for his experiments in interculturalism such as *The Ik* and *Conference of The Birds*, although he continued to direct traditional operas and Western classics. Rather than the experiments with audience participation and social and political themes, alternative theatre artists such as Foreman, Robert Wilson, and The Wooster Group seemed to be moving even further into communication with images rather than traditional narrative and an increasing reliance on technology to produce these spectacular images. National events such as the loss in Vietnam, the widespread distrust and cynicism due to Watergate, and the weakened American economy as evidenced in the energy crisis combined to elicit more formalist and, in some cases, more introspective responses in these theatre artists. In some ways, Serban's *Agamemnon* reflected this trend. In other ways, as with *The Trilogy*, his work stood apart.

Obviously, in a sense, it was a return to the familiar territory of Greek tragedy for Serban, Swados, who again composed the score, and Priscilla Smith, who played the leading roles of Clytemnestra and Cassandra. But it was more than just familiar territory for Serban. At this point in his life and career, he truly had a personal need to stage Greek tragedy. He was still searching for that collective emotional experience for his audience that seems so difficult for modern theatre to achieve. *Agamemnon* also posed a unique challenge. Serban was drawn to the play because it was one of the earliest extant tragedies and therefore, contained more elements of choral poems and emphasized the poetic more than the narrative. Serban was determined to find the essence underneath what many scholars identify as the grandeur and formality of Aeschylus' texts:

> The text is all exposition. It's like a long oratorio, the passages are like those in Homer, a combination of the epic and dramatic. The story can be told in a sentence. But there is *something* underneath the text that we are looking for. After all, the Greeks performed the play many times, and yet they never tired of it. So something else was touched. That something is what we are looking for.[46]

This also meant emphasizing the Chorus more than he had in *The Trilogy*, as the Chorus had over half the written lines of the *Agamemnon* text. Serban attempted to make the Chorus the most important element in his production of *Agamemnon:*

> In our production, the leader of the Chorus (played by George Voskovec) is a sage, a wise man, respected in the community. The Chorus makes a bridge between us and higher possibilities: it is the most important element in the play; it will not only tell the story and bear witness to the action, but is the conscience of the protagonists and the receptacle of the life around them. Their shared collective emotion, expressed through the fullness of their voices, will reverberate to us and, I hope, involve us in their experience. This is what I am searching for in theatre.[47]

Agamemnon was also a very different proposition from *The Trilogy* in other ways. First, most of the play, especially the confrontations between the principals, was spoken in English, using Edith Hamilton's translation of Aeschylus. Some choral sections were spoken in English in juxtaposition with a Swados Greek score. In some ways, because of the combination of English and ancient Greek, the rehearsal and composing process was even more complex for Swados. After first attempting to use an ancient Greek score like she'd composed for *The Trilogy*, then incorporating more modern music, then trying melodies from different cultures, she settled on a score that combined elements of African, Persian, and Arabic story-telling music. These melodies were used for the English sections and were juxtaposed with the ancient Greek text in the original score. Swados explained:

> It was not to cover up the English, but to work out a vibration system so that if the English were going on at the same time, telling what was happening—for that is the function of the Chorus in *Agamemnon*—another score of sounds would be going on, commenting, heightening, dramatizing, and underscoring the narrative.[48]

Second, *Agamemnon* did not have the luxury of a workshop rehearsal situation. Although some actors and singers in the Chorus did a ten week workshop with Swados, the company as a whole did not duplicate the training/workshop atmosphere of *The Trilogy*. Like the 1987 revival of *The Trilogy*, this meant that there were varying levels of training and skill in the cast.

Third, the audience would remain mostly in their seats at the Beaumont Theatre in Lincoln Center rather than following the action around the space as they had at La MaMa. Still, Serban placed a section of audience on bleacher seats on the stage which were movable and parted to reveal the doors of the palace at the extreme upstage end of the Beaumont stage. (See Figure #3) This was Serban's solution for most efficiently utilizing the vastness of the Vivian

Beaumont Theatre. Many critics had considered the space too large and impersonal until Serban's productions of *The Cherry Orchard* and *Agamemnon*. According to Joe Papp, this was the first time they had attempted to use the mechanical revolve beneath the Beaumont stage since the theatre's inception in 1965:

> I ... couldn't get the mechanism working, but decided to put the audience on the stage. It just changed the whole experience. I never liked that theatre too much and I felt I wanted to bash it around a lot. And this is one of the ways ... Because when you are at the Beaumont, you either try to modulate the space (bring it down), modify it, make it smaller or you go all the way with it and simply sail with that ... (Andrei was a) wonderful choice for that space. (As was Richard Foreman when we did *Threepenny*.) ... It was the right place for them. It was for plays and directors who had a sense of scale.[49]

Although it would seem from the above that Serban was compromising on just three aspects of what had made *The Trilogy* so unique, *Agamemnon* added to Serban's reputation for producing Greek tragedy with dazzling spectacle and breathtaking stage imagery. Again, this was due in no small way to his design collaborators in addition to his choices in *mise-en-scène*. Douglas Schmidt's set made use of the ample netting imagery in the text. He essentially created a theatre-in-the-round, surrounding a pit which encompassed a huge, triangular steel cage to which the Chorus often descended. From *The Cherry Orchard* design team, Santo Loquasto again designed the costumes and Jennifer Tipton once more did the lighting. Loquasto's costumes were mostly simple muslin tunics and wraps, more reminiscent of Balkan peasants than conventional Greek tragedy. Tipton's lighting was both spectacular and spare, utilizing everything from spotlights to candles. There was a great deal of torchlight used in the production. So much open flame was used on stage that Loquasto eventually had to fireproof every single piece of clothing worn by the actors.

Serban chose to emphasize some elements of Greek tragedy staging—having the principal actors play more than one role, and using half-masks for them. The masks also aided the double casting of Smith as Clytemnestra and Cassandra and Jamil Zakkai as Agamemnon and Aegisthus. In contradiction to most traditional Greek theatre practice, Serban underscored much of the ritual violence on stage. He opened the play with a 45 minute pantomimed portrayal of the House of Atreus legend, including Agamemnon's sacrifice of Iphigenia and the start of the Trojan War. Previewing the entire action of the play in the manner of Elizabethan dumb show, Agamemnon ceremonially murdered Iphigenia by slowly touching her breast with a scroll. Clytemnestra then used the same scroll in the same fashion to kill Agamemnon before she in turn was executed by Orestis. These brief overall images concluded, Serban then utilized the Chorus to symbolically enact key images in the events leading up to Agamemnon's return to Thebes, all of which are only alluded to in Aeschylus' text. The Chorus had made its entrance from beneath the triangular shaped, steel grating net that covered the pit. The flames of their handheld torches and firepots flickered through the grating, eerily lighting the principal actors from below and playing perilously about their feet. Carrying over the net imagery from the text, Serban made great use of this prop in the prologue. Helen used it as a shawl to entice Paris, Paris used it to rope Helen off to Troy. Serban then staged the sacrifice of Iphigenia in a much more graphic style than the opening dumb show. Iphigenia (12 year old veteran of *The Trilogy*, Diane Lane[50]) was bound, gagged, and raised high in the air before being impaled belly down on the point of a sword. Wearing only a loin cloth (which would reappear on Agamemnon in his death in the bathtub at Clytemnestra's hands) the image was both sexual and Christ-like at the same time. Next came a movement sequence enacting the Trojan War as the Chorus moved about the stage battling with long sticks in stylized slow motion culminating in Menelaus using the same net to trap the Trojan army. Throughout all of these sequences, Swados' original Greek score provided a rich aural counterpoint.

Almost 45 minutes after the opening of the play, the Chorus paraded in a torchlighted procession from the triangular pit to the upstage section of the Beaumont stage. At this moment, the audience bleacher seats on the stage parted to reveal the huge doors of the palace. The narrative of Aeschylus' text began with the watchman's opening speech, the first use of English in the play. Perched way up on a door deep behind the proscenium arch of the Beaumont stage, his throaty whispers were in stark contrast to the cacophony of sound of the prologue. The rest of the play was staged in this more conventional fashion with the action taking place on the stage between the now parallel sections of the audience bleachers on the sides. Still, there were a few more arresting visual and aural images.

For her initial proper entrance, Priscilla Smith as Clytemnestra appeared directly up center in the palace door, high above the Chorus, bathed in a huge spotlight. When the messenger, bringing word of Agamemnon's imminent arrival, began his speech, it was repeated in a musical round fashion by several other chorus members giving an eerie echo effect that suggested the uncertainty of the events of the war. Agamemnon's entrance was deliberately muted. Without any procession, he appeared suddenly underneath Clytemnestra, standing on a small wooden platform, almost as if he were mounting the gallows or guillotine. Serban kept the confrontation scene between the two principals formal and pronounced. Like most of the play following the prologue, the text was delivered in English with occasional fragments of the ancient Greek. Finally, when Clytemnestra persuaded him to walk on the purple carpet, Jamil Zakkai walked backwards up the royal cloth that had been stretched before him into the palace. In Cassandra's vision, audiences witnessed Agamemnon murdered by Clytemnestra in his bath, once again using the same net.(See Figure #4) Apollo descended from the flies on a platform, clad only in a black loin cloth, and prodded Cassandra off to her death with a long spear. The final image of the play was Electra and Orestis standing in the grave of their father staring up at Clytemnestra and Aegisthus in the palace doorway.

Serban was also able to make use of some familiar faces from the La MaMa company in *Agamemnon*. In addition to Smith and Lane, Stuart Baker-Bergen, Jon De Vries, Natalie Gray, Charles Hayward, Onni Johnson, Jerry Cunliffe, Valois Mickens, and Justin Rashid all took roles in the Chorus. Jamil Zakkai, also in the original *Medea*, took over the roles of Agamemnon and Aegisthus when John Cazale was forced to leave the cast because of his illness. (Cazale died of cancer on March 12, 1978.)

The rehearsal period for *Agamemnon* was not always a smooth one. Perhaps it was the fact that Serban and some other members of the company were just coming off the pressure-filled atmosphere of *The Cherry Orchard* and going right into *Agamemnon*. In fact, as soon as *Agamemnon* opened, Serban and many of the very same actors went back into rehearsal for a somewhat revised version of *The Cherry Orchard* which re-opened at Lincoln Center in June, with a few cast changes. In any case, actor Rodney Hudson (Chorus) recalled the final days of rehearsal where tensions had increased to such a point that two women of the Chorus literally had a fist fight on stage at Lincoln Center:

> He (Serban) didn't stop it. He just watched it because it was that kind of primal kind of barbarian quality that was exactly what he wanted. I am not saying that he wanted those people to fight, but this was a manifestation of his saying you are not in New York working at the Beaumont. You are in ancient Greece where they sacrificed, where they will eat their children ... [51]

Still, Serban continued to experiment and improvise throughout the rehearsal period. Many of the striking images of the prologue developed from the company's division into small groups, each group improvising on sections of the House of Atreus legend. Always a keen editor of creative exploratory work, Serban would then select elements to be repeated and revised.

Agamemnon seemed to widen the "Serban split" in the critical community, where again, the issue remained the limits of re-interpretation, if any, imposed upon a director in staging a classical text. T.E. Kalem wrote in *Time*: "Revisionist drama has become the bane of the theatre. It is merciful that Shakespeare, Chekhov, and Aeschylus are not alive to view the bizarre "improvements" inflicted upon their classical works by the whims of directors like Peter Brook and Andrei Serban"[52] while Robb Baker, who had seen virtually every professional production directed by Serban in the U.S., declared it his masterpiece: "Serban is a giant and makes theatre for giants ... His productions are mythic, cosmic explorations ... so much so as to be wholly unaffected by the petty laws of human society."[53]

Agamemnon re-opened at the outdoor Delacorte Theatre in Central Park on August 16. Serban dropped his double casting concept. Now, Clytemnestra and Cassandra were played by separate actors (Gloria Foster and Dianne Wiest) as well as Agamemnon and Aegisthus (still Jamil Zakkai as Agamemnon and Ron O'Neal added as Aegisthus.) Foster had also asked Serban to restore more of the Hamilton English text and the outdoor stage forced a much simpler presentation than in Lincoln Center. Gone, of course, were the moveable bleachers, the audience on stage, and Apollo's "chariot". The steel net-like setting was replaced by the stark palace doors upstage. On the whole, the more conventional staging in the park was received quite favorably. Alan Wallach wrote in *Newsday*: "... director Andrei Serban has restaged the play, stripping away many of the directorial embellishments that had all but buried it at the Beaumont ... The speeches are spoken clearly, and the stark drama unfolds in a more linear fashion than at Lincoln Center"[54] while Mel Gussow observed in the *New York Times*: "... the play regains its passion and terror, the director reaffirms his position as a theatrical innovator *and* respecter of text ... the play is stripped to essentials."[55]

All in all, the summer of 1977 had indeed been a "summer of Serban." In August, *Vogue* had run a feature entitled "The Serban Takeover" calling him "the most robust directing force in the American theatre."[56] Meanwhile, in the headlines of *The Sunday New York Times*, Walter Kerr asked "Why? Why? Why? Why?" in response to Serban's Lincoln Center *Agamemnon*. Kerr's questions revolved around why Serban continuously sought to divert clarity and meaning from language with what the critic considered gratuitous sound and spectacle: "Andrei Serban's production of Aeschylus' *Agamemnon* at the Vivian Beaumont is visually provocative, systematically dehumanized, dramatically sterile; I don't think I've asked as many questions of a staging in the whole of my theatergoing life ..."[57] Two weeks later, in the very same pages, Yale Drama School Dean Robert Brustein defended Serban's vision:

> Mr. Kerr is confused by the loss of clarity in the verbal line, but Aeschylus's early drama is purposely obscure and image-laden; and Serban's use of illustrative dumb-show during the choral speeches, his dazzling transformations of the Beaumont space, and his inter-cutting of the English translation with ancient Greek, give us knowledge of the play where all great tragedy should reach us—in our veins, in our blood. Opinions of any production are bound to differ, but we should be grateful, rather than disappointed, that this one has managed to provoke us into questions.[58]

In fact, Serban spent the next year in residence as Associate Director at The Yale Repertory Theatre directing Strindberg's *The Ghost Sonata* and *Sganarelle: An Evening of Molière Farces* and would later find a semi-permanent home in Cambridge when Brustein founded the American Repertory Theatre. Brustein would be an enormous boost to Serban's career, giving him an outlet in which to work outside of New York.

Agamemnon further enhanced Serban's reputation as an innovative and controversial director. In retrospect, in some ways, it seemed like a more mainstream, uptown event for those who hadn't seen *The Trilogy*. Along with *The Cherry Orchard*, *Agamemnon* also made a significant impact in Serban's professional career. Both productions received enormous publicity, media attention, and heated critical debate in *The New York Times* and many other major newspapers and magazines. Compared to the audiences of 45 and 50 for *Medea* in the original La MaMa basement, they were seen by thousands of people at Lincoln Center.

But *Agamemnon* also represented another step for Serban as an interpreter of Greek tragedy. It was an attempt at producing the play on a far grander scale than he had in *The Trilogy*, akin to the level of opera, or, perhaps, the original Greek productions of 5th century Athens, simply by the nature of the size of the space, cast, audience, and stage effects. In this regard, Serban's *Agamemnon* was a departure from *The Trilogy* and akin to the work of some theatre experimentalists of the 1970s such as Robert Wilson and Richard Foreman working on a larger, primarily visual scale. Aeschylus' text itself is generally considered by many critics and classicists to be material of a more cosmic and supra-human nature than the later plays of Sophocles and Euripides which relate the stories of human individuals. This "more than human" experience which includes the "story of the cosmos, gods, and superhuman forces of which men are one part" is a theatre like the one Artaud proposed centuries later.[59] Hence, *Agamemnon* continued Serban's explorations of Artaud's theories not just through his methods of staging and work with actors, but through the text itself. While the production on such a grand scale left some audiences and critics cold and unaffected, Serban defended it, stating that emotion *was* his main concern and pointing to the large number of audience members who had written letters or visited backstage to report how much they'd been moved. Serban felt he had accomplished even more in this area in *Agamemnon* than in *The Cherry Orchard*.[61] In this sense, Serban's work differed from some of the other alternative theatre artists working on such a grand and imagistic scale in the late 1970s. Through the use of Greek tragedy, Serban remained committed to the exploration of public issues of the community, rather than some private or personal vision, conceived on a grand emotional scale.

It is perhaps in the nature of this emotion where one of Serban's prime legacies in staging Greek tragedy rests. Through his work with the *Trilogy* and *Agamemnon*, Serban had been using every theatrical means at his disposal in striving to *create* powerful emotions, not just *represent* them.[61] Early in his career, Serban had often referred to "the intelligence of emotion" as "trying to avoid the library—the mind, the intellect ... looking instead for the feeling, the emotions behind the works we do"[62] while after *Agamemnon* closed, he offered this on his attempts to use the Greek tragedies to create a direct emotional experience for the spectator:

> After all, what is emotion? What does it mean to be moved at the theatre? Is it to make you cry? A melodrama does that ... many films do that ... Or is it to discover in yourself a new way of receiving an experience through theatre? So unless I am moved in my usual ways—crying, handkerchief—then do I remain cold?[63]

Almost two decades later, Serban mused still on how the theatre can elicit this emotion: "What's the difference between a gesture that is sentimental and one that produces real feeling? What is the gesture that comes from the heart directly into the fingers of the hand?"[64]

It seems clear that in his staging of Greek tragedy Serban was after something larger, something more mythic than the traditional empathy with a character's situation as one might find in a realistic play. Through the use of powerful visual and aural imagery, Serban stirred the collective unconscious of his audience's imagination. He was able to unlock the incredible power in the ancient texts so the audiences could experience them viscerally, "in the life's blood", as Brustein had noted. Often working on a grand scale, and closely examining the role of the emotional aspects of the sounds of the ancient languages, Serban's Greek plays truly did create a sense of terror (if not pity) and awe for many. While the ritual origins of Greek tragedy may be debated by scholars, in some ways, Serban's productions restored the plays to their place as a way for a community to celebrate its relationship to the larger-than-life forces around us, whatever they may be, in a poetic fashion. Serban's Greek tragedies did not represent a linear narrative of the ancient myths and examine the problems of the characters from an informational standpoint; instead they acknowledged the mysteriousness of existence, invoked a sense of ceremony, and explored the possibilities of the powers residing in human speech. Serban was able to create a sense of wonder and astonishment through the plays that, for many, re-awakened them to not only the possibilities of the ancient texts, but also captured in some small way, an organic connection to the experience and an *energy,* for both performers and audience alike, perhaps not unlike what the theatre may have meant to our progenitors in 5th century Athens.

There are other aspects of Serban's legacy in Greek tragedy, of course. As noted Classics scholar Bernard Knox observed, Serban set standards in "richness of music, training of the chorus, ... clear delivery ..., the restraint of the actors ... against which future productions of Greek tragedy will be measured."[65] Too, Serban's ability to stage Greek tragedy using the theories of Artaud and what it meant in the context of the avant-garde theatre of the U.S. in the 1960s and 70s has already been discussed. Like the best work of his contemporaries, Peter Brook, Peter Stein, Peter Sellars, and JoAnne Akalaitis, the *Trilogy* and *Agamemnon* represent the product of a theatre/scholar director's research, conducted with living human subjects in the laboratory of the human stage. In Serban's case, his research and experiment with Greek tragedy had lasted six years from his initial involvement with Brook's *Orghast* in 1971 to his production of *Agamemnon* at Lincoln Center in 1977. (In 1991, Serban returned to Greek tragedy with a production of Euripides' *Hippolytos* at London's Almeida Theatre.)

No doubt there may also have been places where Serban's Greek tragedies fell short—perhaps in the over-reliance on spectacle and effect in *The Trojan Women* and *Agamemnon*, perhaps in an extreme and deep-seated Romantic mistrust of the written word or intellectual experience, or perhaps the emphasis of highly complex and interesting techniques of acting, staging, and music that ultimately distracted from the spectator's emotional involvement with the text in a more conventional sense.

But Andrei Serban's *Fragments of a Greek Trilogy* and *Agamemnon* remain pinnacles of achievement in the modern staging of Greek tragedy. Very few other contemporary directors, especially in the United States, have even attempted to investigate the scope of ancient tragedy in as much depth as Serban. What can a tragedy mean to an audience today? If, as Joseph Wood Krutch discusses in his influential essay "The Tragic Fallacy," that modern humankind lacks the nobility of spirit, confidence in its own greatness, and presumption of a moral order that came out of a celebration of a common belief system of the ancient world, then maybe Serban's distinct achievement with these plays, through the exploration of the ancient sounds and the evocative nature of his staging that emphasized theatricality itself, was to allow a brief glimpse into that world where that spirit *did* exist, where men and women did interact with the gods, and where we might feel some connection, no matter how vague, with the power and emotions that reside in these texts.

Notes

1. Antonin Artaud, *The Theatre and Its Double*, trans. Mary Richards, (New York: Grove Press, 1958) 78, 80, 82, 83.

2. Michael Feingold, "Toward a Pure Theatre," rev. of *Fragments of a Greek Trilogy*, *The Village Voice* 20 January 1987: 85.

3. Peter Brook, *The Shifting Point* (New York: Harper and Row, 1987) 110.

4. Ana Maria Narti, "*Medea*: Andrei Serban's Work on the Tragic Acting," thesis, Institute of Theatre & Film, Stockholm University, 1974.

5. Eileen Blumenthal, "Andrei Serban Makes Dead Languages Live Again," *The Village Voice* 26 January 1976: 107.

6. Robb Baker, "On Theatre: Andrei Serban—The Intelligence of Emotion," *The Soho Weekly News* 17 October 1974: 19.

7. Julius Novick, "Releasing the Cosmic Intensity of the Classics," *The New York Times* 18 January 1976: D4.

8. Arthur Bartow, *The Directors Voice: Twenty-one Interviews* (New York: Theatre Communications Group, 1988) 292.
9. Priscilla Smith, personal interview, 13 February 1990.
10. Narti 10.
11. Narti 6.
12. Narti 20.
13. Narti 20.
14. Smith.
15. Richard Eder, "Andrei Serban's Theatre of Terror and Beauty," *The New York Times Magazine* 13 February 1977: 46.
16. Diane Cartwright, "Priscilla Smith of The Great Jones Repertory Company," *The Drama Review* 20.3 (1976): 79.
17. Narti 16–17.
18. Clive Barnes, "Superb *Medea*," rev. of *Medea*, *The New York Times* 25 January 1972: 26.
19. Henry Hewes, "Subterranean Sounds Surfacing, rev. of *Medea*, *Saturday Review* 3 March 1972: 12.
20. "That's the only college that has invited me," Serban commented. Alan Wallach, "*Romeo and Juliet* Reaches New Heights," *Newsday* 16 February 1972.
21. Baker, "The Intelligence of Emotion," 19. In 1994, Serban added, "Brazil is a land where one can be fed by real magnet-like energy." Andrei Serban, letter to author, 7 June 1994.
22. Mel Gussow, "*Fragments*," rev. of *Fragments of a Greek Trilogy*, *The New York Times* 25 June 1974: 27.
23. Baker, "Catoptromanica," *The Soho Weekly News* 3 July 1974.
24. Theatre Program, *Fragments of a Greek Trilogy*, Cafe La MaMa, 1974.
25. Clive Barnes, "Serban's *Trilogy* is an Event," rev. of *Fragments of a Greek Trilogy*, *The New York Times* 20 October 1974: 64.
26. Douglas Watt, "La MaMa Gives Birth to a Bouncing Baby," *The Daily News* 20 October 1974: 120.
27. Stanley Kauffman, rev. of *Fragments of a Greek Trilogy*, *Persons of the Drama: Theater Criticism and Comment* (23 November, 1974; New York: Harper & Row, 1976): 111.
28. Clurman also expressed some doubt as to the emotional center of *The Trilogy*—especially in regard to the violence on stage and the superb visual and aural effects. He felt the plays were theatrically effective but lacked the ability to touch audiences in an organic way. Harold Clurman, rev. of *Fragments of a Greek Trilogy*, *The Nation* 18 January 1975: 58–60.
29. Smith.
30. Bartow 291.
31. Gussow, "*Greek Trilogy* Returns to La MaMa," rev. of *Fragments of a Greek Trilogy*, *The New York Times* 6 January 1987: C16.
32. Feingold 85.

33. Sylviane Gold, "Catharsis in a Modern Key," rev. of *Fragments of a Greek Trilogy*, *The Wall Street Journal* 20 February 1987: 19.

34. Only John Simon of *New York* remained steadfastly unsentimental, observing: "The trouble with *The Trilogy* lies in Serban's staggering lack of imagination." John Simon, "All Greek to Them," rev. of *Fragments of a Greek Trilogy*, *New York* 2 February 1987: 64.

35. Blumenthal 107.

36. It is possible that no other American experimental theatre group has received as much negative press as The Living Theatre. "Living Theatre bashing" is still much in vogue—a fairly recent example being Michael Patterson's book on German director Peter Stein where again and again they're used as an example of "how not to involve an audience." See pages 43, 94, and 104 in *Peter Stein: Germany's Leading Theater Director*. (Cambridge: Cambridge University Press, 1981).

37. Blumenthal 108.

38. Bartow 290.

39. Narti 91.

40. Smith.

41. Artaud 134.

42. Artaud 83.

43. Cartwright 82.

44. Novick, "La MaMa Rekindles the Fire of Ancient Greek Drama," *The New York Times* 17 November 1974: Sec. 2, 26.

45. Serban, "The Life In a Sound," trans. Eileen Blumenthal, *The Drama Review* 20.3 (1976): 26.

46. Margaret Croyden, "Seeking the Emotions that Stirred the Ancient Greeks," *The New York Times* 8 May 1977: D14.

47. Croyden 14.

48. Croyden 14.

49. Joseph Papp, telephone interview, 13 April 1990.

50. Lane had first appeared in *Medea* at age six—(she was always being killed in Serban's shows!)—and had also appeared as a little girl at the end of *The Cherry Orchard*. Twelve years later, she would take time off from her busy film and television schedule to play Olivia in Serban's production of *Twelfth Night* at The American Repertory Theatre.

51. Rodney Hudson, personal interview, 15 December 1989.

52. T.E. Kalem, "Vandal Sacks Atreus," rev. of *Agamemnon*, by Aeschylus, *Time* 30 May 1977: 76.

53. Baker, *Soho Weekly News* 30 May 1977.

54. Alan Wallach, rev. of *Agamemnon*, by Aeschylus, *Newsday* 18 August 1977: Sec. 3, 18.

55. Gussow, rev. of *Agamemnon*, by Aeschylus, *The New York Times* 18 August 1977: Sec. 3, 18.

56. Leonid Lubianitsky, "The Serban Takeover," *Vogue* August 1977: 152.

57. Walter Kerr, "Andrei Serban's *Agamemnon*: Why? Why? Why? Why?," *The New York Times* 29 May 1977: Sec. 2, 3.

58. Robert Brustein, "Defending Serban's Vision of Aeschylus," letter, Theatre Mailbag, *The New York Times* 12 June 1977: 3, 9.

59. John Herrington, *Aeschylus* (New Haven: Yale University Press, 1986) 12–14.

60. Dean Drury, "Andrei Serban," *Keynote* July 1977: 4.

61. Bartow 287.

62. Baker, "The Intelligence of Emotion," 18.

63. Drury 13.

64. Serban, letter to author, 7 June 1994.

65. Bernard Knox, rev. of *Agamemnon*, by Aeschylus, *New York Review of Books* 14 July 1977; reprinted in *Word and Action: Essays on the Ancient Theater* (Baltimore: Johns Hopkins Press, 1979): 78.

2

Serban and Chekhov

IN 1987, Serban told dramaturg Jonathan Marks: "I will always be nothing less than an artist in exile; and for me, doing Chekhov is like going home. He is very dear, very intimate to me; I see my own family, my relatives, the way I grew up."[1]

Certainly, Serban's Chekhov cycle, beginning with *The Cherry Orchard* at Lincoln Center for The New York Shakespeare Festival in 1977, followed by *The Seagull* at The Public Theatre for NYSF in 1980, *Three Sisters* at the American Repertory Theatre in 1982, and ending with *Uncle Vanya* at La MaMa in 1983, attests to his love and passion for the great Russian playwright. Serban's productions of Chekhov's major plays also did something else. They helped point the way for American audiences, critics, and theatre practitioners to an essentially new way of producing Chekhov: a style which is much more metaphorical than domestically realistic, considerably much more visually lyrical than pictorially illusionistic, and much more humorous, even farcical, than the sober Chekhov that Americans were used to seeing. Often, in Serban's productions, there was a very bold and quite physical acting style, especially in *The Cherry Orchard*. Certainly the designs were much more evocative than representational—from Santo Loquasto's "white" *Cherry Orchard* to the same designer's wooden labyrinth of ramps and platforms for *Uncle Vanya*; this was "Chekhov without walls." Always, there was great and careful attention to the text of Jean-Claude van Itallie's four adaptations in an attempt to penetrate to the heart of Chekhov's poetry in a new and vital way. In short, through his stagings, Serban attempted to find the poetry in Chekhov and, in some sense, freed Chekhov from the "museum prison" of nineteenth century, "heavy" domestic naturalism. Since the first performances of Chekhov by an American company (The Washington Square Players production of *The Seagull* in 1916) this domestic naturalism had been the traditional style in which to stage his plays.

Serban removed Chekhov from the realistic domain of Stanislavsky and placed him in the metaphorical realm of Meyerhold. Visually, this metaphorical realm allowed Serban to develop two other techniques in staging Chekhov throughout his cycle of the four plays: a progressively reductive scenic metaphor throughout the course of the play, and, simultaneously, a more fluid, cinematic approach. The first technique simply means a gradual simplifying and removal of the scenic elements onstage throughout the course of Chekhov's four-act structure, until the last act is played basically an empty stage. The second technique encompasses the first and with the addition of music, tableaux, slow motion movement, and recorded sound allowed Serban to achieve what Peter Brook has called "the beauty of a film ... a succession of natural, true images" in describing Chekhov's poetry. We shall see how Serban developed and varied these techniques in looking at the Chekhov cycle in the order in which he directed the plays: *The Cherry Orchard, The Seagull, Three Sisters*, and *Uncle Vanya*.

The Cherry Orchard —New York Shakespeare Festival, The Vivian Beaumont Theatre at Lincoln Center, 1977

Serban very much felt that he was returning to the spirit of the author's intention with all of the productions of his Chekhov cycle. The best example was *The Cherry Orchard*. Stanislavsky's tragic interpretation in the original Moscow Art Theatre production of 1904, despite Chekhov's insistence that it was a comedy, "in places, even a farce," is well-chronicled. Serban took absolutely seriously Chekhov's direction that the entire fourth act should "be merry and indeed the whole play should be merry and giddy ... An act that ought to take no more than twelve minutes lasts forty ... Stanislavsky has ruined my play ..."[2] So it is ironic that, despite the many good reviews Serban's Chekhov cycle garnered, particularly *The Cherry Orchard*, there were the usual critical reactions that Serban was destroying the plays and intentions of "Chekhov the Master." Serban explained his philosophy in an open letter to *The New York Times*, answering some of the critics of *The Cherry Orchard*:

> With Chekhov's own ideas in mind, I have tried to give my impression of his characters and of that particular moment of change. Because I love Chekhov and the play, I am moved to do it as it strikes me, in a more whole way, not treating it as a museum piece, but as a living, human situation. In this effort to serve Chekhov, I feel an enormous excitement.[3]

Joe Papp signed Serban to direct *The Cherry Orchard* and *Agamemnon* for The New York Shakespeare Festival for productions in the Winter and Spring of 1977. Both plays would eventually be revived, the latter at the Delacorte Theatre as part of the NYSF free summer season in Central Park. As it turned out, *The Cherry Orchard* would have the honor of being the last NYSF production at Lincoln Center as Papp returned his company downtown to The Public Theater in August. In any case, 1977 was essentially "the Year of Serban" as it marked his explosion onto the American mainstream theatrical scene—bigger, more expensive productions, the "best" and biggest facilities, and working with major American "stars" for the first time.

A glance at the cast of *The Cherry Orchard* confirms this. After almost seven years of working with the actors at La MaMa, many of them young, struggling performers trying to make a living in the alternative theatre scene, Serban found himself directing Irene Worth as Mme. Ranevskaya, Raul Julia as Lopakhin, Mary Beth Hurt as Anya, George Voskovec as Gayev, and Meryl

Streep as Dunyasha. Serban did manage to bring in three members of the Great Jones Company—Priscilla Smith would play Varya, and Jon De Vries and William Duff-Griffin would play the small roles of the vagrant and the stationmaster. There was a new "translation" of the play used; the English version was written by Jean-Claude van Itallie, author of *The Serpent*, and former playwright of Joe Chaikin's Open Theatre. The sets and costumes were designed by Santo Loquasto and the lighting was by Jennifer Tipton, again significantly bigger "names" in the design world than Serban's previous collaborators, primarily Jun Maeda, at La MaMa. Incidental music was composed by Liz Swados.

The Cherry Orchard was Serban's first engagement with Chekhov, although Serban had seen Chekhov performed in Romania on a regular basis. Two productions in particular influenced him in regards to how Chekhov should be staged—one Romanian, the other American. The former was a production of *The Cherry Orchard* directed by Serban's fellow countryman Lucian Pintilie which Serban described as "quite revolutionary for its time. It was the first Chekhov staging in Romania to break away from the walls and windows of Stanislavskyan naturalism and see the plays in a more open light."[4] The latter was Chekhov's rarely performed *Ivanov*, staged by British director Ron Daniels and designed by Michael Yeargan at the Yale Repertory Theatre in 1976. Yeargan's semi-realistic set suggested interiors and exteriors through a series of framed doors and curtains and the cast included Alvin Epstein, Jeremy Geidt, and Robert Brustein. "It was a very direct and honest production, one of the most successful Chekhov stagings I've seen," Serban commented.[5]

Most of all, Serban acknowledged the influence of Vsevolod Meyerhold in his production of *The Cherry Orchard*.[6] In Serban's own words, "The production created an enormous controversy among the New York elite, since it was conceived upon Meyerhold's critical observations of Stanislavsky's famous 1904 production."[7] And exactly what had Meyerhold said about Stanislavsky's interpretation? In his 1906 essay "The Naturalistic Theatre and the Theatre of Mood," Meyerhold noted that Stanislavsky had destroyed the overall harmony of Act III:

> The author intended the act's leitmotiv to be Ranevskaya's premonition of an approaching storm (the sale of the cherry orchard.) Everybody else is behaving as though stupefied: they are dancing happily to the monotonous tinkling of the Jewish band, whirling around as if in the vortex of a nightmare ... They do not realize the ground on which they are dancing is subsiding under their feet. Ranevskaya alone foresees the disaster; she rushes back and forth, then briefly halts the revolving wheel, the nightmare dance of the puppet show ... The director (*Stanislavsky) ... makes an entire scene of the conjuring (*Charlotta's trick for Pischik) ... it is long and complicated. The spectator concentrates his attention on it for so long ... he loses the act's

leitmotiv ... The naturalistic theatre has conducted a never-ending search for the fourth wall which has led it into a whole series of absurdities. The theatre fell into the hands of fabricants who tried to make everything "just like real life" and turned the stage into some sort of antique shop.

Earlier, in a letter to Chekhov concerning his own production of the play, just shortly after the Moscow Art Theatre's premiere, Meyerhold observed:

Your play is *abstract* ... a Tchaikovsky symphony. Before all else, the director must get the "sound" of it. In the third act, against a background of the stupid stamping of feet—this "stamping" is what we must hear—enters Horror, completely unnoticed by the guests. "The cherry orchard is sold." They dance on. "Sold." Still they dance ... When one reads the play, the third act produces the same effect as the ringing in the ears of the sick man in your story *Typhus* ... Jollity with overtones of death. In this act, there is something terrifying, something Maeterlinckian ...[8] (italics mine).

So Serban set out consciously to contradict Stanislavsky, who had set the standard for all tragic, sorrowful interpretations of the *The Cherry Orchard*, and return the play to the comic and theatrical vision of Meyerhold. Helping him to achieve this were designers Loquasto and Tipton.

Actually, first and foremost in helping Serban achieve this goal was the enormous size of the Vivian Beaumont Theatre in Lincoln Center. Long considered a "white elephant" theatre with acoustical and sightline problems that had sunk many a previous attempt at repertory at Lincoln Center, Serban and Loquasto, instead, embraced the size of the stage and even accentuated it. They opened up the gigantic stage to its fullest extent and used the maximum depth and height of the stage house. With no attempt at individualizing four realistic environments as had usually been the custom in producing the play, Loquasto and Serban completely covered the huge stage with thick white carpet and a great, white cyclorama at the rear of the stage stretching beyond sightlines. The overall impression was one of an enormous vast, white space, without any walls or realistic rooms. Instead, a few pieces of furniture were brought in for the nursery of Act I, Act II began with peasants hauling a huge plow behind the scrim, the ballroom of Act III was represented by a small, cylinder-like gazebo structure which rotated like a carousel, as Serban evidently sought to make use of Meyerhold's comments on the revolving wheel and the nightmare dance of the puppet show, while Act IV took place on the immense bare, white, blank stage. Each act proceeded through a reduction of physical elements that culminated with the vast emptiness of the Vivian Beaumont stage. Often, there were projections of images behind a scrim, such as rows and rows of cherry trees in Act I and smoky factories and telegraph poles to represent industrialized Russia in Act II.

Serban also staged a series of friezes and images behind the scrim including Mme. Ranevskaya's drowned son, Grisha, walking through the orchard in Act I and a series of articles of furniture in Act IV, held high in the air as they were carried out, the effect resulting in a look of "floating on air" for curtain rods, rocking horses, and even pianos. Serban also made use of slow motion, silhouette figures behind the scrim, asides to the audience while the rest of the actors froze, and a complex "stop and go" waltz in Act III that was carefully choreographed by Kathryn Posin to achieve the whirling, nightmare effect in Meyerhold's notes. Finally, in a breathtaking image that was hotly debated by many as gratuitous, a lovely little girl (played by *Trilogy* veteran Diane Lane) delivered a sprig of cherry blossoms to Firs on a totally empty stage at the end of the play. Serban defended this image as a "metaphor of change."[9]

Joe Papp believed it was Serban's use of the space of the Beaumont theatre that was the single greatest attribute of this landmark production. "He took a small, proscenium play and made it work in a large, unusual space."[10] Serban himself insisted that he was used to such large spaces from the theatres in Europe: "Playing in Europe we have worked in much larger areas. In ruins, in fields. That's how we learned to use space. As soon as I saw the theatre, I knew what I wanted to do. In five minutes."[11]

The entire look of *The Cherry Orchard* was white, snowy, dreamy, poetic, even spiritual; and Serban, in effect, "played against" this very beautiful vision with a very physical, often farcical vaudeville acting style, which was reminiscent of Meyerhold's theories of Biomechanics. Possibly the most famous example of this in the production was Meryl Streep's Dunyasha, considered by many to be a tour-de-force of commedia dell'arte. Streep fainted dead-away when Yasha kissed her in Act I, played a major portion of Act II with her petticoats around her ankles, and literally tackled Yasha to the ground in the final act. Dwight Marfield's Firs was possibly the spryest 87 year old valet ever, making his first entrance improvising a little dance in his 18th century costume; later on in Act II, he spiritedly chased George Voskovec as Gaev around a bench in an effort to force him to put on his coat. Cathryn Damon's Charlotta was "a bizarre Fellini-style governess"[12] complete in Harlequin outfit and clown-white face. As the clumsy clerk, Yepikhodov, Max Wright managed some hilarious business in Act II, entangling himself in his guitar strap while attempting to pull his pistol from his belt. When (Lopakhin) Raul Julia announced that he'd bought the orchard at the end of Act III, he shouted and strode about the stage, tossing chairs, while Irene Worth, as Mme. Ranevskaya, lay full length on the white floor in a black gown, sobbing.

It was Worth who had prevailed upon Papp to secure Serban to direct *The Cherry Orchard* and her performance as the queenly landowner was the centerpiece of the production. In 1977, it would have been hard to find another actress more universally respected in the American theatre community and press than Worth. She was generally acknowledged to be one of America's finest classical actresses, so highly respected, as a matter of fact, that it was widely assumed by some

Anglophile theatre critics that she was British. She was born in Nebraska, grew up in California, but had studied and performed a great deal with The Old Vic and Royal Shakespeare Company in Great Britain. At the same time, she'd often scorned working in so-called "commercial vehicles" and had played Goneril in Peter Brook's *King Lear* with Paul Scofield and also had worked with Brook on *Orghast* which is where she first met Serban. Worth's Ranevskaya was praised even by those who mourned that Serban had desecrated Chekhov's text and Worth always publicly defended Serban's concept and methods.

One of Worth's moments epitomized Serban's ultra-physical approach to the acting style, so clearly a derivative of Meyerhold. At the very end of the play, when she was about to make her final exit from the "house" with her brother Gaev, instead of the usual tearful, subdued departure, Worth slowly began to move around the entire space of the Beaumont stage, gradually picking up speed until it was a full-tilt run; she circled the stage over and over, laughing joyously, literally *inhaling* the space of the "room" for her final goodbye. (See Figure #5) Walter Kerr called this exit one of the at least five images he would never forget from the production as long as he lived.[13] In an interview a month after the play opened, Worth said that she could no longer remember whether this exit was originally her idea or Serban's but commented:

> The last farewell to the room and to the house is almost unbearable for Ranevskaya because it's going to be torn down, and she feels that her roots are gone ... And they will be gone, and she has precious few roots. There certainly are no roots in the love affair. The future's fairly bleak. But I feel that she does leave with a kind of joy, because her daughter Anya says "we can plant another orchard"—meaning life must renew itself, you must not look back, you must not repine, you must go on ... This is how I've chosen to do the last farewell—Ranevskaya hears her daughter calling, she's in despair, she feels her life is at an end ... The very last farewell I give to the room is a kind of farewell to that part of my life which is over with, but I look forward with joy, as my daughter has said. Perhaps it's an unthinking joy that fills her in praise and gratitude for what she has already had. She is a resilient woman ...[14]

Eleven years later, Serban told Arthur Bartow that the image came from the text for somewhat different reasons:

> (The idea) came from my feeling that Madame Ranevskaya knows that death is coming. At the end of the play everything is taken away, there is no house, there is nothing, there is an empty stage. She will only go back to Paris, back to the old lover, back to decay, decadence, death—all the big "Ds". So when she comes back into the room, just before leaving the house, there is this one moment of remembering. It's in the

text. She feels like a little girl looking for her mother. "I feel the steps of my mother. Here they are." As she says that, she starts to walk as if trying to smell traces of where mother would have walked, like an animal. And by doing that she leashes an extraordinary positive energy for a new beginning. Although she is old and not far from death, she walks in a way that brings back all her childhood again. So there is this conflict between defeat and possibility, age and the fact that although Irene Worth was an aging actress, she became like a young person again. It was a very moving upbeat, fresh exit rather than a more traditional, melancholic end.[15]

Both passages are quoted in full, not to attempt to prove "whose idea" it was, but to point out the difference in the motivation of performers and directors and also to demonstrate Serban's ability to stage a scene based on a carefully discovered and justified nuance of the text that most directors simply do not find. In all of the criticism and analyses I've read of *The Cherry Orchard*, and all of the productions I have seen of the play, only Serban discovered the psychological and spiritual connection that Ranevskaya feels with her mother at that final moment and only Serban put it on the stage. Indeed this connection has been building since Act I with Ranevskaya's vision of her mother walking through the orchard "all in white." (Serban also included this moment in his *mise-en-scène*.)

Worth had other moments of great feeling and "psychological realism" in the play. Serban's visual and metaphorical approach did not, as some critics claimed, rob the actors of "their moments." For instance, in Act II, when she tore up her lover's telegram from Paris, she did it so slowly and with such anguish, that many members of the audience involuntarily gasped.[16]

Worth greatly respected Serban's methods of improvisation in rehearsal. She included a moment in performance from an animal improvisation where she had hissed at Trofimov (played by Pulitzer prize winning playwright Michael Cristofer) as a swan: "... I suddenly was a swan on the attack, and I began to peck at him with my beak and chased him around and suddenly I went 'Pssss' ... And I kept that in from the improvisation. I would never have had the courage or the imagination to do that otherwise, and it works, doesn't it?"[17]

Again, Serban's comments eleven years later to Bartow:

She was very sensitive to images. For example, I kept telling her that Meyerhold, being very upset with the way that Stanislavsky produced *Cherry Orchard*, had said that the staging was totally wrong: the third act is a dance of death. The people are partying. They're dancing and dancing, waiting for news that the cherry orchard has been sold. The dance develops into a frenzy which develops into a nightmare. The orchard has been sold! The dance of death! so Meyerhold went on to say, "This is a ceremony. This is something much higher than a small realistic dance in a village. It's about apocalypse." So I told Irene Worth of an image from Meyerhold: I told her she was like a swan, a black swan trying regally to hold her neck up but, in fact, underneath that she was doing a tragic, violent swan dance. She immediately started the improvisation and her body just took off, lifted. It was extraordinary.[18]

"To see Irene rolling on the floor was something," Papp commented on one rehearsal.[19]

Other improvisations used by Serban were an exercise in which the stage managers read the text while the actors mimed the actions, a standard Stanislavsky-type imagination exercise on the given circumstances of everyone's first entrance in Act I ("Who met them at the station? Who did they sit with in the carriage? How did it feel to see the orchard? To smell the orchard?"), and improvising the "fifth act" of the play after the text ends. According to Serban, "Varya becomes a nun, but a *true* nun. Trofimov becomes a Leninist and swallows up Lopakhin. And Yasha becomes a Stalinist and swallows up Trofimov."[20]

Serban later said that none of the actors had any problems with such methods of rehearsal, which, although not terribly unorthodox, were still not the usual fare for a "Broadway, big name" production. Although this harmony has been somewhat disputed by some in the production, the fact remains that, somehow, Serban was able to get these "big names" to be a part of his vision and that most of the reaction, both popular and critical, was euphoric, if not controversial.

There were many who considered Serban's tactics as destroying the purity of Chekhov's text, while others hailed it as a brilliant, innovative and beautiful vision that somehow penetrated the spirit of the play. This controversy was fought in the pages of *The New York Times* and other newspapers, magazines, and journals for quite some time with John Simon of *The New Leader* leading the way for the outraged: "The production is consistently coarse, vulgar, cretinous, and a total betrayal of Chekhov's basic simplicity"[21] and "We are not interested in the truth as a Romanian parvenu pipsqueak sees it. We're interested in the truth as the great master Chekhov saw it"[22] and Clive Barnes defending the production and Serban as "a collaboration of genius, like the cleaning of a great painting, a fresh exposition of an old philosophy ... this lyric poem of Russia on the eve of the revolution has never been funnier, more tragic or more moving ... The State Department should send it instantly to its spiritual home, the Moscow Art Theatre."[23] Even Serban himself joined the battle of words in print, responding to some particularly critical comments in the Theatre Mailbag of *The New York Times* with a letter in which he defended his production, already quoted in the beginning of this chapter.

The Cherry Orchard was revived later in the summer of 1977, after consistently playing to sold-out houses. One summer revival performance was played in candlelight due to the power failure and blackout in the East that summer. Serban re-staged it slightly for the re-opening on June 28. Although some of the cast changes weakened the production, especially Christine Estabrook replacing Meryl Streep, some critics felt that Priscilla Smith and Raul Julia had grown tremendously in their roles of Varya and Lopakhin.[24]

The play was nominated for a number of Tony awards, including Most Innovative Production of a Revival, and Santo Loquasto did win for his costume design as did Jennifer Tipton for her lighting design. Irene Worth was also nominated for Best Actress. Serban was also invited to stage his *Cherry Orchard* at the Shiki Theatre in Tokyo, so in many ways, as Joe Papp noted much later, *The Cherry Orchard* remains one of Serban's strongest and most important productions, simply because it was seen by so many thousands of people, and because of the distinctive use of the space.[25] In a frank acknowledgement of his attempts to stage Chekhov with the fluidity of film, Serban reflected that he had learned from the production to "try to be freer than I was. More cinematic."[26]

And yet, Serban himself seemed somewhat dissatisfied with it a scant three years later.[27] In 1980, Serban saw Peter Brook's production of *The Cherry Orchard* at the Bouffes du Nord in Paris. In his book *The Shifting Point*, Brook writes "It's wrong to conclude that *The Cherry Orchard* should be performed as a vaudeville."[28] Serban was completely won over by Brook's lack of visual effects, the simplicity of the actors, the text, and a completely bare stage and commented: "It was much more powerful because it was the theatre itself. So what you had in that empty space was a group of actors in a direct relationship with the text and the audience and, really, the play was there. You didn't need anything more"[29] and later concluded "I thought that my *Cherry Orchard*, in relation to his, was not all that revolutionary."[30]

Priscilla Smith, who played Varya opposite Raul Julia's Lopakhin in Serban's *Cherry Orchard* also told this story when seeing Brook's production:

> Although I had been in the play for months and months, when I saw Peter's production, it was a revelation. Lopakhin, for example, was the antithesis of the beautiful and charming Raul Julia. He was an awkward, little peasant humbly hoping to buy admission into his own childhood dreams of the good life. There is a moment when Varya throws the keys to the house at his feet. I had always played it as generalized petulance, but in Peter's production, I understood the gesture for the first time. As vulnerable as this girl is—she is adopted and has been little more than a servant—she considers herself above this lumpish man. She is saying, "You may own the property, but don't think I come along with the house." I had never grasped the painful absurdity of this relationship when I played the role. Maybe the audience did, but from my perspective, Raul was just too far beyond the reach of poor Varya.[31,32]

Serban, however, had reached a turning point in his ideas on staging Chekhov. In response to the plethora of "white Chekhovs" that were seen in the late 70s and early 80s in Europe and the U.S., he vowed:

> I never want to do Chekhov like that again. Because looking back on it now, the whiteness creates a false sensation. It really beautifies Russia, and I don't think there's anything beautiful about Russia in that way. I come from Romania and know what the countryside is like—the dust, the mud, the coarseness, and poverty, it's nothing beautiful. It's the beauty of the characters, what they try to achieve, what they try to become. That's where the beauty is, it's not at all in the surroundings. Most of the productions in the last five years have tried to beautify Chekhov, to beautify the set in particular and in general make things more aesthetic. There's no reason to do that.[33]

And yet, Serban's next Chekhov production was also very beautiful.

The Seagull—Shiki Theatre, Tokyo & New York Shakespeare Festival, 1980

Serban directed *The Seagull* twice in 1980. The first was at the Shiki Theatre in Tokyo during the summer. Upon his return to the United States in the fall, he directed it again for Papp's New York Shakespeare Festival now housed exclusively in the Public Theatre downtown. Serban had already re-staged his *Cherry Orchard* for the Shiki Theatre in 1978. When Keita Asari of the Shiki, whom Serban described as "sort of the Joe Papp of Japan," saw *The Cherry Orchard* at Lincoln Center, he insisted that Serban not change a thing in the Tokyo production. He wanted Japanese audiences to see *that* production. Serban noted: "I would have changed a lot if it had been up to me."[34] In a sense, Serban had the opposite experience with *The Seagull*. With this play, he would direct the initial production in Japan, then re-do it in New York.

Although the primary concern here is the American production, some discussion of the Japanese staging is important, not only for its comparative value to the American, but also in regard to the development of Serban's methods of directing Chekhov. (I'm indebted to Laurence Shyer's article "Andrei Serban Directs Chekhov: *The Seagull* in New York and Japan" in *Theater*, 1981, v. 13.1, p. 56–66, for his contribution to this discussion.)

As is so often the case with Serban, he went in "a totally different direction" from the stylized and metaphorical *Cherry Orchard* with *The Seagull* in Japan. Perhaps it was because the play was presented in Japanese which Serban did not speak and therefore there was an emphasis on the physical details of the production. It was almost as if Serban were experimenting with every possible naturalistic method of staging in order to conduct some sort of test on how far one could go in that direction. He and designer Kaoru Kanamuri fashioned a setting of real rocks, real trees, real grass and flowers, and, most realistic of all, a lake in the middle of the stage in which Kanamuri placed a large platform in the shape of a seagull. This is where Treplev's play would take place. Serban was in an unusual situation at the Shiki. There was no lack of funding. Every idea was indulged:

> There was an immense pond of water, perhaps two or three feet deep ... then the whole area was covered with birch trees which were multiplied in a huge reflective wall at the back of the stage. It was all so naturalistic. In the first act, Yakov and the other workmen actually went swimming in the lake and came out dripping with water. There were flowers, real rocks, grass and even dead trees in the water ... I tell you, it was so damn naturalistic there were offstage machines creating waves (in the last act). It really was like a film on stage. It had no mystery, but it certainly had waves ... The lake became blacker and more dangerous ...[35]

Serban's fascination with an abundance of naturalistic detail and the decision to treat the "magic lake" as the primary symbol of the play had its origin in two sources. The first was an aborted project of *The Seagull* at the Yale Repertory Theatre which Serban was supposed to direct for the 78–79 season, before he committed to an exclusive contract for Papp. In the planning stages for the production, Serban seized upon the lake as the central image:

> I was hoping to explore the magnetism of the lake, its power, its depth and the attraction to what we cannot see. Everyone in the play is really hypnotized by the lake. They say, "Oh, magic lake." It's a mystery really, what is at the bottom of that lake and what is hidden in us. So I thought that seeing the lake, seeing the water and imagining its depths would give me, as it might in cinema, the perfect impression.[36]

Though Serban's production at Yale was never realized, Robert Brustein eventually directed the play there with a similar emphasis on the lake as created in a mylar covered stage by designer Michael Yeargan. Brustein directed the entire play as if it were a "dream play" written by Treplev in the manner of Maeterlinck; ironically, Richard Eder in *The New York Times* criticized it for attempting to imitate Serban's *Cherry Orchard*.

The second source for Serban was Stanislavsky himself and his notes in staging the original Moscow Art Theatre production of the play. Stanislavsky had a great influence on Serban's concept of the acting style. Serban did not overload the actors with vast amounts of stage business uncalled for by the playwright as Stanislavsky had. He still felt, as Meyerhold had, that the best way to approach Chekhov's texts was to be very sensitive to changes in the rhythm and musicality of the language. But he did attempt to penetrate to the core of realistic acting with his Japanese actors, using many Stanislavsky based improvisations and exercises in psychological realism in rehearsal. Here Serban expanded upon the types of exercises he had done with the cast of *The Cherry Orchard*. A number of rehearsals were held outside by a real lake, with the actors improvising in character. Treplev and his crew actually constructed the outdoor stage for his play. Arkadina and her entourage made their first entrance, improvising upon the given circumstances along the way to the stage. Serban describes what happened next:

> As they arrived at Treplev's stage, the sun was setting over the lake. It was an amazing moment. It's believed that many of the lakes in Japan are inhabited by strange monsters and we were all strangely touched by that superstition. The moment the night came was so powerful and dramatically charged. There was a sudden change in the light, in the very air and this was reflected in all the actors. But we could never put it on the stage. Our lighting designer was there and he later tried to recapture the remarkable mood but somehow it never worked. That same evening, the actors performed Treplev's play on the makeshift stage by the light of the moon.[37]

A few days later, the actors improvised on the given circumstances of Act II. In an attempt to capture the feeling of the hot, lazy afternoon, the actors sprawled about on a sandy beach, eating, drinking, fishing, and just lazing about. Again, Serban's comments:

> The exercise took about two hours and during that time nothing really happened. But it was most interesting to watch the Japanese actors trying to depict Western *ennui*. They put so much concentration into it that even their boredom became intense and powerful. They did the improvisation very well. Again we tried to recapture the original sensation in performance but were only sporadically successful.[38]

Although Serban seems to have mixed feelings about the Japanese *Seagull* in performance, it was an important step in his Chekhov cycle for a number of reasons. First, he proved to himself once and for all that the three dimensional, naturalistic clutter and detail was not necessary for staging Chekhov. He also plumbed the psychological depths of the characters in a detailed Stanislavskyan sense. Perhaps the language barrier made it even more of a challenge to rehearse in this particular fashion. But it also did something else. It reinforced Serban's feeling that in Chekhov, indeed, in perhaps all theatre, the immediate and sometimes most provoking and emotional messages we receive from a text are primarily non-verbal. Serban recalled that he rarely used his interpreter in rehearsal, instead communicating by gesture and vocal inflection. Once when he faulted the actress playing Arkadina for a speech that just didn't sound right to him, the cast thought it was very funny that Serban should criticize their phrasing: "But instinctively I had been right because she changed the speech and it was much better. You can immediately sense an actor's excellence, it has nothing to do with words, it's something else. I'm convinced that what we receive most immediately is non-verbal."[39]

Choosing to do Chekhov in another language was scarcely an accident. Serban attempted to find the hidden poetry in the text and stage it in a fashion that sometimes did not rely on words. Perhaps the best example of this in the Japanese *Seagull* was the ending when Treplev shoots himself. Instead of being restricted to an off-stage incident, Treplev first tore up all of his manuscripts and then threw them in the lake, turning the water almost completely white from the bits of the torn pages. Then when he killed himself, he fell face down in the lake amongst the bits of torn paper.

Finally, *The Seagull* in Japan, once again, confirmed Serban's cinematic approach to Chekhov. As we have seen, Brook compared Chekhov's poetry with the beauty of film's "succession of natural, true images." Brook continues the comparison:

> Chekhov is a perfect film maker. Instead of cutting from one image to another—perhaps from one place to another—he switches from one emotion to another just before it gets too heavy. At the precise moment when the spectator risks becoming too involved in a character, an unexpected situation cuts across: nothing is stable.[40]

As he had done in *The Cherry Orchard*, Serban searched for and staged what he felt were the visual images that corresponded to the emotions that resided in the text. The difference between the two productions is like that of an impressionist painting and a photograph of the same subject. One is light, airy, and even dream-like and is quite *selective* in the visual detail that the spectator is allowed to see. The other is realistic and, in the words of Serban, contains a "heavy feeling", and shows the spectator everything. Assuming Brook's comparison of Chekhov to a film maker, perhaps Serban's *Cherry Orchard* made greater use of Serban's visualizing of "the cutting of one emotional image to the other" than he did in his Japanese *Seagull*. In response to a question from Laurence Shyer as to whether he would be interested in making a film version of *The Seagull*, Serban answered : "I don't know. A film version of *The Seagull* by a real lake would be so banal."[41] Nevertheless, Serban's Chekhov cycle continued to be cinematic in many ways.

The New York production may have represented to Serban an opportunity to explore the nuances of the language that he couldn't do with Japanese actors. This may explain why some critics were surprised by what they felt was the subdued mood of the New York *Seagull* (especially for Serban!), although it was still visually very beautiful. When Michael Yeargan asked Serban if he wanted to duplicate the setting of the Japanese production, naturally Serban wanted to go in a new direction. The lake was not represented on stage, but instead in the imagination of the actors and audience. (As a matter of fact, the imaginary direction of the lake seemed to shift in Act I from the upstage to the direction of the audience.) Instead, Yeargan designed a simple setting of blond, polished wood plank floor with a raised bridge in the background that was the primary entrance and exit for the actors. In Act I, there were some ferns around the stage floor, plus a few chairs and a small raised stage for Treplev's play. Act II utilized a hammock, a table and a few chairs; in Act III a series of double-door arched flats, a stove, and a couple of tables were used to represent the interior of the house; Act IV contained a few other pieces of furniture with the center arch flats removed, revealing the bridge in the background. All was usually brightly lighted by lighting designer Jennifer Tipton. The polished wood, the use of the bridge which was visually reminiscent of the hashigakari or hanamichi of the Japanese Noh and Kabuki theatres, the small wooden stage for Treplev, also sometimes associated with classical Japanese theatre, the use of the curtain for the small proscenium stage of the Newman Theatre at The Public, and, above all, the overall austere look of the production gave a distinctly "Japanese look" to the play. The irony is that most of the critics assumed that Serban had brought this very Japanese look back intact from his Tokyo production which, in fact, was actually a classic example of Western, three dimensional naturalism. As Serban said, "It's funny but the production in New York was much more Japanese than the one in Japan. So the critics say, 'Of course, he just came from Japan,' but strangely enough, the two productions were not at all alike."[42]

One other element of the New York *Seagull* reflected the Japanese influence and that was Serban's decision to treat Treplev's play in Act I as a Japanese Noh drama. In Japan, it had been played humorously as a Kabuki extravaganza. In New York, on Treplev's wooden platform stage, the use of an off-stage gong and an auto-harp, a Japanese moon, and even on-stage property men was at first also very funny, but the play's mysterious and poetic quality was also reflected in the stillness of Nina's recitation and her stiff, stylized gestures. Serban's choice is actually quite justified in the period context of the play as many symbolic dramas written at this time, particularly those of Yeats, consciously attempted to imitate the quality of Japanese Noh. "I think the play itself is extraordinary if one adjusts to the style of the language. It is, perhaps, the play Chekhov wishes he himself had written ... Treplev's play touches us, like an avant-garde performance ... not through what is spoken but through what is unexplained," Serban observed.[43]

Although the final look of *The Seagull* was beautiful in its simplicity, Serban's original intentions were even more austere. The fourth act went into previews without any walls or realistic semblance of a room at all, but only a rug and a few pieces of furniture on an otherwise completely bare stage, another example of the empty stage for the conclusion of a Chekhov play. However, during previews, Serban and Yeargan decided to use the wall from Act III and break it apart, add a few more pieces of furniture, and the important doors, as called for in Chekhov's text to plausibly explain the logistics of Treplev's suicide. Months afterwards, Serban was still not sure he'd made the right decision:

> I felt the actors needed the doors and the fact that they were inside. They needed some kind of protection from the wind outside. (The breaking of the Act III wall) was almost like breaking apart the original unity of the set, and in a way it reflected what was happening inside the characters ... But I'm not sure that was right ... I'm always changing things and sometimes I think that the final change is not the best one.[44]

In the words of Laurence Shyer, Serban was trying to "strip the stage bare for the final encounter" in the final acts of these first two plays of his Chekhov cycle. In this respect, *The Cherry Orchard* succeeded more than *The Seagull*. Although he might have been later influenced by Brook's bare stage production of *The Cherry Orchard*, Serban's own production of that play came first; so it is quite possible that Serban wants to lead audiences through the play in his usual visually stunning and metaphorical way, only to rely less and less on visual effects to encounter only Chekhov's words for the final images. He would expand upon this idea in his production of *Three Sisters*. For whatever reasons, however, during *The Seagull*, the "final act bare stage image" was eliminated in favor of a more selected realistic look.

The setting was not, of course, the only "last minute" change in the preview period of *The Seagull*. Serban also greatly experimented with the ending of the play. At first, after Treplev burned his manuscript in the stove, an image that Serban says came from Stanislavsky but which also suggested Hedda Gabler burning Lovborg's manuscript, the fire burned brightly, then slowly died out. The burning image was continued with the candlelight entrance of the family, laughing gaily. When Treplev's shot rang out, it was thunderous, almost like an explosion. The lights immediately came to full on stage. All of the actors froze. Their worst fears, especially Arkadina's, had been confirmed. All action stopped until Dorn returned and reported his excuse of the bottle of ether blowing up in his case. Arkadina had to be given a drink afterwards, almost as if she knew without a doubt that Dorn was lying to her and that she was being prepared to receive the news of her son's death. Dorn delivered the last line of the play very melodramatically to Trigorin "Get Irina Nikolayevna away from here. Konstantin Gavrilovich has just shot himself." There was a big pause. The lights faded on Trigorin just as the others were returning to their lotto game. The effect was that no one needed to be told of Treplev's death. The realization of what had happened was on every actor's face the instant they heard the very loud gunshot. It was a shocking, jarring ending, one in which it was suggested that everyone realized what "they had done to Treplev."

Serban felt his second ending was perhaps more true to what Chekhov wanted. The shot was muffled, Arkadina believed Dorn's story about the ether bottle, and the lotto game continued merrily. Dorn delivered the line to Trigorin very quietly. Treplev's death did not have much of an effect. Serban explained his reasons for the change:

> It was a shock ending and a very strong comment. And even though it was effective, I decided I didn't like what it did to the play. The final ending was much less effective but I felt it was closer to what Chekhov intended, that maybe Treplev's death doesn't mean anything ... I mean, Arkadina will have to be told at some point but then life will go on.[45]

Despite Serban's adherence to supposed textual authority, it is possible that his first ending isn't that far removed from Chekhov's own writing. After all, the playwright does include the stage direction that "everyone jumps" or "all are startled" (depending upon the translation). After Arkadina specifically says "Oh, I was so frightened! It reminded me of—", the stage directions then read *She covers her face with her hands* and says "Everything went black for a moment." This seems to be a pretty clear indication that the recent suicide attempt of her son is very much on Arkadina's mind. How implausible is it that she would know in an instant that her son is dead? Instead, it seems that Serban opted for an ending that was perhaps more in line with Stanislavsky's original production, rather than any specifically suggested by Chekhov's text where it is really impossible to come to a definitive interpretation. In this ending, Stanislavsky had the lotto game end merrily and the final sounds of the play were Masha calling out the numbers in a bored voice while Arkadina gaily hummed a tune. Trigorin moved to the table where he struggled unsuccessfully to carry out the doctor's orders to remove her where she wouldn't have to see her son's body. The curtain came down on this image of life monotonously going on, much as it did in Serban's production.[46]

In *The Cherry Orchard*, Serban had applied his understanding of Meyerhold's approach. But in *The Seagull*, Serban's acknowledged debt was to Stanislavsky, if not in the staging, then in the approach to the acting, particularly the rehearsal methods: "What I was attempting with the actors was something very close to the real Moscow Art Theatre. It was my desire to go as far as I could in the direction of that kind of *verité* acting."[47] Serban had a distinguished American cast for this exploration including Rosemary Harris as Arkadina, F. Murray Abraham as Dorn, Christopher Walken as Trigorin, Joyce Van Patten as Paulina, and Pamela Payton-Wright as Masha. The rehearsal period began slowly with many subjective and personal discussions by the actors about their characters. The first readings consisted of each actor reading all of the lines and stage directions for a small portion of the text, followed by another actor's interpretation. This was followed by a period of what Serban called "wild improvisations," using the actors' impressions of the characters as animals or works of art, especially sculptures. Serban reflected on this process:

> Now all these exercises don't really go anywhere but they do give the actor something in terms of freeing his imagination and reminding him that even with a psychological play or a play that takes place in Russia at the turn of the century, he can enter the world of universality and see in himself ... this other character. Of course, we discussed relationships a great deal and got quite stuck in Freud ... But then one returns to the text and sees here Chekhov says "pause" or "through tears" and through these very simple indications we are given relief from the confusion and are brought back by the simplicity of it all, and if one understands this simplicity, one understands something deep and essential about the play.[48]

It is debatable whether the actors were able to communicate this simplicity in a truthful fashion.[49] Harris' Arkadina seemed believable enough in its combination of majesty and pettiness and one really did feel for such characters as Sorin played by George Hall and the irrepressible Medvedenko, played by Richard Russell Ramos. But Christopher Walken's Trigorin was brusque, abrupt, and almost New York ethnic working class as he raced through his "I have to write, I have to write" monologue in Act II. Other characters also contained a certain crassness, almost as if Serban were trying a little too hard to remind us that this is a comedy and that we were not allowed to empathize with them in any Romantic sense. Pamela Payton-Wright's Masha was extremely crude in clumping about the stage in heavy workshoes and constantly chewing a large pipe in her teeth, while Treplev, played by Brent Spiner, (later a star on the television series, *Star Trek: The Next Generation*), was often a boisterous complaining, even whining "would-be" writer rather than the customarily interpreted sensitive soul. The latter was a deliberate choice for Serban: "Treplev has often been played as a romantic type and he's not. He should be a mixture between Artaud and Gordon Craig—a true misunderstood visionary and a nincompoop."[50] Serban was also intrigued by Spiner's physical resemblance to Russian writer Nikolai Gogol: "It was an extraordinary similarity. When I saw him audition I instantly said, 'He looks like young Gogol, let's hire him.' "[51]

While there were many moments of extremely believable and touching moments of acting in the play, overall, there was an impression of bluntness in the acting style of *The Seagull*. Rather than a delicacy, actors used the language in a harsh manner as Serban strove to work against the conventional American perceptions of wistful, tragic Chekhov. In particular, the characters of Treplev and Masha seemed to suffer from this choice. This is possibly an example of Serban deciding ahead of time that these characters were "nincompoops" rather than letting a quality of ambiguity reside in them. Priscilla Smith noted that when Serban phoned her to offer her the role of Masha (she declined it because of another commitment but eventually played the role in Peter Sellars' version of *The Seagull, A Seagull* at the Kennedy Center), he called Masha "an idiot" because she insists on being in love with Kostya rather than her husband.[52,53]

It was definitely the quality of the acting that divided the critics' reaction to *The Seagull*. Some, like Walter Kerr, were puzzled why Serban let his players lapse into "stock Chekhov." Others, like Jack Kroll and T.E. Kalem, felt the acting was admirable, if not exquisite, in the sense that Serban exercised restraint in the production. He allowed the actors room to breathe, something he had not done in *The Cherry Orchard*.

Serban was also praised by many for unabashedly heightening the melodramatic quality of the play, certainly a given in this early play of the still developing playwright who was very much influenced by the popular melodrama around him at this time. This was evident in such instances as the famous "bandage scene" in Act III between Arkadina and Treplev who stalked the stage in long sweeping crosses shouting at each other, finally coming together in a protracted, weepy embrace; and the long narrative of Treplev in Act IV when he recounts the details of Nina's downfall in the year-long gap between Acts III and IV. Some have considered Chekhov's writing to be rather clumsy here; Serban solved it by having everyone pull up chairs around Treplev in a rather stagey tableau to hear the story—in other words, it became a self-conscious admission of the melodrama in the text.

Too, the actors' use of the bridge seemed a conscious staging of a combination of melodrama and ritual ceremony. Many important scenes took place here, often at the expense of more conventionally credible exits and entrances, such as Nina's first embrace of Treplev in Act I and, similarly, Nina and Trigorin's first kiss at the end of Act III, delicately silhouetted by Tipton's lighting. Serban expanded upon this idea of the space being a place for ritual:

> We decided that the front of the stage would define the area of real life intensity with realistic encounters and emotional exchanges very much the way they are in life. But the moment each of the characters stepped onto the bridge, something would happen, it would be another intensity, like stepping into another world. So the crossing of the bridge had to be done just a little off the regular tempo, either faster or slower but different somehow. There were two different movements in the production, two different attitudes, one in front and one at back.[54]

Through these "attitudes," one can see Serban's attempt to put on the stage what Meyerhold had said about rhythm in Chekhov's texts and, similarly, how he had fashioned a more metaphorical visualization of the textual imagery in the upstage portion of the space, as he had done in a more spectacular way with *The Cherry Orchard* owing to the larger space. It is an element of Serban's cinematic approach to Chekhov.

As noted, the acting caused a mixed critical response to *The Seagull*. Frank Rich, newly appointed drama critic for *The New York Times*, in his first review of a Serban play, felt the production was confused and the director's intentions "blurry."[55] While the reaction was by no means all negative, although the always vituperative John Simon of *New York* and Robert Asahina of *The Hudson Review* were particularly vicious and personal, the reviews seemed to surprise and bother Serban: "The reaction to *The Seagull* was very strange. Of course, I read the reviews and was affected by them, I'm not strong enough or detached enough not to be."[56] While Michael Yeargan suggested that the critics were disappointed because they didn't see the Japanese production which they'd heard about,[57] in a way, reaction to *The Seagull* signaled the ending of a critical era of Serban as the "faired-haired *wünderkind*" in the New York press. Clearly there had been a changing of the guard within the critical community in regard to Serban's work. This was, in a sense, the beginning of some consistently mixed and negative critical responses to Serban's work, contrasted to his earlier successes in the previous decade. As a matter of fact, Robert Brustein remains convinced that Serban has not yet overcome this response:

> His *Cherry Orchard* was extremely well received ... this mad, adventurous director was mainstream and critically accepted and that may have been the last time that ever happened. A combination of history and his own development, the changing critical guard, changing fashion and God knows what else made Andrei the subject of a serious critical attack ... which I think took a great toll on him, particularly he doesn't feel he can work in New York anymore ... He couldn't work there, he said.[58]

It is quite possible that the critical community was still wrestling with the idea of Chekhov as true comedies, as the play, whatever its shortcomings, was very funny, especially since Serban took great pains for the audience not to empathize with Treplev. Though Serban was confused and disappointed by some of the reviews, mostly he looked forward to doing his next Chekhov. *The Seagull* had been an important step for him In both productions, he'd tested for himself many of the tried and true theories of how to treat Chekhov's texts in terms of extreme visual naturalism and Stanislavskyan acting. Now he longed to stage a Chekhov play and have the courage to leave the beautiful visual imagery behind: "I want to do Chekhov without any beautifications, without a bridge, without a Japanese platform, without help from production elements—nothing for the eye in that sense ... I want to do Chekhov with only the truthfulness of the relationships."[59] He continued his process of "simplifying Chekhov" with *Three Sisters*.

Three Sisters—American Repertory Theatre, 1982

When I visited the A.R.T. company in the winter of 1989–90 to observe rehearsals of *Twelfth Night*, the members of the company who had been in it or seen it were still talking about Serban's production of *Three Sisters* seven years earlier. These included actors Tommy Derrah (Andrei), Jeremy Geidt (Chebutykin), and Cherry Jones (Irina). Even Robert Brustein believed that not only was it Serban's strongest work at A.R.T., but it was also the best Chekhov he'd ever seen. Unfortunately, not only did the Boston press not share this view, the production was dismissed as wrongheaded, excessive, and silly. Many theatre people, however, found it exquisite. Carey Perloff, the much heralded former Artistic Director of the Classic Stage Company in New York City and currently heading The American Conservatory Theatre in San Francisco, traveled to Boston one weekend to visit some friends. She saw *Three Sisters* on a Saturday matinee and found it so fascinating that she stayed for the evening performance as well.[60] And outside of the local press, respected critics and scholars of dramatic literature such as Jack Kroll (*Newsweek*), Arthur Holmberg (Harvard), Ron Jenkins (Trinity College), and Jonathan Marks (then A.R.T. Literary Director) found the production nothing short of "a revolutionary Chekhov."

What made it so?

It seems that in *Three Sisters* Serban went further than he ever had before in: 1) departing from the sentimental mode that is often mistaken for tragedy in Chekhov productions; 2) making good on his promise to do away with almost all visual effects, without hardly any "beautifications," yet somehow still keeping a cinematic feel for the production; 3) continuing to promote the comic, even farcical mood of Chekhov's plays, despite the fact *Three Sisters* is considered by many critics to be the darkest of the four major plays (it is the only one that the playwright sub-titled "a drama"); 4) concocting perhaps a perfect blend of Stanislavsky and Meyerhold in terms of guiding influence and overall style for the production; and finally, 5) discovering, perhaps for the first time, and putting on the stage the intimate connections between Chekhov and Samuel Beckett—creating a unique blend of comedy and despair that results in a bleak, yet not unfeeling or clinical, theatre poem which investigates both the nature of time and performance itself.

First, Serban's *Three Sisters* was played at a very fast pace, positively breakneck for Chekhov. Jack Kroll called it "the most galvanic, fastest-moving *Three Sisters* you'll ever see."[61] At the start of rehearsals, Serban had caused some controversy by insisting that there was no sub-text in Chekhov and that "depicting Chekhov's characters through method acting leads to self-indulgence."[62] Serban later clarified this statement[63] and it seems in rehearsal that he really does respect Stanislavsky, insisting that his actors be aware of given circumstances and play actions as truthfully as possible. Nevertheless, originally such a pronouncement would have the effect of sweeping away, once and for all, all of the deadly, weepy, sober and agonizingly paced approaches to acting in Chekhov's plays. It would certainly force the actors to "hurry one another."

By the same token, Serban took as one of his major guidelines for the production, Stanislavsky's own words from his autobiography *My Life In Art* in which he formulated the maxim that lifted the Moscow Art Theatre actors out of their despair in rehearsing the original production of *Three Sisters*:

> The men of Chekhov do not bathe, as we did at that time, in their sorrow. Just the opposite; they, like Chekhov himself, seek life, joy, die. They are active and surge to overcome the hard and unbearable impasses into which life has plunged them. It is not their fault that Russian life kills initiative and the best of beginnings and interferes with the free action and life of men and women.[64]

This quote was the first passage one read in the A.R.T. program notes.

More than Stanislavsky, however, Serban continued his practice of trying to realize Meyerhold's ideas of how Chekhov should be played. Meyerhold, who was the original Baron Tusenbach in the M.A.T. production, had once quoted Tolstoi in his essay, "The Naturalistic Theatre and the Theatre of Mood": "One should reveal little, leaving the spectator to discover the rest for himself ... to say too much is to shake the statue and shatter it into fragments, to extinguish the lamp in the magic lantern."[65] Serban's production of *Three Sisters* attempted to put this philosophy into practice. Serban even told Jonathan Marks, "I was trying to understand what Meyerhold wanted, and to use it as inspiration."[66]

Three Sisters was played entirely on almost a completely bare stage with very little furniture and props. Working with designer Beni Montresor, who did the sets, costumes, and lights, Serban and Montresor repeated their reflective stage motif from that summer's production of *The Marriage of Figaro* at The Guthrie. The stage floor was covered with mylar. The only other scenic element was a series of red velvet curtains upstage which could be raised, lowered, and arranged in various configurations. Behind the curtains was a fake cinder block wall which simulated the back wall of the theatre. The overall effect was simple, strangely beautiful, and more than a bit theatrical. It was as if *Three Sisters* were being staged in a theatre itself.

Serban enhanced this theatricalism by his arrangement of the straight-backed chairs for the first two acts. After experimenting with a half-dozen configurations including a box, a circle, and a half-circle, (and, of course, each arrangement necessitated new blocking, thereby never allowing the actors to settle into their movement pattens), on the afternoon rehearsal of opening night, Serban directed the stage manager to line up the chairs in a straight line facing downstage. At first, stage manager Jack Phillips didn't believe him as he and Serban had talked about the idea previously as a joke for the first day of technical rehearsal. But Serban told him, "Jack, it's no joke."[67] Despite the usual Serban "last-minute changes", and this one creating major new movement patterns for the actors on the day of the opening, (see Chapter Four on Serban's need for constant change in rehearsal), the new lineup of the chairs forced the actors into a much more formal, even presentational style of playing for much of the first act. The actors stood in front of the chairs and addressed many of their speeches to the audience. Gradually, throughout the act, the formal line of chairs was broken and for Act II, they were chaotically strewn about the stage.

Act II also saw the introduction of many children's toys into the nursery, symbolizing the gradual takeover of the house by Natasha and her children. Blocks, teddy bears, drums, and toy animals were spread all over the stage floor, constantly underfoot of the actors. For example, after a scene of long philosophizing, greatly impressing Masha, Vershinin delivered the line "I'll slip out here quietly." While exiting to attend to his wife's attempted suicide, he noisily knocked over a castle made of dominoes. Other characters casually played with the toys during their speeches. As Ron Jenkins noted, the effect was "as if they were all in an oversized playpen ... we are left with the impression of endearingly awkward adolescents trying unsuccessfully to find happiness."[68]

For Act III, the red curtains were moved downstage, further enclosing the space. But there were no beds or other furniture as called for in Olga and Irina's room. Instead, they slept on gray blankets on the floor, further visualizing how their mortgaged house is being taken away by Natasha, as their dreams for Moscow and a bright future are also stripped away. Designer Montresor was apparently not completely happy with such a bare look, often asking Serban "What country is this? This is no country in the world" and "Andrei, it's supposed to be a bedroom. Where are the beds?". Serban would always answer with "Beni, it's only a play. It is a play. It doesn't have to be any country in the world."[69]

Finally, for the last act, the curtains were removed, revealing the cinder block wall and the shiny stage floor was covered with autumn colored leaves. (See Figure #6) Various characters lied and rolled about in the leaves, including Irina and the Baron before he exits for his fatal duel with Solyony, while Olga often raked them furiously. The Baron, Chebutykin, and Solyony left for the duel by exiting up the theatre's circular staircase to the flies.

Through this stark, dreamy, and metatheatrical setting, (a mood he was to repeat with *Twelfth Night* many years later), Serban was able to place the character relationships at the center of the play and still not succumb to the heavy naturalism that he felt was so inappropriate for Chekhov. And he still maintained much of the cinematic feel from his earlier Chekhov productions. Serban accomplished this primarily by beginning and ending the play with a taped voice-over of the three sisters speaking. In the opening, the first ten lines or so of the text by Olga were heard in speakers all around the auditorium while actress Marianne Owen's lips moved and eventually began to speak not quite in sync with the tape and then gradually took over. "Father died just a year ago today on the Fifth of May—your name day, Irina. It was snowing then and very cold. I felt as though I should never live through it ... etc." For the ending,

Olga's voice was heard on tape again saying "If we only knew ... if we only knew!" while the three sisters huddled together over the baby carriage, standing amongst the leaves while Chebutykin slowly and methodically ripped up a newspaper.[70]

The effect was a distancing, an alienation in the truest Brechtian sense of the term, i.e., it de-familiarized the personal situation of the three sisters and forced audiences to look immediately at them in a new way: as characters who are confronting memory and as memory confronting characters. For despite the relative quick pace of the production, Serban was able to explore one of Chekhov's favorite thematic motifs, and one where he intersects and pre-figures Samuel Beckett in an astonishingly similar and modern fashion: the passage of time and the timelessness of change. The voice-overs, the autumn leaves on the stage floor, the characters playing with toys, the eerie shadows on the upstage wall, and especially the ending scene with the sisters' confrontation with the baby carriage (the future) and the destruction of current events by the doctor (the newspaper), all were moving and disturbing images of the passage of time for all of the characters. Ron Jenkins analyzes this final tableau and its antecedents on stage:

> Serban has prepared us for this closing tableau with a tapestry of intersecting paradoxes. Kulygin proclaims his happiness as his wife Masha is doubled over with grief over the departure of another man. Andrei smashes his books to the ground in a futile act of defiance that is negated by Ferapont, who follows him around and picks them up behind him. The corpse of Tusenbach is carried by as Irina tries to think optimistically about her prospects. *The intricately patterned succession of events weaves a tangled web of unfulfilled possibilities that connects the future to the past through the illusions of the present.* With a rare combination of visual clarity and emotional depth, Serban has directed a production of *Three Sisters* that achieves timelessness by insisting on immediacy. Avoiding any hint of sentimentality, he sculpts Chekhov's subtext into space and brings it uncompromisingly into the present tense.[71] (Italics mine)

Serban was able to realize this connection between Beckett and Chekhov on the stage. The performances were often farcical, even slapstick, devoid of sentimentality, but never devoid of feeling. Probably the best example of this was the scene in Act III when Chebutykin's (Jeremy Geidt) pants fell down, a moment that disturbed almost every local critic who saw the play. As the drunken doctor delivers his monologue about the patient he's killed, Chekhov's stage directions are to begin washing his hands, weep, then suddenly stop weeping and speak sullenly. Serban staged this so Geidt would bury his face into a wash basin while crouched on all fours (remember there were no chairs in this setting), then drooling like an animal, rub his spittle into the polished reflective floor to get a better view of himself as he spoke about the uncertainty of his own existence ("If only I didn't exist!"); then when he stood up, his trousers came down. Surely this is no accidental quoting of Estragon losing his pants at the very end of *Godot*. The effect is certainly the same—in the very same few moments we experience profound pity, horror, and laughter.

In addition to the Beckettian mood and atmosphere, many such stage actions as those described above removed Chekhov from the ponderous world of the Method and its emphasis on subtext, and placed it in a world of physical actions which were sometimes puzzling, sometimes humorous, but often symbolic of the thematic whole of the play. Again, one is reminded of the repetitious and all-important physical actions of characters in many Beckett plays: Estragon chewing his carrot, Winnie combing her hair, Krapp eating a banana, Hamm wiping his face, and so on. Ron Jenkins called the physical actions of the characters in *Three Sisters* "expressing the subtext in a different mode than we are accustomed to expect in Chekhov."[72] Other examples were Irina spinning in circles as she spoke about the birds flying overhead, Olga raking leaves furiously in order to avoid Vershinin in Act IV, and Chebutykin tearing the newspaper at the end of the play.[73]

Unlike in *The Seagull* or *The Cherry Orchard*, Serban did not make great use of improvisation in the rehearsal period of *Three Sisters*. Perhaps it was an attempt to de-emphasize the sub-textual analysis or what Serban considers the Method's perversion of the Stanislavsky system. In any case, all of the actors I spoke with recalled the rehearsal period with great joy and love, mostly because of what they considered Serban's enormous dedication to the play, his fanatical preparation for the project, and his effusive love for Chekhov. Cherry Jones, who played Irina, spoke at length why this production meant so much to Serban:

> He was so frightened of it because it was such a great play that he had really done his homework and he made us do analysis for two weeks before we ever did a thing with the script. We sat around. He read Chekhov's letters to us and letters to Chekhov and snippets from the biographies and things that Stanislavsky had said and things that Chekhov had said about Stanislavsky and just back and forth and he took us to see *An Unfinished Piece for Player Piano*. (Russian film maker Nikita Mikhalkov's adaptation of *Platonov,* Chekhov's first play.) We would take these field trips too—I think he was hoping maybe we could learn to act like Russian actors if he took us to see these films and get that sort of crazed way the Russian characters can turn on a dime with such total believability because their passion is so great. So that by the time that week and a half or two weeks were up, we were completely in love with Chekhov. He had become a dear friend. So we all approached the work with so much love and so much respect and joy ...

I remember finally ... he started to block. He would have us, this was "the 5th of May", the very beginning of the play and he had us at the window and then he had us crouching on the floor and then he had us embraced in the center and then he had us spread out across the stage. He had these three women in all these hundreds of positions and finally he said, "Oh, we must stop! My mind is in a whirlwind!" He was so scared to really start because he just didn't think he was going to be able to live up to the play!

... there was just a focus about him working on that piece. There was a kind of calm, as calm as Andrei ever gets ... I do think so much of it had to do with the way it was set up. The love that he infused it with from the very beginning ... I remember him saying "I know I can make pretty stage pictures. I know I have got this ability or this talent or this curse to make things clever on stage and attractive and beautiful and stunning." But he really wanted it to be about the words, he really wanted this one to be about what Chekhov was saying and stick to that ... all the beauty he created around it had to come right from the action of the play. And so I think he really tried to discipline himself with *Three Sisters* and he did.[74]

Possibly it was this discipline in Serban's approach to the acting, the design, the *mise-en-scène*, and especially, the text, that made *Three Sisters* perhaps the pinnacle of his Chekhov cycle, and, at least according to his fellow artists, one of his most successful productions ever.

Uncle Vanya—La MaMa E.T.C., 1983

In some ways, *Uncle Vanya*, produced at La MaMa E.T.C. in 1983 at the suggestion of Joseph Chaikin after Serban's proposed *King Lear* was deemed too expensive, was a sort of footnote to Serban's Chekhov cycle. *The Cherry Orchard*, *The Seagull*, and *Three Sisters* had all represented significant forays into Serban's attempt to replace Stanislavsky with Meyerhold as the model for production style of Chekhov. In *The Cherry Orchard*, he'd been especially successful in incorporating a farcical, even vaudevillian acting style and creating lyrical visual images on a grand scale in the vast expanse of the Beaumont Theatre. In both the Japanese and American productions of *The Seagull*, he'd tested the limits of the naturalistic method of Stanislavsky acting as well as intermingling some aspects of the classical Japanese theatre. In *Three Sisters*, he'd finally broken away from the sentimentalism that surrounded many a Chekhov production and to which apparently Chekhov himself was much opposed. In all three productions, Serban continued to experiment with his cinematic approach that included the progressively reductive scenic style that culminates in the bare stage for the final act. *Uncle Vanya* did not really represent breaking new ground in any of the above areas, but it did contribute to Serban's further attempt to free Chekhov from the prison of nineteenth century naturalism.

Uncle Vanya was also a reunion for Serban. It was his first play at La MaMa since *As You Like It* in 1980. It has remained his last. He was re-united with his design team from *The Cherry Orchard* with sets and costumes by Santo Loquasto, lights by Jennifer Tipton, plus set construction supervision by Jun Maeda. In addition, some of the actors had worked with Serban before, including F. Murray Abraham who played Astrov and Frances Conroy (Sonya). Rounding out the cast were Diane Venora, who had recently played Hamlet in a production at The Public, as Yelyena, James Cahill as Serebryakov, and Joe Chaikin, founder and director of The Open Theatre, as Vanya.

In completing the Chekhov cycle, Serban continued to work toward his stated goal of doing Chekhov "without any beautifications", emphasizing the "truthfulness of the relationships," without succumbing to the ossified naturalism of the late 19th century. At the same time, Serban once more attempted to distance Chekhov from the sentimental and semi-tragic playing style which was still a performance standard in this country. And, as always, he emphasized the farce. Despite Serban's proclamation that this one was the least stylized of the productions,[75] *Uncle Vanya* stirred the usual critical controversy, receiving such harsh reviews that Brustein and Richard Schechner both felt compelled to defend Serban in print.

The boldest choice in the production was the setting. Budget limitations notwithstanding, Loquasto's design was a sprawling compilation of platforms, ramps, walkways, and staircases all made of rough hewn, finished wood planking. Serban and Loquasto took their metaphor from Act III of the text when Serebryakov says "I don't like this house. It's a perfect labyrinth. Twenty-six enormous rooms, people wander off in all directions and you can never find anyone." Serban discussed the reason for this evocative design that combined all four settings of the text, including interior and exterior scenes, into one environment: "All the productions of *Vanya* I've seen have been small, following a sense of cluttered naturalism. For us, the house was big and the audience was invited to come inside."[76]

Serban then elaborated on how this production differed from his other Chekhovs:

> This one has the reality of film. The Annex has become like a wasteland barn. The audience is on three sides and is involved in the house, more than in my other Chekhov productions. In *The Cherry Orchard*, the audience looked at a vista from a great distance ... I began the production using natural wood for the scenery—untreated, neutral, with a Beckett-like quality. (The wood was later finished.)[77]

The above comments are significant for two reasons. First, once again, even with this so-called less stylistic approach to Chekhov's texts, Serban was consciously trying to retain some of the cinematic feel from his earlier Chekhov productions. Loquasto's set design allowed the action of the the play to take place in uninterrupted flow from scene to scene, like a well-edited film. And Jean-Claude van Itallie's new version of the text trimmed the play to an intermissionless 100 minutes. Second, this was the first time Serban had publicly acknowledged the connections between Chekhov and Beckett in terms of thematic motifs and overall mood.

The set was used in a variety of ways to underscore the relationships between the characters. For example, Astrov teetered very high up on a walkway, as the doctor balances between an outlook of despair and hope. Serebryakov addressed the household in Act III with his plans to sell the estate on high from a balcony, as if he were a demagogue politician behind a lectern, speaking patronizingly to his constituents below. Vanya's room and workplace was in a center, recessed area that was like a pit, at the center core of this maze-like household. In the final scene, as they sat, doing the accounts, Vanya and Sonya looked like figures in a grave. Throughout, characters often shared the same scene from very great distances in the space and many of the soliloquies, as in *Three Sisters*, were delivered straight to the audience. Too, because of the seating arrangements in the Annex, much of the audience looked down upon the action, almost as if viewing the action of an operating room, reminiscent of the environmental set-up of Jerzy Grotowski's production of *The Constant Prince* for The Polish Lab Theatre.

For all of his talk of intimacy, Serban again worked to create a distancing between the actors and audience and underscored the theatricalism in the production. Revising another cinematic element of *Three Sisters*, Serban began the play with a "live voice-over", i.e., the play opened with Sonya reading her final speech about faith and work out loud from a book. Not only did this immediately distance the actress from the words and the audience from the immediate narrative of the text, it also de-sentimentalized her final speech, as when she did deliver it, it seemed like a memorized text, rather than a spontaneous heartfelt outburst. The only music used in the production was a recording of Bellini's opera, *I Puritani*, which Serban had staged a year earlier for the Welsh National Opera. It was played on a phonograph by the characters at key moments in the text, such as immediately following Vanya's assassination attempt. Again, the effect was to theatricalize and underscore the melodrama in the play, utilized much like a film score.

The acting style contributed most to this distancing and heightened theatricalism, however. On the whole, there were considerably less "physical and vocal pyrotechnics" in this production than in *The Cherry Orchard* or perhaps even *Three Sisters*. Overall, a muted tone of understatement prevailed. Chaikin's Vanya was probably the best example of this. Brustein described his performance as "a sad clown, an aging child, out of silent-film comedy."[78] Even when Vanya discovered Yelyena in Astrov's arms, his reaction was completely deadpan, circling the embracing couple at a distance. Here Serban's staging expressed the voyeuristic sub-text of the moment. Chaikin then quietly turned away without a sound.

One moment of Chaikin's reactions as Serban staged it found criticism from virtually every reviewer but Schechner and Brustein. When Serebryakov announced his intentions to sell the estate, instead of displaying the customary outraged interpretation, Chaikin instead slowly crossed to his rival, sat on his lap, and smilingly and softly registered his protest. The image was that of a ventriloquist and his dummy as well as that of a father and son. Brustein observed, "This is clearly Serban's effort to essentialize how it feels to be a helpless child in a disintegrating household"[79] while Schechner wrote: "When Vanya sits on Serebryakov's knee ... what we have is not a neo-Freudian conceit but hatred boiled down to its sarcastic essence ... an exemplary Brechtian performance—maintaining the tension between what he, Chaikin, is showing us about Vanya and what he, Vanya is experiencing."[80]

Although the other actors were not as low-key as Chaikin, they still possessed what Schechner referred to as a "fire-in-ice" acting style. F. Murray Abraham was a nervous energy, rapid-fire delivery Astrov, twisting his mustache and moving about the maze-like set with great energy, while Frances Conroy's Sonya seemed sincere and restrained in comparison to Diane Venora who played Yelyena in a very flamboyant and bold fashion, constantly striking poses, very aware of the effect she was having on the men of the household. Brustein remarked that it was as if the character were "being played by Mme. Arkadina in *The Seagull*."[81]

The final images of *Uncle Vanya* were quite striking in their combination of farce and despair. Astrov bid his farewell from atop a platform functioning as the desk top of Vanya and Sonya, submerged in their "grave pit." As their pens scratched noisily at their ledgers, Sonya spoke her speech which we had seen her learning at the beginning of the play, while Tyelyegyin strummed the mandolin, dancing and whirling like a dervish.

There is no doubt that the reviews of *Uncle Vanya* were a chief factor in driving Andrei Serban out of New York. (This process was completed two years later with his re-worked production of *The Marriage of Figaro* at Circle in the Square.) Notice after notice referred to Serban as "destroying the classics." Benedict Nightingale of *The New York Times* questioned if Serban had "lost his nerve" as the production seemed to him a cross between ordinary realism and the more spectacular visual effects of *The Cherry Orchard*.

Of course, Serban hadn't lost his nerve. It seems clear that *Uncle Vanya* was simply another step in his process of distilling Chekhov to its essence, a process that he perhaps may have been more successful with in *Three Sisters*. In retrospect, since the actual physical space of the theatre seems to be the overriding performance factor in any Serban play, it is possible that the cavernous La MaMa Annex was perhaps not the best space for Serban at this particular time of his development of the Chekhov cycle. Perhaps he would have been better off in the more intimate space of the Newman Theatre at The Public, site of *The Seagull*. On the other hand, if we apply Peter Brook's litmus test of remaining images to *Uncle Vanya*, what remains with us is the figures of the actors scurrying like rats in a huge maze, certainly not a possibility without the space of the La MaMa Annex.

Even from just the briefest samplings of the thousands of words spent in critical response to *The Cherry Orchard, The Three Sisters,* and *Uncle Vanya*, one can see that the larger issue behind the complaints, attacks, and praise is the question of whether the director has the right to "author" the text in a production with as great a hand as the playwright. In other words, for many critics, the problem was that of the director her/himself, and what the limits or capacities of that artist could or should be. This issue has by no means been solved in the American theatre, but it does seem that it is not as burning an issue in the European theatre where, from Meyerhold on, directors have been expected to treat dramatic literature in a more metaphorical and personal vein. It does seem, however, that because of directors like Andrei Serban, and his productions of Chekhov's plays, as well as *The Trilogy* and *Agamemnon*, that the American theatre had been introduced to this concept. It is now at least somewhat tolerated, if not wholly accepted in some quarters, as the recent critical successes of such directors as Peter Sellars, JoAnne Akalaitis, and Robert Wilson indicate.

It seems clear that Serban has helped to free Chekhov from the "prison" of late 19th century naturalism. In production after production in regional theatres across the country, it is now de rigueur to stage Chekhov without walls, in metaphorical environments, and to emphasize the comedy and distance us from the dangers of sentimentality in an acting style that often seems to combine elements of Meyerhold and Brecht. Just a few recent examples of this are The Goodman Theatre's *Uncle Vanya* in 1990 directed by Michael Maggio, *The Cherry Orchard* at The Arena in 1988, directed by Lucian Pintilie, and Peter Sellars' *A Seagull* at the American National Theatre in Washington, D.C. in 1985. All of these productions attempted to find the poetry in Chekhov through what used to be called a non-conventional style. Many of Serban's methods in visualizing this poetry on stage are on the point of being absorbed into the mainstream of theatre practice. As for Serban, although he hasn't staged a Chekhov play since *Uncle Vanya*, he continues to search Chekhov's texts in an attempt to somehow bring that poetry alive off the page. He likens Chekhov's writing to the technique of a Zen artist, "touching the essence in a few words."[82] In response to a query of where Chekhov's poetry resides, Serban answered:

> In life. Totally in life. If we could see the image of ourselves at this table. Drinking, talking, you holding that glass, me gesturing and the light streaming through the window. In this, in the fact that we are alive now and trying to exchange something, there is poetry. It's in the presence, in the being, in the very substance and vibrations of life.

That's where it is. That's where the poetry comes from. And we don't see it in our lives because we're too taken with ourselves. But he sees it, it's all there on stage—and it's an act of poetry because it's life concentrated.[83]

Notes

1. Jonathan Marks, "Andrei Serban's *Three Sisters*," *Winter Symposium, Literary Managers and Dramaturgs of America* (New York: Columbia University, 9 February 1987) 1.

2. Ernest Simmons, *Chekhov: A Biography* (Chicago: University of Chicago Press, 1962) 604, 623.

3. Andrei Serban, "Serban Defends His *Cherry Orchard*," letter, Theatre Mailbag, *The New York Times* 13 March 1977: D4.

4. Laurence Shyer, "Andrei Serban Directs Chekhov: *The Seagull* in New York and Japan," *Theater* 13.1 (1981): 56.

5. Shyer 59.

6. Several critics who disliked Serban's *Cherry Orchard* also suggested that he took a great deal from Giorgio Strehler's 1974 production at the Piccolo Teatro Di Milano, but it is unclear if Serban did indeed see this production.

7. Arthur Bartow, *The Director's Voice: Twenty-one Interviews* (New York: Theatre Communications Group, 1988) 296.

8. Vsevolod Meyerhold, *Meyerhold on Theatre*, trans. and ed. Edward Braun (New York: Hill and Wang, 1969) 28–33.

9. Serban, 13 March 1977: D4.

10. Joseph Papp, telephone interview, 13 April 1990.

11. Dan Isaac, "A Non-Verbal Approach to Chekhov," *New York Theatre Critics' Review* Spring/Summer (1977): 11.

12. Clive Barnes, "A *Cherry Orchard* That Celebrates Genius," *The New York Times* 27 February 1977: C3.

13. Walter Kerr, "A Daring, Perverse, and Deeply Original *Cherry Orchard*," *The New York Times* 27 February 1977: Sec. 2, 1.

14. Lally Weymouth, "In Order to Achieve Real Wings in Chekhov, You Just Live It," *The New York Times* 6 March 1977: 24.

15. Bartow 297.

16. During one performance, the torn telegram accidentally fell into the first row of seats where its contents were read by a curious spectator. He found such words as "Can't live without you. When will you return? etc." Who says Serban is completely anti-Stanislavsky?

17. Weymouth 24.

18. Bartow 297.

19. Richard Eder, "Andrei Serban's Theatre of Terror and Beauty," *The New York Times Magazine* 13 February 1977: 53.

20. Isaac 11.
21. John Simon, "Deadly Revivals," rev. of *The Cherry Orchard*, by Anton Chekhov, *The New Leader* 14 March 1977: 22.
22. Richard Eder, Henry Hewes, T.E. Kalem, and John Simon, "Critics' Roundtable: *The Cherry Orchard*," *New York Theatre Critics' Review* Spring/Summer 1977: 6.
23. Barnes C3.
24. Other cast changes included Elizabeth Franz replacing Cathryn Damon as Charlotta and David Clennon replacing Michael Cristofer as Trofimov.
25. Papp.
26. Isaac 11.
27. Although, at the time, Serban said he was much happier with *Agamemnon*, the next project he did for Papp. Dean Drury, "Andrei," *Keynote* July 1977: 13.
28. Peter Brook, *The Shifting Point* (New York: Harper and Row, 1987) 158.
29. Shyer 56.
30. Bartow 296.
31. Priscilla Smith, personal interview, 13 February 1990.
32. I also saw Brook's *Cherry Orchard* a few years later in New York with an American cast, but, as much as I was enthralled with the acting and treatment of the text, I cannot agree that it was by any means a definitive production.
33. Shyer 58.
34. Shyer 59.
35. Shyer 60, 63.
36. Shyer 59.
37. Shyer 60.
38. Shyer 61.
39. Shyer 59.
40. Brook 157–158.
41. Shyer 61.
42. Shyer 61.
43. Shyer 63.
44. Shyer 63.
45. Shyer 64.
46. Stanislavsky's ending of *The Seagull* is beautifully described in David Richard Jones' *Great Directors at Work: Stanislavsky, Brecht, Kazan, Brook* (Berkeley: University of California Press, 1986) 71.
47. Shyer 61.
48. Shyer 62.
49. I must confess that I saw Serban's *The Seagull* on videotape at the Lincoln Center Library of the Performing Arts. Therefore, my impressions of the acting may lack a certain immediacy. Nevertheless, they are the only impressions I have.
50. Serban, letter to author, 10 June 1994.

51. Shyer 64.
52. Smith.
53. One is reminded of Robert Brustein's comment about the quality of acting under so-called "metaphorical directors": "If there is a generic weakness in metaphorical production, it is usually found in the acting performances which are sometimes neglected in the directorial concern with visual elements." Robert Brustein, "Reworking the Classics: Homage or Ego Trip?," *The New York Times* 6 November 1988: 16. Also, see discussion of acting in Serban's methods of rehearsal in Chapter Four.
54. Shyer 62.
55. Frank Rich, "Serban Directs Chekhov's *Seagull*," *The New York Times* 12 November 1980: C25.
56. Shyer 66.
57. Shyer 65–66.
58. Robert Brustein, personal interview, 12 December 1989.
59. Shyer 66.
60. Cherry Jones, personal interview, 18 February 1990.
61. Jack Kroll, "A Pair of *Three Sisters*," *Newsweek* 10 January 1983: 70.
62. Ron Jenkins, rev. of *Three Sisters*, by Anton Chekhov, *Theatre Journal* June (1983): 243.
63. He later said "method acting leads to *lifelessness* and acting self-indulgence." Serban, 10 June 1994.
64. Konstantin Stanislavsky, *My Life In Art*, trans. J. J. Robbins (New York: Theater Arts Books, 1948) 373–374.
65. Meyerhold 27.
66. Marks 2.
67. Marks 3.
68. Jenkins 243.
69. Marks 4 and Jones.
70. It is no surprise that Serban didn't hit upon this idea until technical rehearsals just prior to previews. Cherry Jones told me that when the actors questioned him whether they should be mouthing the words along with the tape or just thinking them, he replied: "Don't ask too many questions!"
71. Jenkins 244.
72. Jenkins 243.
73. Arthur Holmberg, rev. of *Three Sisters*, by Anton Chekhov *Performing Arts Journal* 7 (1983): 72.
74. Jones.
75. Gussow, "Serban, His *Vanya* and His Career," *The New York Times* 6 September 1983: C11.
76. Serban, 10 June 1994.
77. Gussow, "Serban, His *Vanya* and His Career."
78. Brustein, "Serban Under Siege," *Who Needs Theatre?: Dramatic Opinions* (New York: Atlantic Monthly Press, 1987) 118.

79. Brustein, "Serban Under Siege," 118.
80. Richard Schechner, "*Vanya* at La MaMa: We Do Chekhov Right," *The Village Voice* 4 October 1983: 121.
81. Brustein, "Serban Under Siege," 118.
82. Serban, 10 June 1994.
83. Shyer 65.

Figure 1. Medea's triumph from *Medea* in *Fragments of a Greek Trilogy* at La MaMa E.T.C., 1974. Priscilla Smith, Jamil Zakkai, & Diane Lane. (From the private collection of Priscilla Smith.)

Figure 2. Priscilla Smith as Electra, with the snake. From *Electra* in the 25th Anniversary of La MaMa revival of *Fragments of a Greek Trilogy*, La MaMa E.T.C., 1987. (Photo by Dan Nutu.)

Figure 3. The audience on the stage of the Vivian Beaumont Theatre. From *Agamemnon* at New York Shakespeare Festival at Lincoln Center, 1977. Setting by Douglas Schmidt. (Photo by George Joseph.)

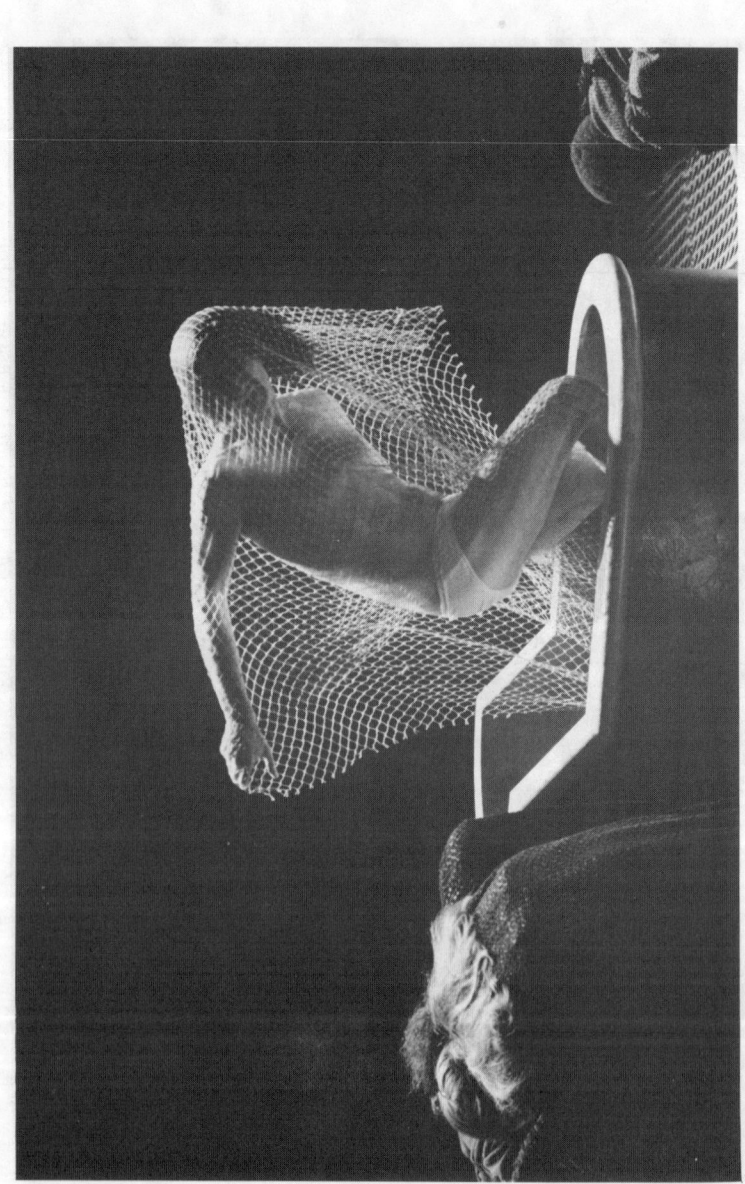

Figure 4. Jamil Zakkai in the murder of Agamemnon in his bath. From *Agamemnon* at New York Shakespeare Festival at Lincoln Center, 1977. (Photo by George Joseph.)

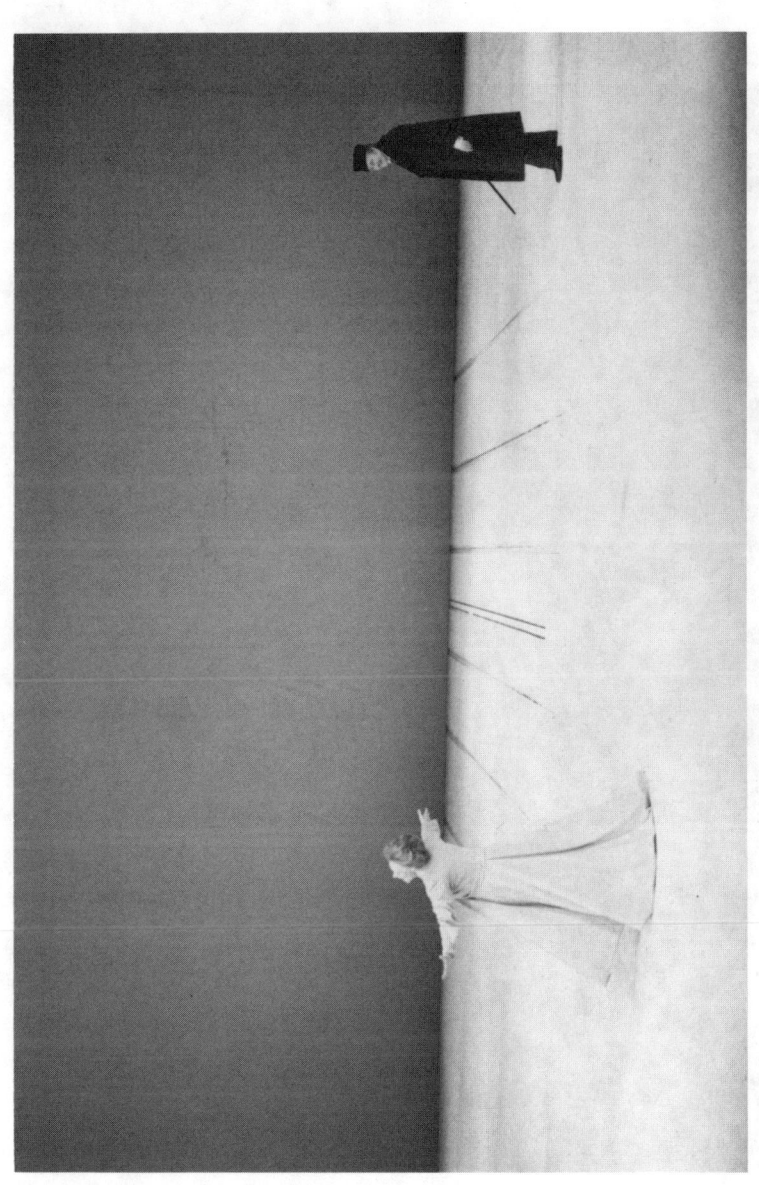

Figure 5. Irene Worth and George Voskovec in Mme. Ranevskaya's farewell to her home. From *The Cherry Orchard* at New York Shakespeare Festival at Lincoln Center, 1977. (Photo by George Joseph.)

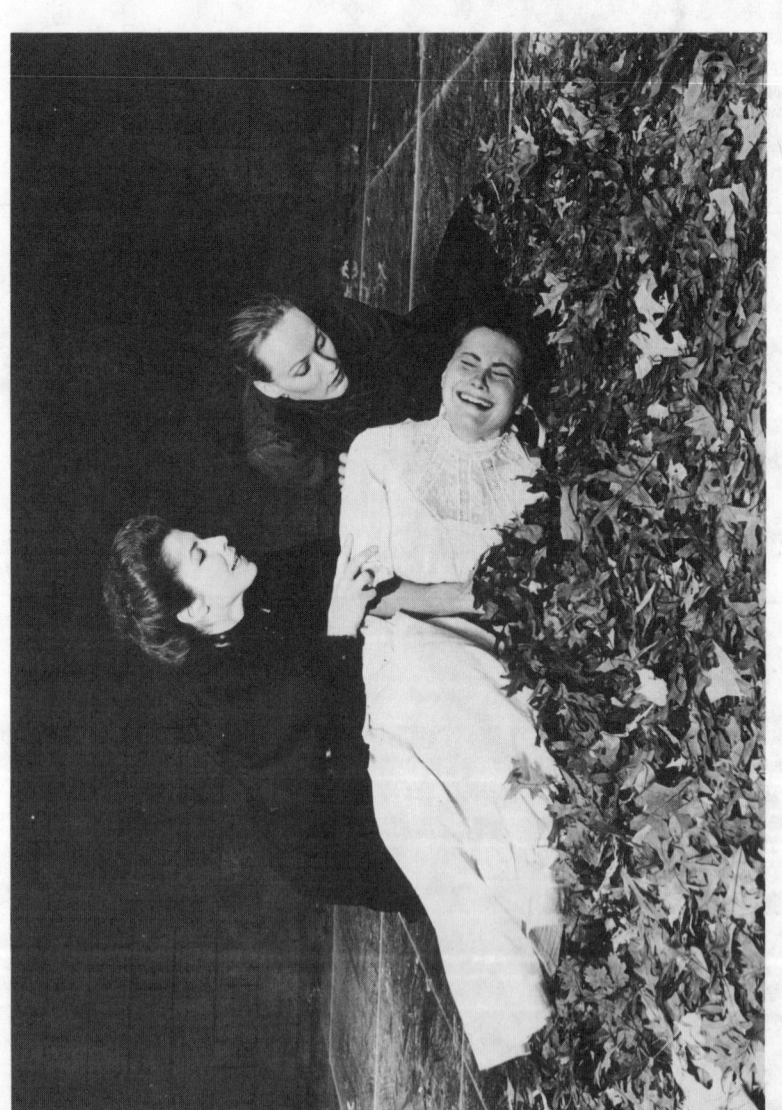

Figure 6. Marianne Owen, Cheryl Giannini, & Cherry Jones as the three sisters in the autumn leaves. From *Three Sister* at American Repertory Theatre, 1982. (Photo by Richard Feldman.)

Figure 7. Richard Grusin and Diane D'Aquila in Tartaglia Observes Angela. From *The King Stag* at American Repertory Theatre, 1984. Masks and Puppets by Julie Taymor. (Photo by Richard Feldman.)

Figure 8. Cherry Jones as Cherestani, the Serpent Woman, in the transformation scene. From *The Serpent Woman* at American Repertory Theatre, 1988. (Photo by Richard Feldman.)

Figure 9. Cherry Jones in Viola's dilemma from *Twelfth Night* at American Repertory Theatre, 1989. (Photo by Richard Feldman.)

Figure 10. Andrei Serban directs *Twelfth Night* at American Repertory Theatre, 1989. (Photo by Richard Feldman.)

3

Serban and "The New Fabulism"

IN REVIEWING Serban's productions of Carlo Gozzi's *The King Stag* and *The Serpent Woman*, *New York Times* critic Mel Gussow coined the term "The New Fabulism." Gussow defined this contemporary form as taking "ancient myths and turn(ing) them into morality tales." Gussow cited such contemporary practitioners as The Bread and Puppet Theatre, The Talking Band, Martha Clarke, Julie Taymor, and Serban himself.[1]

What are the common denominators in the theatrical presentations of such diverse artists?

Shared characteristics include a use of fairy tale and ancient myths, and a bright and colorful visual style that often mixes puppetry, masks, dance, and circus elements in a pageant-like fashion. The New Fabulism also combines theatrical conventions of various Asian theatre forms such as Kabuki or Bunraku and the Italian commedia dell'arte. The acting style is often quite presentational and seemingly improvisational rather than realistic, the themes of the works are similar to that of the fairy tales or myths in that they often present cyclical tales of birth, death, and regeneration, moreover, there is sometimes an overall atmosphere of playfulness, fancy, and fun. This is not to say that darker elements do not exist in the works of the artists Gussow lists above, but, on the whole, there is a quality of celebration of humankind through the cautionary or moralistic "lesson" of the tale. It is also clear that The New Fabulism embraces a wide cultural viewpoint and attempts to achieve a universal effect through the borrowing of performance traditions of many cultures.

This sort of interculturalism is actually a part of a modern tradition in the theatre. For the last century, as the world grew smaller with technological advances in transportation and communication, theatre artists as diverse as Yeats, Artaud, Brecht, Brook, Grotowski, Wilson, and Mnouchkine have introduced elements of Asian and African theatre onto Western theatre stages. Simultaneously, the dramaturgy of Western playwrights, especially Ibsen, has had an enormous effect upon twentieth century theatre in China, Japan, and India. So, just as *Fragments of a Greek Trilogy* had enriched this interculturalist tradition with the use of many different traditions of performance, so would Serban's work in The New Fabulism, a movement slowly inching its way toward global traditions of performance.

Interestingly, another characteristic that distinguishes The New Fabulism is its combination of what Brook identifies as Holy and Rough Theatre. In *The Empty Space*, Brook describes the two forms almost in polar terms. The Holy Theatre is the Theatre of the Invisible, i.e., Grotowski and Beckett, where the spiritual celebration of humankind is enacted in concentrated ritual and ceremony before a select audience. Opposed to this is the Rough Theatre of Shakespeare and Brecht, a truly popular theatre of outdoors and the cabaret, of the street, of smells and color all lacking a consistent style.[2] The New Fabulism is both Holy and Rough. It is an investigation and celebration of spiritual traditions in a popular fashion that mixes many different performance styles, achieving the unity of none.

Finally, The New Fabulism also celebrates theatricality itself. Like many theatrical trends of the twentieth century, the audience is encouraged to take pleasure in the technique of the form rather than succumbing to being swept away by the magic of simulated illusionism. Conversely, a sense of wonder and magic is created by the marvel of the aesthetic beauty on stage whether it be the graceful dance-like movement of an actor, the striking grotesqueness of a puppet, or the imaginative use of a billowing cloth for a storm at sea. The audience is always *aware* that they are in a theatre viewing a performance.

Given this theatrical awareness of the audience, it is appropriate to begin a discussion of Serban's Fabulist productions with Brecht's *The Good Woman of Setzuan* which he originally directed in 1975–76 at La MaMa E.T.C. and restaged at A.R.T. in 1987.

The Good Woman of Setzuan—La MaMa E.T.C., 1975–78, American Repertory Theatre, 1987

Having just established his reputation with the complete production of *Fragments of a Greek Trilogy* at La MaMa in late 1974, Serban and the La MaMa Repertory Company now reformed into The Great Jones Repertory Project. Taking its title from the location of another La MaMa rehearsal site, Serban's company would still be presented by La MaMa but would perhaps be more likely to be funded outside the La MaMa companies.[3] After having worked in Greek tragedy for three years, Serban's choice of *The Good Woman of Setzuan* was deliberate. He felt he needed a break from his long experimental research to do "something simple and light ... Now I feel it is time to let the doors open for a very popular formal theatre."[4] From the beginning, Serban was not interested in an overt polemical treatment of Brecht's text. He sought instead a more comic and earthy approach, similar to Brook's "Rough Theatre." Later on that year, in speaking about his production of *The Threepenny Opera* at the American Conservatory Theatre in San Francisco, his first major guest directorship in the American regional theatre and the ACT company's first encounter with Brecht, he reiterated this philosophy. He described his approach to *Threepenny* as giving the "impression of a bazaar or carnival ... the trick is to find a link between entertaining the audience and knocking them over the head."[5]

In *Good Woman*, Serban treated the play as a fairy tale. With Priscilla Smith in the leading role, and Liz Swados providing the music, *Good Woman* opened on January 30, 1975, as a work-in-progress to generally favorable reviews. In addition to the playful Fabulism of the play, Serban's production had a distinct Eastern flavor which is certainly appropriate to the text. At points, he used highly stylized movement of the actors on the stark two-leveled set constructed by Jun Maeda consisting of revolving screens and sliding doors. Swados' score was neither Asian or like Paul Dessau's original music; it was a conglomeration of modern folk based melodies, jazz, and musical comedy styles. The Eastern setting of the play and Brecht's own deep interest in the Oriental theatre as an alternative method to Western realism are two reasons why perhaps Serban chose *The Good Woman of Setzuan* for his first experiment with the so-called "Fabulist style." In many ways, the development of the alternative contemporary theatre of the West has been dependent on the use of non-illusionistic theatre techniques of the East. But Brecht was also a master showman as well as a theorist and Serban understood that the sense of *fun* and *play* was integral to the staging of his plays. For all of his Marxist beliefs and alienation theory, Brecht was absolutely committed to the idea of entertainment in the theatre. In *A Short Organum to the Theatre*, perhaps Brecht's most complete and organized compendium on his continually evolving and disparate views of theatre, he wrote: "From the first, it has been the theatre's business to entertain people, as it has of all the other arts. It is this business which always gives it its particular dignity; it needs no other passport than fun but this it has got to have ... Nothing need less justification than pleasure."[6]

This "passport" was even more apparent when *Good Woman* opened as a "finished" work on Jan. 23, 1976. It was a celebration of the theatre process itself. The production now had restored Brecht's number of gods to three from the work-in-progress distillation of two and had some minor changes in the cast, but mostly what the play boasted was a solid ensemble of actors who had been working together as a company for some years. Led by Priscilla Smith as Shen Te/Shui Ta and Peter John De Vries as Yang Sun, the disciplined actors of The Great Jones Repertory were able to walk the fine line between a highly mannered, almost "cute" stylized, fanciful Asian folk-tale style and the irony of Brecht's text. Much of the acting was very broad, with large gestures, and movements that were sometimes puppet-like. At the same time, there were touches of pop culture modernity such as Smith's Charlie Chaplin-like characterization of Shui Ta, complete with bowler hat and cane, and De Vries' Yang Sun who, in his pilot's goggles and scarf, looked like a dejected Snoopy chasing the Red Baron. Throughout, the action was supported by Swados' eclectic score in which she herself played piano and guitar and occasionally sang in the chorus. The production was also highly visual as actors darted in and out of the windows and doors of Jun Maeda's set with placards announcing the moral messages of the playwright. Serban also implemented some long wooden rods or poles which were often used instead of the various props that Brecht calls for in the play.[7] They were also utilized as a visual metaphor for the ever increasing burden of the Good Woman throughout the play by their placement on the stage floor in a growing maze pattern. At the end of the play, while the chorus plaintively chanted "Our play is in need of mending" and "How can mankind be good, must human nature change or must the world—well, which?", Smith slowly gathered all of the rods together and clutched them painfully in a startling image of the Good Woman as if pierced by arrows of good intentions.[8]

As in *The Trilogy*, Smith's performance was responsible for much of the success of the production. The title role of Brecht's play has always been a tour-de-force opportunity for a strong actress. In this case, Smith was able to combine the harsh cruelty of Shui Ta the businessman with the sweet naivete of Shen Te, the good-hearted prostitute, with special effectiveness. Aided by the use of a half-mask, another technique from the Asian and commedia dell'arte theatres borrowed by Brecht, whenever she became her "evil cousin," she was able to employ two completely different sets of physical and vocal mannerisms as the two characters. As Shui Ta, she was a hunched over, gravelly voiced figure while as Shen Te she seemed much younger, softer, and even slight, her voice pitched much higher and her agile movements reminiscent of the Chinese classical theatre.

A more playful and relaxed approach was emphasized in the rehearsal process itself. The company could afford to be a bit more experimental in their method as the workshop atmosphere of The Great Jones Repertory allowed for longer rehearsal periods and for the opportunity to preview a production as a work-in-progress before going back into rehearsal for further development. In this fashion, there was approximately a year between the work-in-progress and "finished work" openings. The company also alternated readings and improvisation as they slowly worked their way into rehearsal. Serban's intentions were to recover the street theatre aspects of Brecht:

> *The Good Woman* is not very far away from something I would call very rough theatre—very rough, very popular, and, much more potentially available to a street audience. We talk so much about street theatre without knowing what is possible there, really. Almost any kind of street theatre I've seen does not serve the purpose. The street itself is such a theatrical medium that the problem is to make street theatre in which the reality of the theatre is stronger than the reality of the street. In New York, how can actors really stop a passerby and make him interested in what they're doing? How can we recapture the purpose of an acting company as it was in medieval times, like the strolling players? ... The Brecht work is a little bit working toward that.[9]

Critical reaction focused on the fairy tale musical aspects rather than street theatre approach. In *The New York Times*, Clive Barnes described Serban as making "this caustic fable of poverty, goodness and social exploitation spring into life, like a child's wonderful picture book that ambiguously to the simple is all simplicity and to the knowing is all knowledge."[10] A year later, also in *The New York Times*, Mel Gussow echoed this sentiment: "(Serban) approaches Brecht fresh. In a sense, his is like a child's vision. Where Mr. Serban's tragedies were nightmares, his *Setzuan* is a fanciful folk tale."[11] While the critical reaction was by no means as enthusiastic as *The Trilogy*, the production was highly praised, particularly Smith's appealing and moving performance, and Serban's insight into emphasizing the comic and entertaining aspects of the play in order to highlight the irony of Brecht's text and successfully achieve Brecht's controversial and always difficult to achieve alienation effect.

This very technique was dismissed as facile and lightweight by the Boston press when the production was revived by Serban and Smith eleven years later at the American Repertory Theatre. Earlier in 1987, Serban had re-staged *The Trilogy* to celebrate Ellen Stewart's 25th anniversary of La MaMa so it was ironic that he resurrected another project from his "golden years" of the 1970s. In this case, however, the circumstances were actually very different. A.R.T. was already in rehearsal for a May 15 opening of Soviet director Yuri Lyubimov's production of *The Master and the Margarita*, a stage version of Mikhail Bulgakov's novel which Serban himself had already adapted and staged twice before. The production was abruptly cancelled when Lyubimov had to return to the Soviet Union. Although Serban was already committed to be in London for a BBC filming of his Royal Opera *Turandot*, he agreed to pinch-hit with a version of *The Good Woman of Setzuan* only if Priscilla Smith would once again play Shen Te/Shui Ta. Although Smith was in the midst of a film commitment, somehow she and Serban were able to re-arrange their schedules in order to re-do the play at A.R.T. Serban was actually gone from just before the first technical rehearsal to the first preview performance. Associate Director Charles Otte guided the company through many rehearsals. Serban sat in the audience for the first preview and then somehow managed to re-direct the show between preview and opening night—a period of five days.[12] Serban had also insisted that Liz Swados' original musical score also be used, although some of it was slightly re-written for the A.R.T. actors. He was not permitted to re-create Jun Maeda's original set design, which, according to Smith, was a vital part of the show's original success at La MaMa.[13] Although members of the A.R.T. company felt very good about the play, especially considering the circumstances, and some who had seen both insisted that it was very close to the New York production, the Boston press either couldn't understand or did not accept what they considered such a fun-loving and non-political staging of a major Brecht play. Arthur Friedman's opening lines of his review for *The Boston Herald* summed up the critical reaction with "You know something's haywire when a program note describes Andrei Serban's visually dazzling production of Brecht's political parable play, *The Good Woman of Setzuan*, as 'joyous.' "[14] Nevertheless, given the reactions of the Boston critics, it is interesting to note that Priscilla Smith felt that Serban's "take" on the show was much darker the second time around: "The style, originally dictated by the delicately balanced paper screens of Jun Maeda's set, became more brutal and, in some sense, more mundane—a parody of human behavior rather than a parable about the human condition."[15]

The Good Woman of Setzuan is significant in Serban's development as a director of The New Fabulist style for several reasons. First, it was his earliest effort in the genre. He would use several of the production techniques to even greater advantage in later productions, including the use of masks, the mixture of flavors of Asian theatre and commedia, the eclectic musical and acting styles, and the overall combined mood of color, fairy tale, and morality play. Secondly, although throughout the 1970s Serban would still continue to be best known for his startling interpretation of Greek tragedy, *The Good Woman of Setzuan* did establish him professionally in the United States as a director who was capable of applying his theatricalist vision to a variety of types of dramatic literature. Finally, in keeping with that vision of theatricalism, *The Good Woman of Setzuan* served as an early example of Serban's celebration of the joy of the theatre making process itself, a celebration that would be even more apparent in the *Molière Farces*.

Sganarelle: An Evening of Molière Farces—Yale Repertory Theatre, 1978 and American Repertory Theatre, 1981

In the Fall of 1977, Serban began his appointment as Associate Director of the Yale Repertory Theatre. His first production there was a striking production of Strindberg's rarely performed *The Ghost Sonata*, a perfect marriage of Strindberg's visionary text with Serban's metaphorical and imagistic approach. Strindberg's play is so visual and dream-like itself that Serban's concept did not seem illustrative at all, but actually intrinsic to the text.

At a high-spirited opening night party, Artistic Director Robert Brustein suggested that he now tackle Strindberg's *A Dream Play*, but Serban, like always, wanted to move on to a new challenge.[16] Originally, Brustein and Serban had talked about doing Ibsen's *The Wild Duck* but this was now disregarded as too gloomy for a winter production in New Haven: "... dear God, it would be like coming from a Christmas party into depression!" Serban exclaimed. Brustein also thought that Serban felt the Ibsen play was "too cerebral for his imagistic style."[17]

In his book, *Making Scenes: A Personal History of the Turbulent Years at Yale 1966–1979*, Brustein described the circuitous process by which Serban finally ended up directing one of his biggest critical and popular successes, *Sganarelle: An Evening of Molière Farces*. (As insight into Serban's play selection process, I'm indebted to Brustein's book which is used freely in the following passages.)

For weeks, Brustein and Serban discussed many possibilities—*Ghosts*, *The Imaginary Invalid*, *The Master and the Margarita*, (which he did later in the year for the New York Shakespeare Festival), *'Tis Pity She's a Whore*, and many, many others. Serban would tentatively agree to one, then ultimately reject it. Finally, Serban proposed *A Cabal of Hypocrites* by Soviet playwright Mikhail

Bulgakov. Serban's plan was to present this story of Molière's problem with the royal censors in a grand re-creation of the *Palais-Royal* Theatre with actors costumed as members of Molière's troupe. Despite the technical headaches involved in this concept, especially due to Serban's delay in choosing a script, Brustein agreed. A few days later, Serban had another idea. He wanted to stage Molière's *The Imaginary Invalid* as a curtain-raiser to the Bulgakov play. Since this would have been an impossibly long evening of two full-length plays, Brustein instead suggested a Molière one-act farce. An edition of new translations by Albert Bermel, later to work with Serban on the Gozzi plays, had just been published.

Now Serban wanted to read through every single farce aloud with actors, in order to choose the right one. In the meantime, Brustein was hurriedly auditioning for *A Cabal of Hypocrites*, especially uneasy about casting the key role of Molière on such short notice. At a special reading for Chuck Levin, a recent graduate of the Yale Drama School, to Brustein's horror, Serban didn't even pay any attention to the young actor auditioning.

> When I turned to Serban ... I noticed that he was sitting with his head in his hands, staring at his feet. "What's the matter?" I asked, my mouth getting dry. "We can't do this play" he whispered fiercely. "It's terrible—a melodrama." "But—but ... you liked it when you read it, didn't you?" "Yes," he replied, "but I hadn't *heard* it yet. It sounds *awful*. It's out of the question."[18]

Now Serban required another reading of the Bulgakov play. The very next day with a hastily assembled group of actors, Serban rejected the play as "too heavy. No style."[19] Instead, he proposed to do the short Molière farces they'd been reading all week and string them together under the title *Sganarelle*. Still, Serban insisted the play reading sessions must continue in order to choose the right ones. He eventually chose three plays: *The Flying Doctor*, with Mark Linn-Baker, then a second year acting student at the Drama School, to play Sganarelle; *The Forced Marriage*, with Brustein himself in the Sganarelle role, (eventually replaced by Eugene Troobnick) and the third play was itself titled *Sganarelle*, as yet uncast (eventually played by Michael Gross). Brustein then convinced comic actor Bob Dishy, of Second City fame, to read for the role. Serban wanted him immediately, but Dishy suggested he play the Sganarelle role in the full-length play *The Doctor in Spite of Himself*. Serban, fearing he would lose Dishy otherwise, agreed.

Now there were three farces plus a full-length play to rehearse with opening night only three weeks away. Instead of rehearsing on their feet, Serban and Dishy quarreled over the existing translations of *The Doctor in Spite of Himself* which was not included in the Bermel volume. They began transposing a new translation. After a full rehearsal's work, they produced the opening speech of the play.[20]

Then Serban had the cast work for three days in the costume shop—trying on various pieces that he hoped would help them find their characters. Dishy refused to participate in this, preferring to study his lines. The next day when Serban asked the actors to improvise in gibberish, Dishy complained that they were wasting time.

Serban's response was to quit the show. He suggested to Brustein that Dishy direct the play. Then he admitted to Brustein that he had "lost his inspiration. He was not a machine punching out productions. He could not create under the pressure of time."[21]

But Brustein was able to get Serban and the production back on track. He let Dishy go (who was apparently relieved), postponed the opening one week, dropped *The Doctor in Spite of Himself*, and re-cast some other roles with younger members of the company.

Serban's concept was for the company to play the farces as a traveling street troupe in every available space of the theatre, including the lobby and downstairs lounge. Although this was eventually abandoned because of New Haven Fire Department regulations, he did manage to add a fourth piece after all. Based very loosely on *The Doctor in Spite of Himself*, it was a fast-paced slapstick farce with all of the actors speaking a carefully orchestrated nonsense text invented mostly by Liz Swados. While the actors beat each other and shouted such phrases as "Pimnikkika" and "Shatapupu", occasionally placards with crudely scrawled English translations would drop from the flies. *A Dumb Show* was the unqualified hit of evening, along with Mark Linn-Baker's gymnastic performance as The Flying Doctor, where he literally seemed to be in two places at the same time.

With a simple but effective white set design by Michael Yeargan, and bright, outlandish commedia costumes by Dunya Ramicova, *Sganarelle: An Evening of Molière Farces* was a perfect blend of commedia dell'arte and the Rough Theatre as described by Brook. It was also a huge success for the Yale Repertory Theatre—so much so that, along with *The 1940s Radio Hour*, it was chosen to tour to Boston and New York at the end of the year. Brustein had long resisted this temptation as he didn't feel transferring productions to New York should be a goal of resident theatres.

Critical reaction to both the production in New Haven and the tour in Boston and New York was highly favorable. There was praise for all of the acrobatics and vaudevillian techniques of all of the actors, but almost every major critic conceded that the real star of the evening was the imagination of Serban. Mel Gussow pointed out that Serban was no stranger to comedy in his productions of *Good Woman* and *The Cherry Orchard* and called him "a universal clown,"[22] while even John Simon called the production "a sometimes anachronistic but always ebulliently laugh-filled whirligig."[23]

Three and one-half years later, when Brustein and a good portion of the Yale Rep company had moved to Cambridge to create the American Repertory Theatre in residence at Harvard University, Serban was engaged to re-stage the Molière farces. Thereafter, it toured Chicago at The Goodman Theatre and also the D'Avignon Festival in France where it was greeted enthusiastically by the French. Jeremy Geidt, who acted in the A.R.T. revival, fondly recalled:

> To play Molière in English with an American company ... and get the notices that he did is fantastic. He found a way into Molière that the French responded to immediately, not being the Comedie Francaise way. People would say it has to be these damned Americans who will tell us how to act our national monument and they were totally impressed ... a way into Molière that was not the French way.[24]

This was similar to the Greek audiences viewing *The Trilogy* in Athens a few years earlier. Serban's production restored life to a time-honored, culture specific theatrical institution in a new way—with an American company.

Despite Serban's usual disinterest in revivals,[25] the *Sganarelle* revival was an important project for him. Because of its enormous critical and popular success, and with the strong support of Brustein, Serban eventually found a semi-permanent home at A.R.T. It became the primary outlet for his American non-opera work in the '80s. Although he wasn't completely through with New York, there's no doubt that Brustein's company gave Serban a critically safer and supportive non-commercial environment in which to experiment. Brustein's company also became the primary American outlet in the 80s for such other avant-garde directors as Robert Wilson, Peter Sellars, and occasionally Ann Bogart and JoAnne Akalaitis. Serban was hired not only as a Director for the company but as a faculty member for the Advanced Theatre Training Institute at Harvard (in conjunction with A.R.T.), teaching Acting and Directing. By 1984, Serban had married and bought a home in Cambridge, not far from the theatre in Harvard Square.

The *Sganarelle* revival would have been difficult to mount even if Serban hadn't been committed to simultaneously opening Verdi's *La Traviata* his American opera debut, at Juilliard. As has been described, much of the show had been improvised by the actors in an extremely concentrated rehearsal period almost four years ago at Yale and the nonsense language of *A Dumb Show* had to be reconstructed from an audio tape finally located in a Yale library.[26]

Besides being a classic example of Serban and his collaborators being able to turn near disaster into inspiration, *Sganarelle* was a breakthrough because he felt he had been incorrectly labeled by critics as an intense, solemn director of tragedies (*Good Woman* notwithstanding): "I enjoy laughter. In Romania, I did many comedies. But in the U.S., I have played three years of Greek tragedy. So it was time to do a broad, rough farce."[27] Specifically, in regard to The New Fabulism, *Sganarelle* also demonstrated Serban's commitment to exploring possible models for the commedia dell'arte acting style, certainly a valid choice for the early Molière texts. He would explore his next model even further with the texts of Carlo Gozzi.

The King Stag—American Repertory Theatre, 1984

Serban turned 40 years old in 1983. Though he was entering middle age, in many ways, he felt he was still considered an *enfant terrible*:

> I never meant to be—even when I was 20. To my complete surprise, I found I was creating an uproar. I don't do things to provoke. Life is full of negative steps, why be negative in the theater? ... The commercial zone is closed to me. The new playwright zone is closed. So I go to Europe and do operas. It's the new fashion to use theatre directors.[28]

With these words, to Europe Serban went. For most of 1984, he did not direct any plays. Instead, he mounted four operas—and not all of them in Europe. First was *Il Trovatore* at Opera North in Leeds. Then came *The Merry Widow* for the Welsh National Opera. Next was a re-staging of *I Puritani* at the Netherlands Opera. In the summer, Serban scored one of his biggest successes—Puccini's *Turandot* for the Royal Opera, first staged at the Olympic Arts Festival in Los Angeles. This production was later produced in London in September, at the same time he was doing Prokofiev's *The Love of Three Oranges* for the Geneva Opera. Both the Puccini and the Prokofiev operas are based on the Carlo Gozzi tales for the theatre of the same names. It is here that Serban ostensibly found the fuel for his next major projects in the theatre. Actually, he later acknowledged Armenian director Arby Ovanessian for introducing him to Gozzi's so-called "mystery plays."

Serban himself called 1984 his "year of Gozzi." In Gozzi's *fiabe* or fairy tales for the theatre, which the Italian author had introduced to late 18th century Italian theatre as a counter-attack to Goldoni's "reform" of the commedia dell'arte tradition into a more legitimate and literary form that would appeal to the rising Italian middle class, the most famous example being Goldoni's *The Servant of Two Masters*, Serban found a near-perfect expression in text for his own ideas about the essence of pure theatricality. Gozzi's tales freely mix traditions of the commedia dell'arte, elements of Italian and Asian fairy tales, and a sprinkling of the 18th century French "fairground theatres." Gozzi restored the masks, the low comedy, and especially some of the improvisation that Goldoni had removed from the commedia dell'arte. Moreover, all of Gozzi's tales are interwoven with a mood of magic, exoticism, poetry, and the wonder of children's theatre simplicity. The essence of the Gozzi/Goldoni conflict was that Gozzi believed that the theatre should "imaginatively re-express the world"[29] rather than copiously imitating it as Goldoni did. Serban felt that this age-old aesthetic argument had also divided Meyerhold and Stanislavsky. There was no doubt with whom Serban sided on this artistic issue! Serban expanded on Gozzi's appeal to him in the program notes of the A.R.T.'s production of *The King Stag*:

What Gozzi wanted to affirm is that the theatre's truth exists only within the theatre; that the theatre's function is not to copy or mimic any sort of reality; and that naturalism is a perversion of art. This is equally true of opera, which is in its very essence an art of convention and of imagination—by the simple fact that in opera one expresses oneself in song.[30]

Serban was by no means the first director to be drawn to Gozzi's theatricality. It is certainly no accident that Meyerhold produced some of Gozzi's tales in his revolt against the naturalism of Stanislavsky. According to then A.R.T. Literary Director Jonathan Marks, Meyerhold "claimed Gozzi as his guide in the search for a pure, magical theatre, divorced from the humdrum of reality."[31] Serban even felt that the quarrels of Gozzi and Goldoni were renewed in the disagreements between Meyerhold and Stanislavsky, the essential conflict being to celebrate the theatre's very theatricality itself or to imitate reality. In passionately arguing for the former, Serban called for a "naive style of playing, like that of children's theatre ... almost like a Punch and Judy show" and summarized:

> Here the theatre is king, joy bursts forth, gestures crackle, agitated by a kind of organic pulsation that must be made to surge from the story— perhaps finding along the way the path to the "Biomechanics" Meyerhold talks about; in other words, something like an energy, a pattern of rhythms, a system of gestures.[32]

It is as if through Gozzi's work Serban was able to articulate many of his ideas about art, theatre, and acting that he had been working on throughout his career.

The King Stag opened at A.R.T. on November 29, 1984, completing Serban's "year of Gozzi." By all accounts, it was a tremendous artistic, popular, and critical success. As always, no small measure of the credit went to Serban's collaborators—a new English version by translator Albert Bermel, scene design by old friend Michael Yeargan, lighting by Jennifer Tipton, another Serban veteran who had lighted *Cherry Orchard, Agamemnon, The Seagull,* and *Zastrozzi,* music by Elliot Goldenthal, actors Priscilla Smith, Thomas Derrah, and Rodney Hudson, but especially Julie Taymor, for her spectacular costumes, masks, and puppetry.

Making use of rod, bib, kite, shadow, and just about every other conceivable type of puppet, Taymor and Serban were able to convey the magical atmosphere and complex action of the kingdom of Serendippo. Deramo, the good king, has finally selected the lovely Angela to be his queen because she loves him for himself and not for his money or power, when he is tricked by his evil prime minister, Tartaglia, into divulging his secret of being able to pass his soul into the bodies of wild animals or other human beings. Tartaglia uses the power to transform his own spirit into the body of the king while relegating Deramo to a stag. Angela, however, is not fooled by the lustful prime minister's intentions. Eventually, all resolves happily when the good magician Durandarte breaks the spell and Deramo is re-united with his queen. Such wonders as a huge flying bear, (See Cover Photo), graceful, leaping deer, and a quick-witted, swooping parrot were all accomplished with stunningly beautiful craft in a manner not unlike the Japanese puppet technique of Bunraku, in which the operators manipulate the puppets with great precision in full view of the audience. Many characters in the play, including the king stag and an old man were played by puppets with the operators on stage and the actors supplying the voiceovers.

Yeargan's set combined a scrim background for much of the shadow play, such as the royal hunt scene in the forest, a floor that lit up like a scrabble board, the announcement of each individual scene with titles on colorful banners, and a thrust stage further extended into the usual auditorium of the Loeb theatre, while Elliot Goldenthal's eclectic musical score utilized everything from African thumb piano to Chinese percussion instruments.

Serban also made use of the commedia half-masks and Eastern style full head masks, a bold, acrobatic, and presentational acting style with some improvisation and interaction with the audience to complete the picture of whirling color, breathtaking magic, and childlike naivete of the possibilities of such pure theatricality. Individual actors such as Harry S. Murphy as the wisecracking Brighella, often improvised in a contemporary fashion ("Where did you get your license—K Mart?") and commenting on the old man who was killed by Tartaglia in the King's body ("He probably didn't have tenure") while Thomas Derrah as the King often executed some Kabuki-like dance moves as did Diane D'Aquila as Angela, daughter of Pantalone, in love with the King. The play began with many of the actors dancing on stilts in front of the huge face of the statue that is one of the King's secrets.

Every major critic from *The Boston Globe* to *The New York Times* wrote of the magic of Serban and his collaborators. As noted earlier, the production caused Mel Gussow to coin the term "New Fabulism" while Jack Kroll of *Newsweek* called it "one of Serban's most magical productions."[33] For the remainder of the decade, *The King Stag* was the most enduring and popular of A.R.T.'s touring productions. The combination of such bold Asian, Brechtian, and commedia techniques was something that Serban had been experimenting with as far back as his production of *The Good Woman of Setzuan* for La MaMa in 1975. Nine years later, he perfected the combination in what will surely remain as one of his most theatrically effective and beautiful achievements as well as his perfection of the form of The New Fabulism.

The Serpent Woman—American Repertory Theatre, 1988

On November 30, 1988, Gozzi's *The Serpent Woman* was the opening production of A.R.T.'s 10th anniversary season in Cambridge. Serban enlisted many of the same talents from his previous collaborators on *The King Stag* including translator Albert Bermel (along with Ted Emery) for this particular English version, composer Elliot Goldenthal, and actors Thomas Derrah, Jeremy Geidt, and Harry Murphy. However, Julie Taymor was not available to design the costumes, masks, and puppets. Instead, these items, along with the set, were designed by one of Japan's leading designers, Setsu Asakura, who had met Serban in 1978 when he'd first visited Japan. Although Asakura is an extraordinary artist in her own right, Taymor's absence ultimately hurt the production, according to Brustein, because the Japanese designer's busy schedule simply didn't permit her to be in residence for the entire rehearsal period. "It didn't have the delicacy of *The King Stag*", Brustein recalled.[34]

Nonetheless, Serban had been preparing the A.R.T. Company for some time for the production.[35] As a faculty member of the Institute for Advanced Theatre Training, Serban conducted a number of workshops and exercises in exploring commedia dell'arte techniques for both the Institute students and the members of the company. In February, a full seven months before *The Serpent Woman* went into rehearsal, he organized a three week workshop in text and improvisation as they would relate to the play. Nor was this the extent of his preparation. In the summer of '88, Serban invited an old friend and classmate from Romania, commedia specialist, Nikolaus Wolcz, to conduct a mini-course at A.R.T. The class explored the standard elements of commedia dell'arte with an expert who had devoted his life to the study of the behavior of the stock characters, the classic lazzi, masks, and gestures of this tradition.[36]

Serban was determined that *The Serpent Woman* not be "*The King Stag* Part Two." He wanted to go in a new direction with his study of Gozzi. In an interview with Arthur Holmberg, he explained what the play and its author meant to him and, coincidentally, made some very telling comments on how he felt about the state of modern theatre:

> It works on several levels. Children will see it as a fairy tale; adults as a parable. It's a mythical fable of union, separation, and reunion ... The avant-garde today is caught up in sociology. It confuses the accidental with the essential. The theatre I'm interested in is in search of the miraculous ... In this play you have princes and princesses and a heroic romance. But you also have the commedia dell'arte characters who challenge, question, and mock the values of the main plot ... Like all good fairy tales, Gozzi's play has an important message. It's a positive, hopeful message, but it isn't a facile or simplistic one. Great theatre reconciles you to life, not by running away from the difficult problems, but by facing them and searching for the ideal ... Much modern theatre is like a room that is locked up and sealed off from anything that can sustain life. Look at Dostoyevsky ... there is always in that dark prison a little window above, and through that window one can catch a glimpse of a tiny streak of light. You know there is something to hope

for, to strive for ... But modern theatre is trapped in a room without windows, and we sit around in the mud, accusing and complaining without looking up. I believe that art is here to clarify something about our existence, not just to embrace the confusion. That's not enough. Art must acknowledge the prison wall, but also the window in the wall.[37]

In *The Serpent Woman*, Serban attempted to achieve Gozzi's dialectic and contradiction in the form of the commedia clowns who would often break character, interact with the audience, and otherwise interrupt the complex plot of the play. In the play, while on a hunt, Prince Farruscad (Derek Smith) meets Princess Cherestani (Cherry Jones), who has been transformed from a doe into a beautiful woman. They marry on the condition that he never attempt to learn her name. When he is overcome by curiosity, wife, palace, and children disappear. In order to win them back, he must be put to a severe test and never curse her. Farruscad breaks his pledge and Cherestani is transformed into a serpent. Only after enduring even more horrible tests such as fighting a bull and a giant, and ultimately kissing the mouth of the serpent, is Cherestani transformed back into a princess and they are reunited with their children (played by marionettes manipulated by hooded figures).

Unfortunately, the overall effect of the commedia clowns continually mocking or distracting from this action was one of self-conscious forced humor which often fell flat.[38] Despite one brilliant bit of byplay where actress Ellen Kohrman, playing the lovestruck servant Smeraldina, literally seduced a man in the audience and exited the theatre door with him, much of the actors' improvising and interacting with the audience simply wasn't funny. One can grow tired of the actors exhorting the audience to "Turn around—it's okay!" in order to watch a piece of action behind them in the house of the theatre.

Asakura's designs were much more Japanese flavored than the more eclectic *King Stag*. Many of the puppets were constructed in the pure Bunraku style with white faces and controlled by the long sticks of hooded manipulators. Costumes were more influenced by the Kabuki style, using some traditional blue and white patterned fabric and rich Japanese brocades pierced with gold thread. Asakura noted that "the costumes are mostly made from Japanese kimono fabric, but the shapes are those of the commedia characters."[39] Asakura's scene design attempted to make use of a combination of proscenium and Kabuki effects to create the various environments in Gozzi's text such as the desert, a palace, and an underwater fairy kingdom, but according to one performer in the play, there was a lack of budget, and ultimately, there was a spare "space staging" look to the show. Even the rock where Princess Cherestani was to disappear almost instantaneously as in the Kabuki theatre eventually was modified as the performers and technicians were unable to achieve the immediate effect.

Despite some absolutely stunning scenes, such as Cherry Jones' nude transformations into a serpent and back again, (See Figure #8) images similar to

The Trilogy in beauty and impact, *The Serpent Woman* was dismissed by the Boston press as forced, confused, and generally not as inspired as *The King Stag*. Kevin Kelly of *The Boston Globe* called it "huff and puff stuff with cultural pretensions" and determined the production excessive,[40] while Carolyn Clay of *The Boston Phoenix* asked "Is *The Serpent Woman* snake-bit?"[41] Only Mel Gussow of *The New York Times* reviewed it positively and this was perhaps due to the fact that he saw it late in the run when it had tightened up considerably.[42] To add to the difficulty of an already tense rehearsal period, for a while, Serban had wanted to stage Gozzi's *The Green Bird* as part of the evening as well. He had actually created a similar Gozzi double bill with *The Love of Three Oranges* as a crude curtain raiser for *The King Stag* in its original production. Serban also considered performing both *The Green Bird* and *The Serpent Woman* on alternating nights. This time, Serban was persuaded not to overload the company or himself, and instead to concentrate on just one play. Still, the rehearsal process seemed more difficult than usual, with Serban blocking even more slowly than normally, trying to make up his mind on what to do with the clowns in the play. In the always strenuous technical rehearsal period, Serban seemed particularly manic, often reprimanding the cast and crew. As he often does, Serban continued to work on the show after it had officially opened, and finally began to pull back on some of the improvisation. The company, too, inevitably began to relax into the performance, and according to Brustein, "to feel like themselves and grab a hold of the play and realize what Andrei wanted them to realize ... it became a very beautiful experience and I think one that Andrei felt was realized according to his original dream."[43]

The Serpent Woman remains Serban's last "official" foray into the style we have defined as The New Fabulism. It was a significant contribution to the form for several reasons. First, it was one more example of Serban finding a model for a contemporary use of commedia dell'arte acting techniques, especially in the use of masks and improvisation. Second, because of the nature of Gozzi's material, it provided Serban and his collaborators an opportunity to fuse specific Asian theatrical techniques such as Bunraku and Kabuki into the performance. Finally, together with *The King Stag*, Serban's staging of these two productions perhaps rescued playwright Carlo Gozzi from the dusty shelf of theatre history academia and began the process of restoring his work to the vibrant world of the stage, although only time will tell of any measure of sustained impact. During rehearsal, Serban confided to Albert Bermel that he would like nothing better than to devote himself to working on Gozzi's plays for the rest of his life.[44]

While Serban hasn't devoted himself exclusively to Gozzi's tales, he has carried much of the mood and atmosphere of the form with him in future productions, if it is appropriate to the text. (See the next chapter for a description of Serban's 1989 production of *Twelfth Night* at A.R.T.) Moreover, there is no question that Serban's New Fabulist productions have provided fertile ground for the work of other artists, the best example being Julie Taymor and Elliot Goldenthal's 1988 production of *Juan Darien: A Carnival Mass* in which many of the characters were played by puppets and mingled with live actors in this magical tale of transformation based on the short story by Horacio Quiroga.

The Fabulist style has been a perfect marriage of form and Serban's own vivid imagination. The power of these Brecht parables, Molière farces, and Gozzi tales has been primarily *theatrical*—a power that resides in visual and aural imagery rather than the spoken word. Obviously, this has always been one of Serban's greatest strengths as a director. His Fabulist work has also allowed him to explore the magic of the theatre through its most basic element: the immediacy of the actor. In each of these works, Serban evolved an acting style that was very physical, bold, and often improvisational--in short, a commedia dell'arte equivalent. Finally, The New Fabulism has allowed Serban to pursue his own ideals of achieving on stage the naivete of children's theatre. It is in this simplicity, this innocence, this magic that Serban finds any hope for contemporary theatre at all. If we look further at his final remarks on Gozzi, they ring of an artist striving for a faith in an innate goodness in life and attempting to construct this vision on the stage in the face of enormous current cynicism: "Art has a responsibility to explore the essence of life, and this also includes virtue and goodness. Art must carry man's craving for the ideal. It must inspire hope and faith. But in our time, trying to provide spiritual weapons and directing people toward goodness is difficult to achieve, maybe impossible."[45]

Serban is undoubtedly an unabashed Romantic at heart. He sincerely believes that to make theatre is to celebrate and communicate an essential goodness in ourselves in a mysterious way. At the same time, he recognizes the need for the ugly and the vulgar and perhaps this is why he can't resist adding what many see as excessive or unnecessary humor or downright foolishness to otherwise extraordinarily beautiful productions. This combination of lyrical beauty and good natured foolishness seems to be at the heart of The New Fabulist style.

Notes

1. Mel Gussow, revs. of *The King Stag* and *The Serpent Woman*, by Carlo Gozzi, *The New York Times* 12 December 1984: C19 and 30 December 1988: C3.

2. Peter Brook, *The Empty Space* (New York: Atheneum, 1968) 42, 65–66.

3. Jan Hodenfield, "Romania's Gift to the Theater Here Raises Repertory Sights," *The New York Post* 31 January 1976: 36.

4. Robb Baker, "Andrei Serban: The Intelligence of Emotion," *The Soho Weekly News* 17 October 1974: 19.

5. Stanley Eichelbaum, "Staging An Upside-Down Opera," *The San Francisco Examiner* 8 April 1975: 27.

6. Bertolt Brecht, "A Short Organum to the Theatre," *Brecht on Theatre: The Development of an Aesthetic*, trans. and ed. John Willett (New York: Hill and Wang, 1964) 180.
7. Perhaps this idea was left over from "the sticks exercise" which was eventually cut from *The Trilogy*.
8. Ross Wetzsteon, "Who Ever Heard of a Cute Brecht?," rev. of *The Good Woman of Setzuan*, by Bertolt Brecht, *The Village Voice* 2 February 1976: 107.
9. Eileen Blumenthal, "Andrei Serban Makes Dead Languages Live Again," *The Village Voice* 26 January 1976: 108.
10. Clive Barnes, "La MaMa's Prolific Virtues Crown *Good Woman*," *The New York Times* 4 February 1975: 24.
11. Gussow, "A Fresh Brecht," rev. of *The Good Woman of Setzuan*, by Bertolt Brecht *The New York Times* 27 January 1976: 28.
12. Bonnie Raphael, personal interview, 15 December 1989.
13. Priscilla Smith, personal interview, 13 February 1990.
14. Arthur Friedman, "*Good Woman* Has Faults," rev. of *The Good Woman of Setzuan*, by Bertolt Brecht, *The Boston Herald* 26 May 1987: 35.
15. Smith.
16. Robert Brustein, *Making Scenes: A Personal History of the Turbulent Years at Yale* (New York: Limelight Editions, 1984) 252.
17. Brustein, *Making Scenes* 255.
18. Brustein, *Making Scenes* 256.
19. Brustein, *Making Scenes* 256.
20. Brustein, *Making Scenes* 258.
21. Brustein, *Making Scenes* 258.
22. Gussow, "Molière Farce Staged by Serban," rev. of *Sganarelle: An Evening of Molière Farces*, The New York Times 8 June 1978: 113.
23. John Simon, "French Without Tears," rev. of *Sganarelle: An Evening of Molière Farces*, New York 10 July 1978: 66.
24. Jeremy Geidt, personal interview, 15 December 1989.
25. Cherry Jones noted that he spent a lot of time in rehearsal reading the paper! Cherry Jones, personal interview, 18 February 1990.
26. Jonathan Marks, "Born Again Sganarelle," Theatre Program, *Sganarelle: An Evening of Molière Farces*, American Repertory Theatre 1981, n. pag.
27. Andrei Serban, letter to author, 10 June 1994.
28. Gussow, "Serban, His Vanya and His Career," *The New York Times* 6 September 1983: C11.
29. Ted Emery, "Carlo Gozzi in Context," Introduction, *Five Tales for the Theatre*, by Carlo Gozzi, trans. and ed. by Albert Bermel and Ted Emery (Chicago: University of Chicago Press, 1989) 5.
30. Serban, "Taking the Imaginary Seriously," Theatre Program, *The King Stag*, by Carlo Gozzi, American Repertory Theatre 1984, n. pag.
31. Marks, "Five Characters Who Found an Author," Theatre Program, *The King Stag*, by Carlo Gozzi, American Repertory Theatre 1984, n. pag.

32. Serban, "Taking the Imaginary Seriously."

33. Jack Kroll, "In the Kingdom of Serendippo," rev. of *The King Stag*, by Carlo Gozzi, *Newsweek* 17 December 1984: 79.

34. Brustein, personal interview, 12 December 1989.

35. I include this account mostly to counter the notion that Serban only creates on the spur of the moment in rehearsal.

36. Hafiz Karmali, "Andrei Serban and the Meaning of *The Serpent Woman*," *A.R.T. News* IX No. 1 November 1988: 1, 4.

37. Arthur Holmberg, "Interview With Andrei Serban," *A.R.T. News* IX No. 1 November 1988: 4.

38. I personally felt that the humor was self-conscious because of the theatre space itself—the large, proscenium arrangement of the Loeb Drama Center of A.R.T. As I watched the play, I wondered if the overall ambience of the clowns would have been more successful at the La MaMa Annex with the actors and audience in a more environmental space.

39. Iris Fanger, "Japan's Asakura is Hot Commodity in World of Theater," *The Boston Herald*, 2 December 1988: S22.

40. Kevin Kelly, " ART Season Off to Excessive Start," rev. of *The Serpent Woman,* by Carlo Gozzi, *The Boston Globe* 5 December 1988: 12.

41. Carolyn Clay, "Hiss and Tell," rev. of *The Serpent Woman*, by Carlo Gozzi, *The Boston Phoenix* 9 December 1988: 6.

42. Brustein, personal interview, 12 December 1989.

43. Brustein, personal interview, 12 December 1989.

44. Albert Bermel, "Afterword," *Five Tales for the Theatre*, by Carlo Gozzi 309.

45. Holmberg 4.

4

Serban in Rehearsal:
Twelfth Night at The American Repertory Theatre, 1989

IN DECEMBER of 1989, I observed Serban "tech", preview, and open *Twelfth Night* at The American Repertory Theatre in Cambridge, Massachusetts. Thanks to the kindness of the A.R.T. company, particularly Artistic Director Robert Brustein, as well as the many actors, designers, technicians, and administrators of the company, and Serban himself, I was able not only to observe rehearsals and performances, but to speak with as many people as I could regarding Serban's methods.

In almost all cases, everyone in the company was more than willing to talk about their experiences with Serban. In order to re-capture the atmosphere and nuances of the rehearsal period as accurately as I could, I decided to record them in journal form below.

The First Day of Technical Rehearsal—Tuesday, Dec. 5

Upon arriving on the afternoon of the first *Twelfth Night* technical rehearsal, I'm ushered into the dark house of the Loeb Drama Center. As my eyes slowly grow accustomed to the dim light, I make out a tall figure at the front of the house continually running on and off the stage showing the actors exactly how to execute a shift of scenery, including tossing several suitcases onto the stage from the wings. It is Andrei Serban speaking in a high-pitched, intense, but not unhumorous tone that I will grow very accustomed to in the following days.

My initial impression is that Serban is in complete control of the technical rehearsal. He gives the light cue counts, the sound cue counts, calls for an exact amount of smoke from the fog machine, and gives instructions on how fast the front curtain should be raised and lowered. He often shouts to the designer and technicians in the sound booth—"Don't do *anything* until I tell you to do it!" This meticulousness seems to extend even more to the actors to whom he routinely gives exact line readings, pause counts, and demonstrations of specific movements. Serban seems to get almost instantaneous results from all of the members of the A.R.T. Company, many of whom have worked with him before. For example, Serban seems to be confused by the inclusion of composer Mel Marvin's *(Tintypes, A History of the American Film, Yentl)* score on the house sound system for the first time. This is the company's first rehearsal on the Loeb stage—for six weeks they had been in a rehearsal hall across town.

Within minutes of Serban demanding that they go back to the rehearsal tape he was used to, a technician has plugged it in for him on a portable cassette player hastily arranged in the house. Serban seems to be thinking about every detail of the show constantly—all at the same time. In a given minute of rehearsal time, he gives notes on the curtain, the lights, the music, an actress' shoes, and the pace of the action on stage. He gives directions to his actors like "Don't rush; be much softer," "It's an emotional moment," and "It's a cruel act." He shows the actors *exactly* what he wants them to do, often re-blocking entire scenes now that the actors are finally in the performance space. No scenes are "run," rather there is a continual "stop & go" for every moment of every scene. Serban appears to be fascinated with props in this production—the throwing of the luggage in Viola's arrival on the sea coast of Illyria in Act I Sc. ii, Sir Andrew and Sir Toby watching cartoons and Lawrence Welk on television in Act I Sc. iii, and Olivia's ladies-in-waiting each presenting the disguised Viola with a rose in Act I Sc. v.

Some very quick and immediate impressions of this *Twelfth Night*—the set is a white marble box, complete with a ceiling that looks somewhat classical and rather sterile. The first scene of the play takes place with a narcissistic Duke Orsino (Kario Salem) looking like a spoiled rock star, lolling about on a bed while his portrait is being painted, his hushed, melancholy voice "If music be the food of love, play on" amplified by a hidden body microphone. In the next scene, Viola (Cherry Jones) lands at the sea coast with cut-out waves being pulled horizontally back and forth in the fashion of Italian Renaissance scenic effects. Before Viola changes into a man's clothing, she pulls a Polaroid snapshot from her bag (presumably her twin brother Sebastian?). As if in answer, a silhouetted figure of Sebastian rises from the waves all the while accompanied by Marvin's absolutely wondrous and haunting score of harps and synthesizers. Act I Scene iii takes place in a huge empty living room, save a couch and a tiny television on the floor. Sir Toby Belch, Sir Andrew Aguecheek, and Maria (Jeremy Geidt, Robert Stanton, and Lynn Chausow) seem muted and even desperate in this sterile atmosphere, rather than the customary comically robust interpretation of these characters. When Malvolio (Jim Lally) appears in the next scene, a tall, thin man dressed in black and a bowler hat, reading a newspaper while leaning against the proscenium arch, he reminds me of an image from a Magritte painting. This is definitely not the usual festive interpretation of this play!

The Second Day of Technical Rehearsal—Wednesday, Dec. 6

As I arrive early for today's noon rehearsal call, I find Serban already in the theatre working with the technicians and designers. In the coming days, I realize that Serban always arrives early, leaves late, works through the two hour dinner and shorter breaks, and rarely leaves his place in the house, not even to use the restroom. His usual schedule as far as I can determine is about 9:30 am to 1:30 am everyday with no breaks. Occasionally, he is joined by his wife, Alexandra, and two young sons, Nicholas and Anthony, ages 4 and 2, who bring him soup and otherwise play in the house and on the stage during the rehearsal! (Cherry Jones would later tell me that this is one of Serban's calmer technical rehearsals, at least compared to last year's *The Serpent Woman*. "The reason why he gets that way is that when he gets really obsessed he doesn't eat and he doesn't sleep."[1] On the other hand, lighting designer Howell Binkley offered that Serban didn't seem to sleep much when he finally did leave the theatre early every morning: "He stays up all night thinking and studying the process of the show.")[2]

This morning Serban is working with a huge, yellow cut-out helicopter that flies up and down and apparently will be used for the Duke's entrance later in the play. Stenciled on the side of the helicopter in very official, almost bureaucratic letters is the word "Duke" (a reference to then Massachusetts governor Michael Dukakis?).

The rehearsal begins with the actors. Antonio and Sebastian (Rodney Hudson and Stephen Skybell) make their first entrance on a large, cut-out ship that rolls in from the stage left wing, with Antonio perched high on the mast. Serban runs the scene over and over, looking for the exact right amount of puffs of smoke from the fog machine to simulate the ship's motor. He tells both actors "I want to make it much more stylized" and shows them how to walk, very slowly with many designated pauses in the movement. A comment to Sebastian is telling: "Look straight ahead—don't make it naturalistic!" Finally, Serban cuts the smoke from the scene altogether and moves on to Act II Sc. ii, a short meeting between Viola and Malvolio. Viola (now disguised as Cesario) makes her entrance circling gracefully about the stage on a bicycle. I immediately think of Serban's 1982 production of *The Marriage of Figaro* at The Guthrie in which each major character traveled on wheels, from skateboards to shopping carts, but somehow here, the effect, as accompanied by the repeated bubbling musical theme of Marvin's score, is magical, not gimmicky. After Malvolio leaves her the ring, the curtain comes down and Viola steps in front of it for her "I am the man" soliloquy. The curtain coming in and out for the scene shifts surprises me, as it is a custom that is now generally associated with an old-fashioned method of producing musical comedy. Too, the actors are often bathed in follow-spots for soliloquies, or even within scenes with other actors. The impression is very presentational—I'm not quite sure what Serban is after, yet. Meanwhile, Cherry Jones is thus far a very earnest Viola. She doesn't play the laugh lines, of which there are many in this soliloquy; instead, she appears to be genuinely upset and even frightened by the possibilities of her love for Orsino, Orsino's love for Olivia, and Olivia's attraction to her. (See Figure #9)

Serban spends a lot of time on Act II Sc. iii—the "famous drinking scene" in which Sir Toby, Sir Andrew, and Maria hatch their plot against Malvolio after he reprimands them for a bout of all night drinking. Of course, this scene is treated very differently in this production! We are back in the sterile living room of Olivia's house. This time, amongst the very spare modern furniture, the curtain rises on a burning trash can in the center of the room. Sir Andrew and Sir Toby sit about listlessly, speaking their lines very slowly and softly, staring at the flames. One can't help but be struck for a moment, no matter how fleeting, of an image of the homeless, so many of whom are outside this very theatre in Harvard Square and the surrounding city of Boston in this cold winter. When Feste, the Fool (Tommy Derrah) enters, he carries with him a large emblem of the "We Three" he refers to and all three actors enact a feeble "See no evil. hear no evil, speak no evil" pantomime. The Fool sings the "O Mistress mine" song very softly and slowly. The effect is one of melancholy—there is no joy or mirth here. I see Serban construct a brilliant moment on the spot—he has Sir Toby come downstage to challenge the audience with his line "But shall we make the welkin dance indeed? ... Shall we do that?" But with lighting designer Howell Binkley's shadowy lighting for this scene, the actor shouts these line in almost total darkness. The silhouette image is very disquieting. The "Hold Thy Peace" song is also sung very softly, almost innocuously. These people are not having fun, they're not making that much noise—all is muted. Serban works *against* the text, instead of trying to accommodate it. The result is the opposite of most "festive reveling" that we often see in conventional productions of Elizabethan plays. Maria joins the two would-be revelers and Malvolio is finally awakened after a somewhat more lively song of "Tilly-Vally Lady", a carefully choreographed, rather gymnastic "choo-choo train" dance which Serban runs over and over again, much to the actors' consternation. Sir Toby drunkenly "moons" Malvolio (and the audience), holds up a lighted miniature Christmas tree on the line "the twelfth day of December", and finally passes out on the couch while Malvolio lectures. The scene is funny, but in a disturbing way. It is not the usual hearty laughter I've felt with this scene in previous productions. One last observation on this scene: Serban instructing actor Bob Stanton (Sir Andrew) "Don't play sad—be the opposite. You're full of hope!"

We now return to the Duke's palace where Orsino is once again in bed, surrounded by his attendants. His head pops up from beneath a shroud with the line: "Give me some music." When Viola/Cesario enters, the Duke invites her/him right into his bed. This dialogue is also whispered on the body mics and lit with a very tight pin-spot. The atmosphere is very sexual, although it is not clear how much the Duke really wants Cesario since in a short while, he will once again request s/he bear his love to Olivia. On the other hand, some aspects of the text actually resonate even further with Viola/Cesario huddled in the Duke's arms in his bed, such as the Duke's advice to marry an older woman. Women are discussed as pets and toys in the exclusive, possibly homosexual male-bonding world of the Duke. Still, a little later, Orsino literally violently hurls Cesario from his bed, raising the question of why Viola would love a man like this in the first place. I'm reminded of the continual charges that Serban excessively illustrates the text, sometimes at the expense of credible character relationships, instead of "trusting the words." Serban eventually removed this violent piece of business, apparently at the suggestion of Brustein and A.R.T. Literary Director Robert Scanlan.[3] When The Fool is called in to sing, a painting of a death image is utilized. Once more, the song is sad and melancholy, at least, at first. It soon becomes very indulgent, with Feste moving all over the stage like a Las Vegas entertainer singing a schmaltzy melancholy love song. We even see one of the attendants unabashedly spreading the smoke from the fog machine around the stage like a bad special effect from a Hollywood awards show production number. The scene finally ends with Viola alone on stage seeing another vision of Sebastian cross the stage in a candlelit procession of attendants. Much later, upon further reflection, I realize why this image, unlike perhaps those earlier in the scene, makes perfect sense and is vital, rather than gratuitous: Viola has just told Orsino about her family background—"I am all the daughters of my father's house, And all the brothers too—and yet I know not." Serban visualizes on stage the inner monologue of Viola's love and connection with her twin. It is an image based upon a careful reading of the text.

I notice for the first time that Feste the Fool is costumed like a Beckett tramp—he could be Estragon or Vladimir from *Godot*. The knapsack on the stick he constantly carries even reminds me of Death's scythe.

This afternoon's rehearsal only covered two scenes, with Serban's constant stopping and going, particularly repeating the procession scene over and over. I wonder if the pace of the tech will pick up with an audience due at the first preview performance on Friday night and over half the play still to go. I assume at some point there will be a run-through of the show?

I have dinner tonight with an old friend, Bill Finlay. I didn't realize that he was the fight choreographer on this show, nor did he know I was watching rehearsals. Naturally, I ask him about working with Serban. Bill makes two comments which will stick in my mind. The first is "He's a smoothie." He goes on to explain how Serban "smoothed over" Finlay's ruffled feathers when Serban ran a fencing scene (the fight between Antonio and Sir Toby in Act III Sc. iv—actually most of the combat is between Antonio and Fabian in this production) before Finlay had a chance to finish choreographing it or bring it up to speed. Without Finlay present at the rehearsal, Serban asked them to do it closer to the real timing. Luckily, no one was hurt but a sword was broken, due to an improper hit. When Finlay presented Serban with the broken sword, the director was properly ingratiating, thus Finlay's comment! No matter. As a director himself, Finlay has the utmost respect for Serban as an artist, if not his understanding of stage combat. He said he'd been given a tremendous amount of freedom by Serban in his interpretation and staging of the fights. I mention my impression of Serban in control of the technical rehearsal at every moment—literally like a painter with his canvas, only using text, actors, scenery, light, sound, etc. as his palette. Finlay nods. "When he's in the house watching tech—he knows exactly where everyone in the theatre is at any given moment ... and how they can help him."

Tonight's rehearsal—all five hours of it—is devoted entirely to Act II Sc. v. In this exterior scene, supposedly Olivia's garden, a huge cut-out cactus appears up center while a strip of green felt is diagonally laid out across the stage. Fabian (Dan Nutu) makes his first entrance in a white gangster's suit with sunglasses—a Mafioso type. Serban instructs Malvolio to speak directly to the audience in this scene, not unusual staging for this letter reading scene. The letter is placed in every possible position by Sir Toby and Sir Andrew before Malvolio sees it—a very funny, old-fashioned bit of slapstick. This tone continues with the way Fabian, Andrew, and Toby peek out from behind the cactus and watch Malvolio speculate on the letters M, O, A, I and the yellow stockings. Serban works so specifically with Jim Lally that he even turns a somersault exit himself so Malvolio could imitate him. I overhear a brief discussion after midnight as I'm leaving—Serban seems to want more dry tech time (without the actors) which appears to be hard for the A.R.T. crew to build into the schedule because then they lose stage time for focusing lights, painting, re-building the sound tapes, etc. As it turns out, Serban and the crew end up working together every morning from about 9:30 until the 12 noon actor call.

The Third Day of Technical Rehearsal—Thursday, Dec. 7

I didn't fully realize it last night (possibly because *I* was so tired—try to imagine how the performers and technicians feel!) but we have finally come to the intermission point in the play, after Shakespeare's Act II Sc. v.

Feste ends Part One by hitting a huge gong. Serban divides up Shakespeare's next few scenes a bit differently. The first part of Act III Sc. i, the dialogue between Feste and Viola takes place in front of the curtain. As Serban instructs The Fool to leave through the curtain and "be more mysterious—I'll be your friend from now on", (another example, by the way, that Serban indeed does think about character motivation when coaching actors!), it begins to finally dawn on me that Serban is fascinated with the curtain as a physical symbol of all that is mysterious about the "show" of the theatre—from Broadway to 19th century entertainment. Characters peeking into and out of the curtain, as they do throughout the production, give a metatheatrical quality to the play that is further enhanced by the spotlights, cut-out scenery, and eclectic costumes. Some might call this style postmodern (as indeed Frank Rich did later in *The New York Times* although, interestingly, no one at the A.R.T. ever used this term when discussing the production), others might find it metatheatrical, or the theatre commenting upon itself, and still others might find it confusing or even gimmicky. To me, it's fascinating in both a thoughtful and visceral way, but I'm not exactly sure why. In other words, it's pure Serban.

Despite the provocative and unusual visual effects, Serban continues to pay attention to the language most of all (even in a supposed "technical rehearsal"). " 'Wit' means talent, Cherry! It must *mean* something! Every word counts,

Cherry!" Serban implores her. She is incredibly patient, I think, as is the entire A.R.T. Company.

The curtain opens on a fairly bare stage when Sir Toby and Sir Andrew enter. Sir Andrew uses a translation book when Cesario speaks to him in French—a pretty funny bit of business, actually. While waiting for a sound cue, Serban asks the actors to practice a bit of blocking. He absolutely hates to wait—he is constantly striving to make best use of the time. (Later that evening, Serban becomes so impatient he refuses to wait for the stage manager to write down a cue count. Even when Brustein implores him to be reasonable as the crew won't remember it unless they write it down, Serban explodes with "Let them write later!")

When Viola meets Olivia (Diane Lane), the action switches inside to a sort of Hollywood mansion look. (This is still all Act III Sc. i.) Outside Olivia's palace a cut-out palm tree is seen in silhouette against a red sky. Olivia greets Cesario in a contemporary sexy evening dress, heels, and a cigarette holder. Serban gives Diane Lane this last accouterment on the spot and she resists at first. "We want a Hollywood image," he insists. The atmosphere is indeed very Hollywood—a seductive quality of looking out at the Pacific at sunset in Santa Monica. His other directions to the two actresses include "Soft hands! God! Like this!" (he demonstrates) and "This scene is more emotional than sexual." Cherry Jones and Diane Lane may be the two consummate Serban actresses, with the exception of Priscilla Smith. Jones has played leading roles in *Three Sisters*, *Sganarelle*, *The Miser*, *The King Stag*, and now this, while Lane was an original member of *The Trilogy* when she was six years old! She literally grew up acting for Serban on the *Trilogy* tours.

The emphasis Serban is placing on sexual ambiguity in the play is finally coming into focus for me. Instead of playing this scene for the laughter of mistaken identity and disguise, the attraction between the two women is very real and anguished. The scene is sexy without being graphic. At one point, Olivia presses Viola's hand against her cheek. In all of the *Twelfth Nights* I've seen, for the first time I believe that Olivia truly loves and wants Viola/Cesario.

Serban continues to have sound problems in this scene. He wants most of the sound cues in the house speakers, not in the backstage speakers. "It's much more aggressive—like an invasion." My heart continues to go out to beleaguered sound designer Maribeth Back.

The next scene (Shakespeare's III-iii) eventually turns out to be the most controversial in the production—the one that makes the purists say "Shakespeare is rolling over in his grave." For the meeting of Antonio and Sebastian, a scene that is often hurried through in a purely informational sense so we can get back to the stories of Viola and Malvolio, Serban places them in the bar that they speak about—The Elephant. Traps open from below the apron of the stage upon which the actors lean, sipping their beers while a neon Michelob sign flies in from above and a lilting lounge piano is heard. Both Antonio and Sebastian speak very softly and seductively on the amplified body mikes. The scene is very soft and sexy—so intimate that one is embarrassed to be eavesdropping and watching. Not content, Serban adds another actor to the scene, a handsome young man in a muscle tee shirt, in order to get Sebastian to speak even softer and not be overheard and "to add a sense of humor." As the new character sips his beer and watches the other two, suddenly the scene turns into a gay bar and Antonio's relationship with Sebastian makes perfect sense. Later on, Antonio will fight ferociously for Sebastian and be stunned when Sebastian (actually Viola) will not return the money he's loaned. The scene is, of course, very funny and will draw the biggest laughs every night from the audience. Still later, Serban will add two women at another table to the side who watch the action and drink and smoke (to counter the image of the gay bar?) and *still* later, after the show is in previews, Serban adds the biggest sight gag and, at the same time, the most metatheatrical and openly postmodern element to the production: an actor who looks just like Shakespeare sitting at another table in the bar watching the entire scene and writing it all down with a quill pen. In one scene then, again one that is virtually ignored in many traditional productions of *Twelfth Night*, we see two very possible lovers in perhaps a gay bar, drinking beer, observed by patrons of the bar, all the while being observed by an image of the author watching and noting what is being done to his text! It is Serban's way of acknowledging the author's presence in dealing with any text, but it seems especially appropriate with Shakespeare given the numerous interpretations of his texts. It is a brilliant piece of directing, most of which was evolved on the spot at the technical rehearsal. Serban places the scenes in environments we recognize, instead of letting a scene be in a neutral setting, but more important, as Assistant Director Paul Walker was to tell me later, the locale of the scene evolved out of the intimacy between the two actors in rehearsal. The setting of a gay bar came later—it was not imposed on the text at first. It was a question of "what universe would hold that kind of conversation."[4]

Serban finally moves on to the next scene (III-iv). Olivia is primping for Cesario in spiked heels in front of a mirror. When Malvolio arrives in his crossed garters, he looks like a punk rock star gone awry—actually, a bit like rock star Billy Idol with a teased blond wig and huge leather boots wrapped tight with yellow garters. Now comes one of the most disturbing parts of the play. As Malvolio listens to his boom box radio, very pleased with himself with the impression he believes he's made on Olivia, he is threatened and beaten with chains by Sir Toby, Fabian, and Maria. As he is whipped, The Three Stooges theme blares out of the radio. On the afternoon of opening night, this will be changed to a portable television set and a religious Jim Bakker type theme song. Malvolio screams as he is beaten, then jumps off the stage and exits through the audience on the line "Go hang yourselves all! You are idle shallow things; I am not of your element" as the houselights are abruptly bumped on. Fabian then comes directly down center to the lip of the stage and quietly speaks the line "If this were played upon the stage now, I could condemn it as an improbable fiction." Immediately, the house goes down and we re-enter the world of the stage. Instead of just playing a joke on old Malvolio, we see a very cruel act (which will become even more so when Malvolio is imprisoned) intermingled with a theatrical self-consciousness that, to me, is consistent throughout the play.

Unfortunately, there are many intricate sound cues in this section with Malvolio and the others turning the radio on and off. Finally, after many missed cues, Serban stops the rehearsal completely and shouts for A.R.T. General Manager Jonathan Miller to come into the theatre from whom he will demand new sound technicians, "real professionals." Miller somehow manages to placate Serban and the rehearsal continues, but I wonder if the folks in the sound booth can remember about now why they were first attracted to this art of make-believe.

A few minutes later Serban is waving to his children who are lying on the stage while he works. The scene continues. Finlay gets a few minutes of stage time to work on the fights. The Antonio/Viola confrontation over the money is deadly serious and not just a funny plot device of mistaken identity. The officers enter in a cut-out police car with siren, rotating red light, and the insignia "Illyria PD" on the side, handcuff Antonio and take him away. When Sebastian enters and fights with Sir Toby and Fabian, Serban stages Olivia's rescue in a very romantic and traditional manner. She literally draws him into her house, moving in seductive slow motion as the music sensuously underscores, partially undressing on the way, while Sebastian can scarcely believe his good fortune. When Diane Lane complains to Serban that it isn't credible for her to leave her wrap on the ground, Serban answers her with "For sex, you leave everything."

The company refers to the next scene as "Malvolio's Outhouse" and now I see why. Malvolio is held prisoner in a giant outhouse that rises up from the floor. He is sitting on a toilet, bound and gagged with toilet paper. As Sir Topas, Feste dons a long black gown and a mask (he looks like Il Dottore, the quack doctor from the commedia dell'arte), and climbs on the roof of the outhouse to taunt Malvolio. Serban's direction to Feste is "It's a very strange ceremony. Ritual—a voodoo." Later in the scene, the outhouse descends once again, returning Malvolio to the bowels of hell? (or a sewer?) We hear Malvolio on a mic way down below, completely out of sight, while Feste continues his conversation with him on a brightly lit stage that is oddly disconcerting. Suddenly Malvolio's hand pops up from below the stage, as in Brian De Palma's *Carrie*. This scene will be significantly edited after preview, although the outhouse is still used. One thing is certain: Serban is going out of his way to show the cruelty that is enacted upon Malvolio is much more than he deserves.

The next brief scene (IV-iii) of Sebastian and Olivia making plans to marry is almost played "straight" by Serban on the bare stage, but in Sebastian's opening soliloquy, we hear Malvolio's unearthly screams from below.

It is now almost midnight when Equity regulations require the company to stop. There is one more scene left to tech—the long denouement of Act V Sc. i. There will be no run-through before tomorrow night's preview audience. (I find out later that this will be the first non-stop run-through *ever* of the entire play.) The company gamely begins this long final complicated scene. First, Feste reads Malvolio's "letter" which is actually a crumpled up piece of shit-stained toilet paper. Then the Duke and his henchmen make their long awaited entrance in the yellow cut-out helicopter. A cheap Italian love song plays while each of the Duke's attendants saunter about in white jackets and dark sunglasses—like a bad foreign film. It is now 11:55 pm and everyone, actors, designers, technicians, etc, are exhausted, except, of course, Serban. Or if he is, he sure doesn't show it. He's still going strong—insisting on seeing Olivia enter in her wedding dress. Where on earth does he get his energy from? A final thought as I trudge wearily out of the theatre: as noted earlier, Serban authors the entire production like a composer, then conducts it note by note using actors, text, lights, scenery, and sound. If we could only find the proper notation for it, then it wouldn't be just inside his head and everyone could read it. It might certainly make this process easier. The only problem with this, besides being impossible, is that Serban often "composes" on the spot. By the time someone could get an idea down, he'd already be off to ten others.

The Fourth Day of Tech—Friday, Dec. 8 (First Preview tonight at 8 pm)

I'm very curious to see how Serban ends the play. Like many Elizabethan comedies, *Twelfth Night* seems to "end forever" with a lengthy denouement explaining the various disguises and relationships.

The first element of note in the final scene is that Sir Toby is really *hurt* and very bloody when he makes his final appearance. Next, the recognition scene between Viola and Sebastian lives up to its advance billing throughout the play. Actors Jones and Skybell act out a mirror exercise, then while everyone else disappears behind the slowly entering cardboard waves, they seize each other's wrists and roll together on the floor, joyously shouting their lines. As the couples are paired off, Viola and Orsino, and Olivia and Sebastian, there is an uneasy sense of a "foursome." It is clear with Viola's farewell kiss to Olivia that she is not sure she is getting the best partner after all. Rather there is a strong sense of succumbing to social convention. Then, Malvolio is hoisted up from below through a very, very long rope descending down into the trap. A bedraggled, completely broken figure, his final threat "I'll be revenged on the whole pack of you" is delivered very slowly as he is literally dragged off the stage. A minute later, he is back—slowly crossing from upstage left to right, carrying a suitcase. After Malvolio's exit, it begins to rain and thunder. There is an ending tableau of umbrellas that Finlay has described as "very Magritte." Each duo of lovers (Viola/Olivia, Viola/Orsino, Viola/Sebastian, Sebastian/Olivia, Olivia/Orsino, Sebastian/Antonio, and Andrew/Toby) have a "moment" together before pairing off with their correct partner. Attendants hand off the umbrellas which are opened at the back of the stage silhouetted against the cyclorama in this very slowly choreographed ending. All the while, rain continues to fall, with an occasional roll of thunder and the whistle of the wind, while one continuous note is played on a synthesizer and The Fool very slowly and softly sings "When that I was and a little tiny boy/With hey, ho, the wind and the rain." It is an exquisite, if protracted final image. The very final image is a scroll that unrolls on The Fool's back with Shakespeare's face super-imposed on a map of England. (This is later cut.) The curtain-call is a simple lineup, an ensemble call. Now for an audience!

This afternoon there seemed to be a real air of uncertainty, as if no one knew "whether the ship would sink or float." Finlay told me that Brustein confided "that they are usually farther along at this time." And yet, I feel confident of a fairly smooth preview (I'm sure it won't be for Serban.) I have confidence in A.R.T.'s professionalism and the experience of the cast and crew. All along I've sensed from everyone in the company, but particularly those who have worked with Serban before, an incredible patience and an attitude that this is "business as usual" and if they can just get past the usual tension and challenge of any technical rehearsal, they trust that they and Serban can pull a great production from this enormous stew of ideas, technical marvels, and long rehearsal.

But perhaps I'm wrong. When I leave at 5:20 pm this afternoon, there is a frenzy of technical and clean-up activity in the theatre with Serban still giving notes to the actors. I discover that the company has a betting pool on the running time of the performance time tonight, since there's never been a run-through. My guess is three hours.

First Preview Impressions—Saturday, Dec. 9

Well, I was wrong. The show ran just about four hours with an intermission—from 8:15 pm to 12:10 am. Brustein gave a very witty curtain speech about this being the first run-through of the show so they weren't sure how it long it was! In a sense, the audience was privileged to see "the complete and unabridged version." He also spoke of Serban's imagination and "chutzpah."

The performance went fine considering the circumstances—a few glaring technical errors, mostly sound. I estimate out of a house of approximately 500, there were about 30 walkouts—mostly babysitter problems I'll bet! Most audience members seemed to "go with it" and enjoy it very much. There was very long applause at the end, although some seemed puzzled. (One young student even asked me if I knew what was going on.)

The general feeling amongst the company is that there is a great play somewhere in these four hours and that it simply needs to be cut. Brustein told me right before the performance started "Now he *really* starts to work—to edit, once he sees it before an audience." Robert Scanlan would later say the same thing: "He listens to the audience. Directors in previews seldom make full use of the audience. Andrei does."[5]

Serban and the crew have been at rehearsal this morning since 9:30. It appears he has many cuts ready. At first, he seems rather dissatisfied with last night's preview: "Last night was a fuck-up—don't talk about last night!" But I notice that he doesn't say this without humor or a twinkle in his eye.

Serban is very interested in the reactions of the audience—especially the response of children (He arranged an audience of exclusively children when he was previewing *The Marriage of Figaro* at The Guthrie). He also wants to know how many people walked out last night vs. the first preview of Robert Wilson's marathon *CIVIL warS*, part of which was presented at A.R.T. in 1986. Serban's intention is to cut 30 minutes in tonight's second preview. This is the first time I've seen Serban smoke. He asks a technician for a cigarette. Several members of the company are coming down with the flu—Cherry Jones in particular is very ill while Serban himself looks a bit under the weather.

The company gathers for a note session in a circle of chairs in the West Lobby of the theatre. There is an atmosphere of accomplishment, even relaxation that I haven't perceived in the last 72 hours. Serban begins his address very slowly.

> First of all, congratulations. You made it through. Technically, they (the crew) accomplished miracles. In spite of this endless epic, it was an absolutely unique night—it will never be repeated. Although it was long, some people were never bored. It is very interesting to sustain this for four hours. There is a specialness about entering this time—a time of its own; a first run-through before an audience has a fragile quality and the innocence of a flower that didn't fully blossom, yet invites a special attention.
>
> *Twelfth Night* is not really a comedy. It is instead a look at the human condition. What is love? What is sexuality? What is the relationship between men and women? This is unsafe territory. It is not an easy evening. This is not a *Twelfth Night* after-dinner show where everything is reconciled.There are elements of disturbance—a mirror to life, a mirror to what we all are.
>
> It's great that you didn't try to provoke laughter—laughter comes anyway, but not via shtick, only through the paradox and contrast in the play.
>
> The danger starts tonight. Last night was completely pure—because we didn't know the sense of timing and try to manipulate. Now we will never be naive in that way. It's up to you to provoke in a fresh way every night. Last night was honest ... Helicopters, police sirens—all of the cheap tricks create the sublime and ridiculousness ... We must always be confronted with a surprise ... an amazing mixture of modern and old. Shakespeare allows that.

The problem that we have is how to transmit this to the audience. If I were Artistic Director (of A.R.T.), I'd take the risk of doing it (not cutting the play). It's painful for me to do this, I hate to do it.

How do we make this proposition clear to the audience? The scenes are so ambiguous. What is the polarity of this attraction? It is very hard for the audience to know who to "vote for." They want to know where the goodness is. Here it is extremely difficult to say. One is left with subtlety, interesting but disquieting. All I would like to have established is a sense of humility and recognition that we are all celebrating on the stage some forces in ourselves—bringing to light what we know very little about! Don't play for laughs. Everything must be unexpected.

Then Serban gave an example of the audience having an ironic laugh on the priest's line—"a contract of eternal bond of love" noting "It's a beautiful line but the audience laughs because today it's almost an irony to believe in that!"

Serban's formal address completed, rehearsal begins once more. Serban lets his assistant, Paul Walker, circulate amongst the cast giving acting notes, while he works major moments on stage, mostly technical. To begin with, Serban has Feste swing his mallet, but *not* hit the gong to begin the play. Already in the opening seconds of the show, it's not what we expect to happen. Serban tones down the physical attraction Orsino has for Viola/Cesario; it becomes less homosexual, more ambiguous. He speeds up several scenes giving directions like "Like silent cinema—like vaudeville—so fast!" Others, he slows down even more: "Do not feel obliged to speed up. That will be catastrophe. That's conventional tempo I'm not interested in. Even slow has rhythm in it, like music."

Serban also gives many cuts in the text. Many are made in the "Sir Topas" scene with Malvolio and Feste. Others are in Sebastian and Olivia's scene after they've made love (IV-iii). Serban trusts some actors to make their own cuts—especially Jeremy Geidt who plays Sir Toby.

I can see Serban's sense of humor today. He's more relaxed and joking with members of the company. Ever patient stage manager Annie King asks him if he has cut a musician in a scene. He laughs and says "No, but that's very good!" Later on, I ask Serban where he watches the show from every night and he replies "They lock me in a cage to make sure I don't jump on stage and say 'Stop!' " (Actually, the light booth).

Second Preview—Saturday, Dec. 9

The play runs 3 and one-half hours. It is much tighter, much more focused, but as Serban said, already becoming safe. The biggest change, besides as an overall growing sense of confidence and polish in both the acting and technical departments, is a downplaying of the erotic love between Viola/Cesario and Orlando. As Serban intends, it is now more ambiguous. The Sir Topas/Malvolio scene in IV-ii ("Malvolio's Outhouse") is also much shorter. The play seems to be working in a multi-leveled fashion—of sexual ambiguity, the sterility of modern life, and the metatheatricality of The Fool peeking behind the curtain and the cut-out scenery. For me, what is not working yet is the urgent sense of what the characters are trying to *do* to each other—and why—especially in Part Two. Why does Sir Toby deceive Sir Andrew in setting up the phony duel with Cesario? This is an intriguing question especially in the way that Serban has staged it. Although the scene is funny, there is an absolute fear in Viola's actions—she actually retches before facing her opponent. It is all very cruel. The same goes for why Malvolio is tortured and even the long denouement in the final scene. There lacks real confusion in the identity mix-ups since the entire world of the play has been in chaos from the start. But then, perhaps this is what Serban wants. He has no wish to return to "order" as in a traditional comedy.

Equity off-day—Monday, Dec. 11

I've now seen four previews. The official opening night is Wednesday. Last night's preview, (there were two yesterday with Sunday's matinee), was by far the best show so far. I was really listening to the actors, perhaps for the first time, and involved with the actions and problems of the characters. Everyone in the company, including Serban, seems more relaxed and confident. The running time is now three hours and 35 minutes. There have been so many small adjustments in the performance since first preview I'll just mention a few: Olivia now tries to take off Viola's jacket in Scene III-i (the company calls this scene "Olivia Gets Hot"), the spotlights have been removed in the final scene where the lovers are all matched up, and Shakespeare has made his appearance in the bar. When Serban arrives at the theatre with his son, he is very gracious: "This man has been waiting to talk to me for days!" We sit in the house and I manage to keep Nicholas entertained with drawing and non-sugar lifesavers while I ask questions of his Dad. I reproduce the interview below since it is not only the key interview in the scope of this study, it is also the best insight into Serban's theatrical methods.

An Interview with Andrei Serban—Dec. 11, 1989

I'm speaking with Andrei Serban, director of Twelfth Night on Dec. 11, 1989.

And he has a cold.

And he has a cold. How did you happen to select Twelfth Night. I know it is your first Shakespeare since As You Like It, right?

Yes. *Twelfth Night* is a play I never wanted to direct. All the productions I have seen of it seem uninteresting and I thought maybe the play is a kind of banal comedy with no other implication but just to create laughter and make people have a nice evening after dinner in the theatre. When Brustein persuaded me to look at *Twelfth Night*, I read it again and saw that are some elements of darkness and of emotion which exist in the play that I have never seen in a production. So I thought maybe it is a challenge to try and discover a *Twelfth Night* that hasn't been discovered before .

Did you see the Théâtre du Soleil version? (a much celebrated production directed by Arian Mnouchkine in Paris, 1982, which incorporated Japanese and Indian theatre techniques).

Yes, I saw that and although it was very beautiful, I don't think it had much to do with the play. I mean it was an exquisite production, but it left out the whole dark substance of the play, the whole feeling of despair and loneliness, cruelty, sarcasm, ambiguity of the sexes, and the difficulty of love. All those very important themes were left out—just a long evening of enjoyment of commedia dell'arte and Eastern techniques and it was a theatrical evening of great charm and imagination but it was not presenting the play.

What do you do differently when you are working with the text on a Shakespeare?

I just study more carefully than if I work with lesser playwrights. If it is true that in any Shakespeare line there are seven levels of meaning, at least I hope to discover two, if not more.

What about all the so-called traditional methods of dealing with the meter and the scansion?

Sure, that is important and at times we try to follow that up like a kind of very good guide, and at times we try to dismiss it, like, for example, in the bar scene. Although that scene is written in verse, it is usually a short scene, a transition scene which happens between Antonio and Sebastian and in a regular production, you don't even notice it. In this production, I think you remember it because of its slow pace established by the mood of people talking quietly in a *cinéma-verité* fashion. So that is why we took the liberty to break the pentameter. I think that because we do this the way we do, we don't try to go against Shakespeare's words, but somehow the words themselves are heard much more than if we would have done it in a kind of fast pace, respecting the pentameter.

Do you work with the actors in any particular way because it is dealing with verse? Differently than your work on Chekhov, for example?

In Chekhov, people talk apparently like in life. But that is not so. They talk like in life, but they use fewer words. In Shakespeare, the poetry and the rhythm apparently call for a larger-than-life approach. But this is also not so. Because in both Chekhov and Shakespeare, although they use different techniques, they reach the same impression: life as essence, life distilled. How can an actor use his own materials which come from life and heighten his own concentration and his own quality of attention to a higher level? So there is an effort which the verse obliges the actor to come up to, to rise up to the occasion and, at the same time, to be totally truthful to himself.

Are there particular exercises you do with the actors to get what you want?

Yes, in the first two weeks we did a lot of exercises on language, on verse, and on the movement of the stanzas in the line. All those exercises were apparently purely technical, but they were not. They were also trying to connect the meaning, the emotion, and the mind, in a way that all these three elements participate at once when the verse is spoken. So something which does take place is quite extraordinary in which one's voice is involved, one's intelligence is not asleep, and one's body is active and not lazy. One cannot do Shakespeare unless one is completely there. One cannot really correctly give justice to this *extraordinary* poetry which has such amazing depth of wisdom, subtlety, and power unless one is really making an effort to go beyond the ordinary. That is the type of exercise we try to do.

Can you give me an example of one that you felt worked really well?

There is a Cicely Berry exercise called "the two point exercise." (Berry is the Voice Director of the Royal Shakespeare Company and has also worked often with Brook.) One puts on the floor two marks six feet apart and one starts on one point and says the first word in a speech, one word only. It doesn't matter if this word is a short word, a verb, a noun, an "and" or an "or" or short connecting word. It doesn't matter what the word is. But you just say one word at a time. And for the next word, you move to the next point and say the second word. And so forth, back and forth moving between words and saying the word on each point. The next exercise is to try to say one thought, one sentence in one point, and then move on the next sentence or the next thought. Then you try to go to the end of one line or one verse, then move. You get to the next point, you say the next line. Then what you try to do is make the connection. So it is very subtle. It is almost as if one tries to dissect, to go into syllables, so every syllable in a word, every letter, every syllable, every constant, every vowel, to discover how they are connected—the connection between one word to another.

Why one word is necessary in the middle of a sentence and how the sentence would be without that "or" or "and." How is it important? Or a very short "if?" How that changes the thought. How that takes us in another direction or how an "and" completes or adds to a thought. What is the movement in the pentameter? What is the reason the verse stops and what is the new energy which brings the new sentence or next verse up? All those exercises were there only to awake in the actors the extraordinary power that is within the written text that when spoken, so many echoes could come to life.

How do the images take place in your mind? How did it happen for this play?

I just start with an interest that I cannot explain. I truly don't have this clear idea in my mind of how it should look. And then slowly, as I read the play two or three times, and then I let it rest for a while, and then I come back to it again, just fragments of images come to my mind. Just from a fragment, just from one image and something connects to something else and, for example, in the *Twelfth Night*, I want to do something which, although the set is a kind of classical set with columns and so on, somehow has a feeling of the beauty of an Illyria which is imaginary, but could be somewhere on the Mediterranean rough coast. With that I try to bring in all kinds of echoes—old and new. That is why the bar scene is a contemporary image or the police car or the helicopter mixed with Grecian urns and neoclassical splendor. So to really mix up images from all these times is to just create something which is timeless—to bring the past into the present.

Do you see those as you are rehearsing or even before rehearsals begin?

I see little before we begin and sometimes I see a lot after rehearsals begin. I really don't know the play well before opening night. I learn the play as I am doing it. I start to understand the play with the actors. Perhaps before we begin rehearsal, a little bit, but much more so during rehearsal. That is why I change a great deal until the last moment.

There was a time when it seemed that you were very interested in working with Artaud's theories and putting them on stage. I think of The Trilogy and The Ghost Sonata which I saw at Yale years ago. I am not seeing that so much in work that you had done lately.

One can't really apply Artaud to everything. There are materials that just can fit Artaud's energies and inspirations greatly and there are some plays which that is very difficult. To apply Artaud to Chekhov is to eliminate the usual sentimentality. To apply Artaud to Shakespeare is possible and in some moments of *Twelfth Night*, you can see the Theatre of Cruelty. It is not directly Artaud, but one can see that one read Artaud.

You are very interested in putting a duality on stage. You mentioned somewhere you like to mix the sublime and the ridiculous.

Let's take Shakespeare. As Brook says often, Shakespeare, more than anybody, has the Holy mixed with the Rough from one minute to the other. Take the first three scenes of *Twelfth Night*. The first scene is a palace, perhaps the palace of the Borgias or the Medici. The Duke has his friends, artists sculpting, and his Raphaels painting all around him, like a gathering of the elite art in Italy at the time, trying to create music and love and poetry that is refined. That is why "if music is the food of love, play on" is as if music and life are connected together. Then the second scene, it moves on to the sea coast—a completely different feeling, a different setting. It's a romantic sea coast with tempest and wild movement in nature. And then the third scene takes us into a domestic situation where two people are sitting down in front of a television set, talking nonsense about sex. In the first three scenes, it takes you to all the levels, all the possible levels of mystery, romance, art, love, sensuality, yearning, longing, and the most trivial talk. Already in the first twenty minutes the levels, the scope is extraordinary! That is what I try to be sensitive to, instead of making all these three scenes like one, following in a fast pace one after the other. I try to really take time with each one and establish in each the exact atmosphere and individual quality in the rhythm of each scene. Each of the first three scenes is almost a miniature play in itself. The first one is the sophisticated court. The second one is like the wild mysterious sea—nature has its unknown mystery, its yearning. Viola comes in as a woman, the only time you see her as a woman. You see her sense of confusion of being lost and her desire to belong somewhere. And then in the third scene, you see two people, Andrew and Toby, watching TV and being bored, not having any aim in life. Out of boredom, they decide to start this game of cruelty, a joke which becomes cruel and that will destroy Malvolio at the end of the play. They will just destroy somebody out of boredom.

As I watched that, there was a great sense of sterility in that scene on this set.

Exactly. It is like a desert. See that palm tree there. Like in a dry land where cruelty comes out of boredom.

There is the culture watching the television, it is all so clear. The thing I want to ask you about this kind of duality, where in the same minute you laugh or cry, that seems to inform a lot of your work. Your interest in Chekhov seems to be about that. And I thought about it when I saw The Serpent Woman last year. When he was battling the monster at the end, it was actually quite comic in a way, even though it was a spiritual quest. This kind of yin and yang thing is almost the same split you perceive between Gozzi and Goldoni and even Meyerhold and Stanislavsky. Could you comment even further on that?

It is true. The most extraordinary possibility for the theatre is the thing that makes us feel most alive in our life—and that element is the element of the surprise. I feel that nowhere else other than in the theatre is this possible. Like cinema or television or any other art, the surprise comes through kind of a manipulation of effects. In the cinema, perhaps Spielberg's movies apply that kind of surprise, but it is a different kind. It is not really the surprise that I am yearning for when I was a child and wanted to be surprised freshly. In the theatre, it is the fact that it is unpredictable. So often when Brook talks about the Deadly Theatre, what is missing is that there are no surprises. There are elements of being cultural, being aesthetic, being entertaining, respecting the rules of show biz, but not being taken for a ride "somewhere else."

Now in this production we have the element of the use of the curtain. The fact is, in theatre history, the curtain was taken away for good reasons, because the curtain was kind of an artificiality. It was keeping the audience and the actors separated somehow. To take the separation away, we threw the curtain away. But in some ways, when we took that away, we took away the element of surprise. As children, we always want to know what is behind the curtain. We wants to know what is hidden on the other side of the curtain and what will happen when the curtain goes up.

Yes, and I've seen you playing with that in rehearsal.

And that is why, in a way, I was very eager to re-introduce the curtain in *Twelfth Night*, just because it is something with this extraordinary expectation. I want to be taken on a journey and I want to verify my believing it.

How is it different than when you work with the playwright when s/he is there, rather than Shakespeare or Molière?

I will be so happy to be able to work with somebody that I can ask questions of—what does this line mean or what were the intentions? Starting to work with Ribman, (Ronald Ribman, author of *Sweet Table at the Richelieu*. Serban directed the world premiere at A.R.T. in 1987), it happened at the beginning. There was a very good collaboration because he really did come and explain. I wanted him to be around and to be at the rehearsals and to help with all kinds of suggestions. In that sense, I am very much for working with a living playwright. The problem is that anytime I work with a living playwright, I have bad luck in the final period, especially with a play that hasn't been done before, the playwright is more nervous than all of us put together. If in the beginning, he is there with us in the front row, as the opening approaches, he goes further and further back. And by the last day of rehearsal, he is somewhere far away in the last row, and kind of a slight figure in a chair, shrinking with fears, doubts, and defense. And somehow, instead of him asking "can you help?," what he does is just doubt every choice of the production, every choice of the direction. I wish then much more to work with Shakespeare or Chekhov!

Are there any living playwrights you are interested in working with?

There are a lot of living playwrights—I would love to do their plays. But somehow, they never offer them to me, because they are afraid I am going to do something crazy with them just because I use my imagination.

What are your feelings on having a company of your own and being what you call a Gypsy director. I read somewhere that you wake up and you don't even know what country you are in. I know you have an incredible schedule. You are going to be in London and then California and then France and then Chicago. What is next? How would you like to get beyond that to have your own company?

It is just impossible. It hasn't been possible yet and it doesn't look like it will ever be possible because first, the economics, and second, somehow I think people look at me as a threat. If they would interview me, they would find that my ideas are too dangerous and somehow they would rather go with a much safer choice. (Three years after this interview, Columbia University found Serban's "dangerous ideas" to their liking and hired him to head their Hammerstein Theatre Center and M.FA. Acting program.)

And so you are just a Gypsy.

Forced unwillingly by circumstance. I would like to stay in America because I like working in America much more than Europe in the theatre because I like American actors and I like the speed of improvisation ... and openness that American actors have. They have very few hangups which European actors have. Because they come from a culture and because they have a tradition, European actors are rigid. They know much more or they think they know much more than in America. Here there is such little tradition in acting, because nobody truly knows ... Fake some stuff here, fake this or fake that. There is nothing real in the teaching of acting in America, unfortunately. Or fortunately maybe, because here, people are much more fresh or much more open to try anything, rather than say "well, I only know this method." One doesn't even know what "method" is! Here everything can be experienced or tried as it is on a zero ground. So I like the spirit of pioneering and openness which is in America still, but the financial support is so poor that I just don't know where to do this seriously. That's the problem.

The Final Rehearsal and Final Preview Performance—Tuesday, Dec. 12

After yesterday's day off, the company once more gathers at 12 noon to begin rehearsal. Tonight is the final preview performance with the official opening on Wednesday. Serban continues to work moment-to-moment—right now, he is working on the Duke's scene in Act V, where Antonio is beaten by the cops. I'm still noting how much he literally gives to actors—such as "Laugh louder! Faster! Ha! Ha! Ha! Ha! Ha!"

Serban surprised me yesterday when he asked me what I thought of the show, particularly if I thought it was too long. Apparently, he is still arguing about the length with Brustein. He's been asked to cut another 30 minutes to get the play to a more conventional length of 3 hours. Serban responded with "Go get Michael Kahn!" He doesn't want to cut more and doesn't know where he could. Again, Serban is not interested in a conventional, well-paced show.

Other small adjustments in the final scene: a loud thunder crash now begins the rain sequence, a faint foghorn now replaces the wind as the very final sound of the play, and the spotlights on the "final four" characters have returned. The Shakespeare map and face have long been cut. Serban shows Jim Lally (Malvolio) step-by-step how he wants him to walk for the final exit. Lally played a small role in Serban's New York version of *As You Like It* in 1980. He has very fond memories of the production, although Serban had to be reminded of who he was when they began *Twelfth Night* rehearsals! Serban also fixes how the umbrellas are passed off for the final tableau, it got an unwanted laugh the other night. The adjustment, with the umbrellas already opened, is less comic.

Odd occurrence—Kario Salem (The Duke), noted that he shouldn't dance with Olivia immediately in the final scene; instead he should be amazed she is in her wedding dress. Serban agrees at once, then asks "Who told you that?" Salem replies "Robert." (Scanlan? Brustein?)

Opening Night—Wednesday, Dec. 13

Both Brustein and Scanlan perceive Serban as a "major refresher of classical texts" and feel very strongly that this *Twelfth Night* represents some of Serban's strongest work. Brustein, in particular, is in a position to make such a statement, having seen most of his major American productions from *The Trilogy* on. He also spoke very highly, though not completely uncritically, of Serban's work with actors and designers in the major productions he has created under Brustein here at the A.R.T.—especially *Three Sisters* and *The King Stag*. Whatever their artistic differences, it is clear to me that Brustein has the highest possible respect for Serban as an artist and that he is in no small way responsible for getting his work out to an American audience. Brustein is also responsible for developing the audience he has here at the A.R.T. There aren't many theatres in the country that have an audience that would "go with" (or maybe "stay with") this *Twelfth Night* for 3 and one-half hours (four on first preview!)

Serban makes his last major adjustment in the final rehearsal this afternoon, changing Malvolio's music from Three Stooges to the Jim Bakker type religious theme. This sequence is run a number of times along with a host of other minor details in various other scenes. Other changes from the final preview performance last night: Serban has added a toy dog to Malvolio's outhouse that barks and Fabian and Feste have to clean up some imaginary dog shit, Olivia now throws a spoiled, rich girl fit on her lines "Ay me detested! How am I beguiled!" in V-i and there is now a significant amount of blood on Antonio's feet in his final exit of the same scene. He is now really beaten and thoroughly humiliated. This is an image of absolute intolerance for the outsider of society—in this case a homosexual. Because Rodney Hudson is the only black actor in the cast, the image is further enhanced. He is an outsider in an all-white society.

Before this afternoon's final rehearsal began, Serban gathered the company together one more time for a final opening night note session. Once again, everyone assembles in the West Lobby, sitting silently in a circle for some time, waiting for two actors. Serban sits completely still, eyes closed. He almost appears to be meditating. Many of the actors still have colds. Finally, when everyone arrives, Serban begins to speak. Later, Rodney Hudson, who has worked with Serban as far back as *Agamemnon* in 1977, tells me he's heard many sections of the speech before.

Serban's Notes to the Company on the Afternoon of Opening Night

We do feel, after 7 or 8 weeks now, closer to appreciating and understanding *Twelfth Night*. We're trying to really be the vessel—the medium for the text to come through us to the audience, to create, if possible, a circular level of attention. This is best when the silence of the audience is very acute. The silence is so vibrant, one can hear it. This is when it works the best.

The responsibility is again and again to transmit the text in all its openness. Every audience member then takes what they want—each according to his/her own potential. Therefore the true title of the play is *What You Will*.

The play itself works on so many levels. From the second to the seventh level of meaning, I still don't know what this play is about. It's a riddle. Although Shakespeare was a Renaissance man, he was much closer to a medieval man. *Twelfth Night* has its roots in an early medieval mystery play—like the 11th/12th century morality plays. It's connected to this tradition rather than the progress of the Renaissance.

Then the question is: how to bring the past into the present? How do we use helicopters and these other modern props and still feel the wisdom of an old morality?

Don't miss this opportunity to feel that something is open to experience every night. So take this. Don't only give, but *receive* something. The art of theatre is a give and take, back and forth, a boomerang. The most successful theatre must do this—a circular movement. We receive something that is higher as well as giving back what was filtered. It's so important to really change the attitude towards acting. We must get this subtle relationship. What is an actor? We are just like the audience. We are part of them. There is no difference if we all get equally high on Shakespeare!

Serban then spoke in specific terms about the production itself:

The comedy is working well. It's great when laughs are unexpected. It's better when it's unpredictable.

The serious part is the delicate part. One must be truly, deeply personal to really feel it—not manipulate. This will make a difference in the listening/reception of the audience. In the serious part, we still need to grow—to be more real, more risky, less acting. This is hard—private. Not even to family or friends can one say these things. You must say these things on stage—the things that cannot be said in private.

In terms of acting, it is at its best when all the calculations have been made, like a chess game. But then try to forget about technique and have trust in one place only—intuition. The 19th century actors were inspired by the Muse of Intuition. There must always be a touch of improvisation. This is real creativity. It's exactly how we planned it, but just a little different. Where this comes from, we don't know. It's an intelligence that doesn't come from the head. There is no name for it—the surprise that is the most important element in the theatre: you ride the horse, but let loose the reins.

That's why things seemed too slow or too fast—because we spoke from the head. It's not right to speak slowly just because "Andrei told me." It must be absolutely organic, absolutely right. Trust the subconscious.

(Long pause)

Every night there is a different audience. An attentive ear can sense that before the curtain goes up. There is a way the audience comes to the theatre. Some people are noisy and energetic—their outer energy is bubbling. Other times, they're much quieter—they read the program. That *already* tells you how the night is going to be. There is a sense—a connection in the air before it evens starts.

How we work with this is a question of fine tuning. If we can feel this right away, (that perhaps this audience is more attentive), we can make the quieter passages even more quiet. If they are ready to laugh, be less sensitive, we must know that too. Audiences will always be more or less sensitive. If they are responding to the sex jokes as well as the mysterious moments, one can choose how to act everything. The extraordinary thing about Shakespeare is that he's vulgar and refined in the same expression. Nothing stays the same as evidenced by the construction of the play—how he builds the play. It starts with a beautiful palace; then a wild sea coast; then a domestic scene watching TV. These images come from the text like three different plays. One must play three different texts. We are all made up of Sir Toby and Viola. We all have these levels. The audience must recognize every single character as aspects of themselves or we are lost.

Regardless of reviews, we must do this. Reviews will be devastating—written by people who are ignorant like we are. Often, critics, with some exceptions, are failures—failed actors, directors, playwrights. They write articles out of frustration, not because they love the theatre. When there is bitterness, there is no respect for craft. Pay no attention to it. Even if they are good, they don't know what they are saying.

Do our work—the opportunity with this extraordinary play. Every night we have the opportunity to start again—fresh, unique, just for tonight.

The Day After Opening—Thursday, Dec. 14

There really is something magical about an opening night—everyone expectant, everyone "dressed to the nines," etc. One feels significant just being there—glamor, thrills, etc. It is the best evidence of sex appeal in the theatre.

The play was very well-received—then again, it was a packed house of A.R.T. staff and supporters. Ellen Stewart was here. Serban raced to her first as soon as the curtain came down. I sat across from Ann Bogart, former Artistic director of Trinity Rep, who didn't crack a smile all night. All the Boston papers were here. *The New York Times* will come later. There were a few walkouts, but on the whole, the audience seemed to listen very well. There were lots of laughs. The scene with Shakespeare in the bar got the biggest comic reaction. No major technical problems, except for some sound flubs and some headset instructions accidentally heard in the house.

At the reception afterwards, Serban gave notes to some of the actors waiting in line for food. I overheard reactions ranging from "The best Shakespeare I've ever seen" to "distracting—gesture was working against the text ... sexual gestures too obvious, unnecessary."

I remained at A.R.T. only two more days and saw the second performance of *Twelfth Night* on Thursday. On Friday, the rotating repertory schedule returned with a performance of the two Ionesco one-acts *The Bald Soprano* and *The Chairs*. During that 48 hours, I interviewed as many members of the company as I could—including actors Tommy Derrah, Rodney Hudson, Jeremy Geidt (and much later, Cherry Jones), designers Howell Binkley, Derek McLane, and Cathy Zuber, A.R.T. Vocal Coach Bonnie Raphael, and Assistant Director Paul Walker. I also viewed videotapes of some of Serban's previous shows at A.R.T. (*The King Stag, The Juniper Tree, The Good Woman of Setzuan* and *Sweet Table at the Richelieu*) and spent a good portion of time going through the A.R.T. publicity files for materials on Serban. I will attempt to bring as much of this information into focus as possible in discussing three final elements of Serban's rehearsal methods (especially in relation to *Twelfth Night*) to close out this chapter: his relationship with text, his relationship with actors, and his relationship with designers.

Serban and His Text

Many of the theatre artists at A.R.T. thought that *Twelfth Night* was one of Serban's strongest efforts in terms of working with text. Bonnie Raphael even felt the production was a "very big departure for Andrei. I don't know whether it is because of Shakespeare or (if) he is in a different place right now, but this is as strong as I have seen his work in terms of text."[6] Robert Scanlan, while noting the highly visual quality of the production, said: "At the same time, I get Shakespeare handed to me on a silver platter. I get the kind of attention to Shakespeare that I do when I read it and that is extremely rare in production."[7] Cherry Jones recalled the first day of rehearsal:

> ... and we all knew that it was just going to be extraordinary because he was so excited and had 82,000 different books on his table of interviews and a lot of reading of Peter Brook and different English voice coach notes and he was absolutely obsessed that we should be able to speak it properly.[8]

And on that first day Serban himself told the company that as Brook noted that there are at least seven different meanings of any Shakespeare line,[9] they were going to attempt to find as many meanings as possible.

Clearly Serban was more prepared to explore the text thoroughly than he had with his last Shakespeare, *As You Like It*, originally produced in France in 1976 and revived in New York in 1980. In that production, there had been many cuts in the text. Originally staged outdoors in the French countryside, Serban pantomimed much of the action behind the speaking characters, even staging many offstage actions only referred to in Shakespeare's text, such as the young men flocking to see the banished Duke in the forest and Le Beau's description of a wrestling match. Serban explained that "All those little adventures, those little imaginary tales are very important. We have to see all the little embroiderings."[10]

In *Twelfth Night*, Serban felt a responsibility to attempt to discover Shakespeare's every word, hence his reluctance to edit in the preview period. Up until then, Serban had not cut one word of the play. And although much of the staging was highly visual, including moments that are only referred to in Shakespeare's narrative, it was based upon a careful reading of the text. These moments were staged for a greater clarity of action and character rather than for gratuitous effect. Act I Sc ii is a good example. After Viola confides to the Sea Captain her feeling for her brother and we see her interest in Olivia's mourning for her own brother, at the conclusion of the scene Sebastian rises from the waves—an image of sibling connection that has dominated the scene and will continue to haunt the play.

In *Twelfth Night*, Serban's fertile imagination served the words more and more. Certainly he was committed to the actors ingesting the words in their own bodies throughout the rehearsal period. Bonnie Raphael described many of the Cicely Berry exercises that Serban used in the early rehearsals such as the "Two Points" exercise that Serban spoke of: "They were an attempt to get the actors to get physical about the language, get specific about the language, understand the images, understand the arc of the language." Serban also used six or seven different texts of the play simultaneously to make sure that all of the nuances and possibilities of different line readings surfaced. Raphael also recalled: "... he would not let the actors get off of a line unless they could paraphrase it exactly and knew exactly what they were talking about which I respect him for. A lot of Shakespearean directors I worked with don't bother to do that in a show."[11]

Is this respect and attention to text, the very lack of for which Serban's detractors criticize him, a new phase in Serban's continuing development as a director?

I would answer with a tentative "yes," only if we see it as part of his long-standing evolution as an artist. Serban has never really been an anti-literary director or disrespectful of text. Even in *The Trilogy*, he was penetrating to the core of the ancient texts in a visceral way, and in a way that was genuinely innovative for American theatre. The same is true for *The Cherry Orchard*. Serban and his collaborators truly believe he is serving the text. Of course, he is a highly visual and metaphorical director. But, at least in *Twelfth Night*, most of the images and the "departures" from the text were actually intrinsic to it. Again, Scanlan remarked:

> The text is the last thing that should be paid attention to. It is actually the result of everything else and the worst possible directing of theatre is text rhythm ... read it off the page and you get all your ideas off the page ... The language (should) happen last as it does in life ... Text

deserves attention at the end. It is like the leaves on the tree. It is the first thing you see, but, in fact, the last thing that grows ... In fact, that is the way I think Andrei approaches the play. The irony and the paradox of working on a play is when you are handed a script, it is the only entry point. You have to build your way back into the core of the play and then re-invent the stage event and Andrei does that instinctively. He has a profound instinct of the stage that puts language in the proper relation to the theatre. He gives it its full due.[12]

One is reminded here of Paul Walker's comment that Serban "finds the right universe" for the characters to say these words to each other. In the bar scene with Sebastian and Antonio, and many other scenes in *Twelfth Night*, Serban is indeed, "re-inventing the stage event" so that the words resonate in a way that is vibrant, vital, and even new. On the other hand, others still find this method "distracting" and "illustrating the text" rather than "trusting the words." Raphael again points to this as perhaps a function of Serban, a non-native English speaker, working with English texts:

I think he could trust the text more than he does. Again, I think it has to do with the fact that English is his third language. First is Romanian, second French, and English third. So I think he does work around the text a whole lot ... I think the difficulty is not only doing a play in a language which is not native to you, but a play in an esoteric form of that language ...[13]

Perhaps what makes Serban truly a successful global director is his ability to visualize texts in meaningful fashion for all audiences, whether they can understand the original language of the text or not. Surely this must be at least part of the reason why he is a successful director of operas, where often the libretto is in a tongue foreign to the audience's ear. This ability to "cut-across" the barriers of language is inherent in Serban's own unique international makeup, as Raphael has noted, and was no doubt also strengthened in his early years at La MaMa, with the emphasis on multiculturalism there.

Although Serban is a voracious reader in three languages and devours book after book of criticism in preparation for production, he works from very few notes, never uses a promptbook, and writes very little down in the course of a rehearsal. He is always working in the immediate moment—intently watching and listening to his actors and attempting to engage them in all of the possibilities suggested by the text.

From the Greeks to Chekhov to Shakespeare, one of Serban's primary goals has always been to communicate the non-verbal essence of the text—what Brook calls the invisible. This does not mean the Serban is contemptuous of the playwright, merely that he wants to embrace the work in all of its sensory imagery and not merely to "faithfully translate" it off the page in a literary fashion. From the very beginnings of his career, Serban has been committed to "the intelligence of emotion," to "discovering the life in a single sound," and "the hidden vibrations of language."[14] Because Serban's theatre strives for the miracle of the constant surprise and unexpected for his audience, and because his theatre does not embrace what he calls "small, psychological realism," he probes the text for the images beneath the literal meaning. In the best of his productions, whether it be Euripides, Gozzi, Chekhov, or Shakespeare, the viewer is engulfed in the world of the text as filtered through Serban's fertile imagination in a fresh and powerful theatrical experience.

Perhaps Brustein says it best with his comments "There are really two Andrei Serbans":

> There is the Andrei Serban that really sits down and reads the play, often with the help of a dramaturg, if it is a translation. The reason he wants a dramaturg is because he wants to find out where it has been mistranslated ... He wants to get to the original meaning of that text. He will do the same thing with an English text. He wants to get the original meaning of the text before it was filtered through and debased by convention and tradition. So he is a Romantic in that regard, but he is also traditional. He wants to get the original energy of the text.
>
> Now that is the Andrei Serban who gave us that sublime *Fragments of a Trilogy*. There is another Andrei Serban who is probably making the` same effort, but he is being led off into gesture and illustration ... In *Twelfth Night*, for example, the final moment, not the final tableau which is exquisite, but the final moment when Feste comes out and drops a map and the map is of England with Shakespeare's face on it. Now that is the second Andrei Serban. It is unnecessary. I think it is rather obvious ... It is illustrative. It is not poetic. (Again, this business was cut after the first preview performance.)[15]

It seems evident that *Twelfth Night* was a result of mostly "the first Andrei Serban" but Brustein's point is well-taken. We find a similar dichotomy in his relationship to actors.

Serban and His Actors

Brustein once said that "It's a mystery how Serban gets his results."[16] Serban seems both autocratic and flexible in working with actors. He is at once a taskmaster and an improviser. He sometimes doesn't explain things to actors. Brustein recalled Serban asking him to talk with an actor he was unhappy with in the original *Sganarelle* because he didn't want to,[17] while in other circumstances, he overwhelms the actor with very specific images that leave no doubt as to which direction he wants them to take the character. (Throughout *Twelfth Night* rehearsal, he kept reminding Cherry Jones as Viola to "turn the other cheek—like Christ."[18]) Tommy Derrah, veteran of twelve Serban productions, offered two general approaches to Serban's work with actors:

> One is extremely choreographed and sometimes the process will be that way throughout the rehearsal period. Other times a lot is born out of improvisation; actors are sent off to corners of the room to explore sections of the play. Sometimes it's a combination of both. Andrei is a brilliant editor as well as a director. His imagination is wild so I never know what I'm going to get into whenever I start any project with him.[19]

In *Twelfth Night*, Serban was working with what Derrah described as the first approach. The work was all very carefully choreographed moment-to-moment and was pure Serban. As a matter of fact, it was not uncommon for some performers to ask questions at the beginning of the scene such as "Andrei, do you need me by the wall?" or "Andrei, may I light the cigarette here?" This condition is what Scanlan referred to as "some actors getting gunshy" and "chopping up their attention to the point where they can't do creative work ... there is no real will involved. That can cause frustrations in trained artists."[20] In other words, Serban has such a strong vision that he becomes a puppetmaster.

On the other hand, there is evidence of the second or improvisational approach even in a play like *Twelfth Night*. It was certainly evident in *Sganarelle*, *The Ghost Sonata*, and *The Marriage of Figaro*. In many of those rehearsal periods, Serban would break the actors into groups, give them a task upon which to improvise, and send them off. In 1982, while rehearsing Beaumarchais' *Marriage of Figaro* at The Guthrie, Serban had the cast improvise a children's theatre version of the play and later arranged for their first run-through in front of an audience of children.[21] We have seen how he used improvisation in *The Cherry Orchard*, *Fragments of Greek Trilogy*, and other plays. For Serban, improvisation is a way for the actors to explore the world of the text in a fresh manner without pre-conception. So, ironically, Serban is simultaneously perceived by some as both a dictator and a wild improviser.

In *Twelfth Night*, many members of the company noted that there was a great sense of freedom and improvisation in the early and middle stages of rehearsal and that it is only in the tech period that Serban begins to choreograph moment-to-moment. And for all of the actors who would never work with Serban again, there are just as many who are devoted to him and feel his demands pull the best work from them as actors. Here are two who feel that way. The first is Cherry Jones who talked at length about her feelings on working with Serban. Her response to a question on how she dealt with the famous Serban last-minute changes:

I loved it because it always made perfect sense to me. It wasn't like a director who will tell you to do something and then the next day give you a direction that has nothing to do at all with the character or with any human being who has ever lived. That is so arbitrary and so false! But Andrei, when he throws something out the window, the next thing he gives you is even more fascinating, I find. And if it is not, he realizes it even more quickly than you do and if you are willing to go along with it, you are going to be taken on a fantastic ride! If you fight him, uh-uh, he doesn't like that even though he says he does! He needs actors who are willing to take a leap of faith and just go where he goes and it is so great when you do. A lot of actors don't like to move into a world where the director's concept is the key. What they don't understand is that in the right moment, the right director, and with the right company, it can be the most fulfilling experience in the world. He challenges you. Just what he did with *Twelfth Night*. He raised the stakes to such a degree that everywhere I turned, it was so overwhelming on every level with every character. You walk on stage into Andrei's plays and you are in a world that has never been seen before which is what all actors like. You get to move and he never boxes you in. He's spoiled me for other directors.[22]

Rodney Hudson put it even more succinctly:

The only star of an Andrei Serban show is Andrei Serban and you have to give yourself over to that ... You give up your own active ego ... I think that an actor worth his salt will be able to see that there is something going on and they will give themselves over to it ... And in that regard, he has given me such "actorly" moments ... It's just so wonderful what he has given me to do. (As Antonio)[23]

Perhaps Serban and other "concept" directors such as Robert Wilson require more discipline in the performer to follow the structure of an abstract form, but conversely, the result is a liberating freedom within the performance. In other words, the director, using the text, composes a strict score of actions, movements, and moments that is not unlike the score of musical notation. Having the score so specifically composed frees the actor to perform it as a musician might use her/his instrument. Brustein elaborates:

Now, I think the real breakthrough and the major change is *Twelfth Night*, because Andrei, who is often accused of being a puppeteer, putting the actor on his mark and expecting the actors to perform exactly as he wants, found a way to liberate the actor through very careful moment by moment, gesture by gesture intervention directing. And there are some actors who feel, I'm sure, that their liberties are constrained under these conditions, but I think that most of the actors felt that they had been liberated and that they found a freedom within form, a freedom within structure that was very important.[24]

Of course, many actors, perhaps particularly many American actors to whom "freedom" and "input" means so much, are not going to respond to such methods, but Serban's treatment of actors is certainly not as rigid as Robert Wilson's, who often requires all his performers to count out every movement, nor is it as disciplined as some other Asian theatre forms, for example, the Japanese Noh. Jeremy Geidt, who has been in eight Serban productions, had this to say:

> A lot of people tend to categorize certain directors as sort of dictatorial or fascist and I have never found Andrei that way. There is a way he wants things done, but if you want to come up with an idea, he will listen to you and he will be ready and accessible to different things ... I have never found anything with him that is not stimulating and I have never found him unopen to suggestion.[25]

Perhaps a key to working with Serban is for actors to find a way to express themselves personally within all that Serban has given them. Tommy Derrah notes that even if Serban says "Just move one finger, I will move one finger; but I will change it a little bit. Not that I am being contrary, I can't just ape the movement, I have to make it mean something to me."[26] Rodney Hudson also spoke of "re-interpreting it," to make it truly the actor's contribution and not just fulfilling the instructions of the puppetmaster. Hudson insists that this is the *actor's* job, not the director's and implied that it is required in working with any director.

> You can't get out there and just do Andrei Serban's stuff. You have to re-interpret it. You have to find the motivations to do that and to re-interpret and that is where a lot of people get mixed up because they can't. They can't re-interpret what he says in his blocking or his acting style, and they hold onto their own things to the point where they falter ... I find him extraordinarily confining on one hand and, paradoxically, I have such freedom. But you have to know what he wants and you have to re-interpret what he says to make it fit you. That is part of the actor's job. It is not a directorial thing.[27]

An example where Cherry Jones was able to "re-interpret" as Viola was in Act V Sc i. The Duke has just said that he will kill her and as she's exiting had to answer Olivia's question "Where goes Cesario?" with the lines "After him I love/More than I love these eyes, more than my life,/More, by all mores, than e'er I shall love wife."

> Now, it is a very simple thing in any other production as she is simply saying "I am going with the guy I love." But in this production, it was "I am going to make myself go with him because I *cannot* love a woman." And I saw so clearly where he (Serban) was going with the blocking and I remember when I would get to those lines in particular I could never say them—I was having trouble getting there. I would say, "Andrei, I know what you want. I just can't get there yet." We have worked together enough that he usually left me alone pretty much. He knew that the blocking would get me there eventually ...[28]

In other words, Serban gave the actor the framework and let her make the choices that made it truthful for both her and the audience. This moment as played in performance was an agonizingly beautiful one in the production. There is no question that Jones' sub-text was clear to the audience.

Another argument for Serban eventually re-establishing his own company is that he seems to coax such wonderful performances out of the actors he's worked with before. The "Serban veterans," so to speak, can read Serban well in rehearsal, they know what he wants, even if he is not direct with them, they know that they must somehow "fill it" emotionally, and above all, they are incredibly patient with him as the pressure of opening night draws nearer. In other words, they respond to Serban's methods because they trust him. And because they trust him, their own work takes on greater resonance. (This also true of designers who have worked with him before.) Rodney Hudson even speaks of an actor's first show with Serban as basic training and Bonnie Raphael adds "If you start second guessing him, whether you are a designer or an actor or anybody, it really diminishes the possibilities for the performance."[29] On the other hand, Tommy Derrah, who, again, has been in more Serban plays than anyone, gave the impression that if Serban would sometimes take the time to explain why, "we are trying this because I just want to see what it looks like," it might avoid some misunderstandings in rehearsal.[30] Serban definitely doesn't coddle actors, although judging by his record of achievement, he knows them very well.[31]

One final issue in his work with actors is Serban's continual habit (some would say need) of adjusting elements and moments in the production very late in the rehearsal process, as we have seen on the afternoon of the opening of *Twelfth Night* with Malvolio's music. A more extreme example was his re-arrangement of the chairs on the set the day *Three Sisters* opened. Does Andrei Serban have a need to work from chaos—to keep everyone on edge so that the actor never feels s/he can settle into a deadening habit?

Bonnie Raphael thinks so:

> Andrei has said to me that he believes that actors do their best work when they are uncomfortable and he believes that comfort is the bugaboo. It works against, it mitigates against an actor's greatest

creativity so he creates tension in his rehearsals on purpose. He creates that edge, throwing everybody off, that monkey wrench in the works. He does it on purpose, because he feels that if actors are off balance, if he can throw something in their path, if he can disorient them, he feels it gives an edge to their performance that he wants.[32]

Hence the lack of run-throughs, or even running of scenes until there is a preview audience and the addition of so many elements comparatively late in the rehearsal period. These examples in *Twelfth Night* are minor examples of "creating tension" to keep everyone on edge compared to the incident that Rodney Hudson referred to in *Agamemnon* when two members of the Chorus fought during rehearsal.[33]

Though we hate to think of directors whose work we admire as manipulative, the fact remains that directors are in extremely psychologically powerful positions, especially with individuals who are dependent on them not only perhaps emotionally, but even financially (a fear of losing a job or not being hired back the next season, etc.). Even Cherry Jones, who among the actors who have worked with him is undoubtedly one of his biggest supporters, said that "If he feels like a person needs to be more like a victim on stage, he will make a victim out of them ... he will play all sorts of psychological games to create that."[34] The "chaos" then that Serban creates might actually be pretty carefully constructed.[35]

One more very real possibility exists that Serban continually challenges his actors with fresh ideas at any point in the rehearsal process because he simply has to *see* his ideas enacted by the actors. For such an imaginative man of the theatre, he is unable to "direct in his head." As Bonnie Raphael observed, "he directs with live breathing bodies doing things." And Scanlan remarked "He doesn't store ideas." Serban has the actors immediately act upon his ideas and then decides if he wants to keep them. This can be difficult for actors who haven't worked with him before who may feel that it is their fault that Serban rejects an idea. He is simply rejecting the idea; it is not because the actors have done it poorly. Serban watches his actors with tremendous concentration. Raphael noted "Watching him watch is just exhausting. Then he decides whether he likes it or not and if he doesn't like it, he has no problem with re-staging it, even if tomorrow is opening night."[36]

This familiar theme of always being willing to change, never "falling in love" with any bit of business, never "being married to anything" because Serban will change it at the eleventh hour was echoed by literally every actor I spoke with at A.R.T. and also all of the designers. Before moving to that discussion, however, perhaps these words of Cherry Jones best sum up how an actor must feel in order to flourish under Serban: "It is just like being five years old and going over to Andrei's house to play and they are all his toys! And so you have to play what he wants to play and you have to play with all his toys, but he is such a great kid, you are happy to do it!"[37]

Serban and His Designers

Priscilla Smith once said that Serban's real genius lay in his working relationship with designers, not actors; Robert Brustein says that he has "a nose for collaborators." Certainly Serban's collaborations with such designers as Jun Maeda, Julie Taymor, and especially Michael Yeargan have been extraordinary. Much of the success of *Twelfth Night* seemed to stem from his collaboration with Derek McLane (Sets), Cathy Zuber (Costumes), and Howell Binkley (Lights). Like his work with the actors, Serban is known amongst designers as the director who is known for continually adjusting, changing, and re-ordering his ideas about the play: Apparently this is what caused such unhappiness for designer Santo Loquasto who designed both sets and costumes for *The Cherry Orchard*: "Andrei would see white and say "Let's make it black." For him, not to change is to rule out the possibility of improvement. This is both interesting and very difficult to deal with. It leads to a kind of chaos and it costs a lot of money."[38] Ostensibly for this reason, Loquasto only did costumes for *Agamemnon*. Yet, in 1983, Loquasto once again designed for Serban—*Uncle Vanya*.

It is precisely this reason why Michael Yeargan and Serban have had so many successful projects together: "Flexibility is half the battle when you're designing with Andrei" while Serban admires Yeargan's ability to "throw this away and start again." Yeargan, like Serban, believes the design process evolves in rehearsal.[39] For the *Twelfth Night* designers, flexibility seemed to be a given in working with Serban: "Constantly changing things and experimenting" (McLane); "He wants to try everything. He starts to feel sad that there is only one way—he doesn't want to miss anything" (Zuber); "You can't be married to anything"(Binkley).

As a director known for his striking visual sense, one assumes that Serban has a great deal of input into the design decisions of his productions. By all accounts, this is true, but it is also true that Serban seems to work in a truly collaborative fashion with his designers in the process, perhaps more so than his work with the actors.

His work with Derek McLane supports this notion. For their first project, *The Miser*, McLane made 17 or 18 rough paper models, often creating them on the spot while Serban sat in the same room, voraciously reading French criticism of Molière's play:

> ... finally when I was ready, I would say Andrei, you can take a look and he would say, you ready? I would say, yes. He would say okay, and put his book down and no matter what it was he would look very intently, even if it was something he didn't like, he would look at it, I would say, for sometimes five minutes, sometimes 20 minutes. But he would really sit and look at it and ask me questions about it and sometimes he would say "it is interesting." If it was interesting, that

meant it was a contender and then if it wasn't, he would say "I don't think it is so good" and it would get set aside, because nothing got destroyed. So we kept on working like that.[40]

Serban studies his design possibilities with the same intensity as he watches a scene in rehearsal and then makes his decision. The collaborative model-making on the spot, by the way, is a technique that Yeargan and Serban have often used, especially in their opera work.[41]

For McLane, his process with Serban was often non-verbal and a mixture of intuition, trial and error, and quality time. For *Twelfth Night*, although he didn't make as many rough models as he had for *The Miser*, he visited Serban at his summer home in France that July and stayed with him for eleven days while they worked on the designs: "That was kind of a wonderful situation because we were in an isolated place where the only distractions were the beauty of the landscape and his family ... no one called. There was nothing else to do and we got to just work and concentrated on this for eleven days which is a wonderful way to work."[42] Again, for McLane, it is definitely a two-way street in the design process:

> He will always indulge any idea you have. He will never discourage you from an idea, so if you ever suggested one to him, his immediate reaction would be try it and see ... the thing I find exciting working with him is that he never stops exploring and so the infuriating thing is it never lets you rest and everything you have done can be called into question at any moment. So sometimes you feel like it is impossible to make progress and sometimes you feel like you work hard and suddenly it is useless; but on the other hand, what is wonderful about that is, as an artist, you are always being pushed to be better, to always question everything—which I think is wonderful. [43]

For Cathy Zuber, "sketching on the spot" was unusual and certainly different than her work with other directors. The process of designing within the evolutionary process of the entire production continued with the first day of rehearsal: " ... we brought tons of costumes over for each character, based on the sketches, to try things on. They were all from stock. These adjustments were made to the final designs."[44] (This is reminiscent of Serban's three day "costume party" to begin actual rehearsal for the original production of *Sganarelle*, even though opening night was less than three weeks away.) Zuber added "It's a real challenge because of the eclecticism. The production is not like a kit—like it is with other directors—adding water."

Howell Binkley came into *Twelfth Night* with the most experience of working on Serban's shows, having previously designed the lighting for *Sweet Table at the Richelieu*, *The Good Woman of Setzuan*, and *The Miser*, all at

A.R.T. For Binkley, working with Serban means tossing out a lot of preconceived ideas about what constitutes "good lighting":

> Sometimes conventional lighting is being able to see people's faces. Andrei really enjoys shadows. He enjoys directional light coming in from a weird angle ... Andrei is not really into color, although it depends upon the production. It is always white: "Make it bright, bright!" You have to lose all your conventional ideas—faces, color, atmosphere. You have to put those in the dusty dumpster outside before you start going to draft ...[45]

Binkley corroborates McLane's feeling about the process of inspired collaboration with Serban and, like several of the A.R.T. actors, felt he had more freedom with Serban than Robert Wilson:

> Usually I will sit in rehearsal and he will share ideas with me. As far as references to photographs and things like that, I have done that a lot with other directors and there are certain images they really want to produce with a certain pastel color or something like that, but with Andrei, we make our own pictures and usually I get my ideas when I am in the rehearsal process, even if he is just working on one page and he spends five hours on it. I get a lot of my ideas just like that ... Andrei lets me provide a lot of my own decisions ... I have the utmost respect for him and what he does ... It is difficult sometimes for people to go and change things. When I know that it is going to be for the best, I am willing to do that. It is a good process. It triggers you to do more, to produce more, but you have to go into it as a learning process. You can't be married to anything.[46]

However it happens, having seen much of Serban's work since 1979, I can honestly say that somehow, Serban is able to bring out the absolute best in lighting designers. Such plays as *The Ghost Sonata* (lights by Thomas Skelton), *The Umbrellas of Cherbourg* (lights by Ian Calderon), and Binkley's *The Miser* and *Twelfth Night* remain the most bold and vivid examples of light I've seen used on the stage. In *The Ghost Sonata*, the Strindbergian demon-characters of the "ghost supper" were eerily lighted from below the stage. The light for *Umbrellas* seemed to spray a colored mist all over the stage and especially through scene designer Michael Yeargan's movable Plexiglass panels. Huge shadows were cast from the brilliantly backlighted gigantic doors of *The Miser* set, while the solid orange glow of the cyclorama silhouetted the cactus and palatial setting of Olivia, underscoring the aridness and sterility of the court world of *Twelfth Night*.

Treating the design process as an evolving and flexible component of the production as the acting is treated is obviously not a popular concept with many designers and producers in the professional theatre. It bucks "the system." It has the potential of losing a lot of time and money. And yet, since at times the results can be extraordinary and truly exciting, it is a fortunate circumstance that there are some adventurous institutional theatres like the A.R.T. where that process can take place. And, of course, that there are designers that are flexible and bold enough, to risk it.

Aftermath—Friday and Saturday, December 15–16

The Boston reviews appeared on Friday and were mostly laudatory. Kevin Kelly of *The Boston Globe* called "Serban's *Twelfth Night* dark and stirring ... Serban's work here ... is stylistically consistent and oddly powerful."[47] Despite Serban's warning about reviews, there appeared to be a sense of relief in the company, as if by luck, Serban had received the recognition he deserves. Mel Gussow of *The New York Times* would not be so complimentary—accusing Serban of turning a comedy into a "problem play."[48]

I am a bit sad to leave the company after almost two weeks and deliver many thank-you notes and cards. On my flight back to Michigan, I ponder what the future may bring for Serban, the Dangerous Gypsy, who will shortly be winging his way to London. Will he ever indeed have his own company like in the golden years at La MaMa? In the meantime, many of the images and impressions of Serban in rehearsal are indelibly etched in my mind:

—Serban's kids crawling all over stage while he works.

—Annie King, stage manager, patiently calling for actors Jeremy Geidt and Robert Stanton (Sir Toby and Sir Andrew) to take the drinking scene "one more time, gents."

—Mel Marvin constantly roaming throughout the house with folded arms, giving his support to harried sound designer Maribeth Back.

—Serban *always* selecting one or two more individuals to work with ten minutes more after the rehearsal has officially ended at 5 pm or 12 midnight.

—Serban *never* leaving the house (or hardly ever). He works around the clock from 9:30 am to 1:30 am everyday.

—Serban using his full palette of text, actors, light, sound, costume, and scenery to *create*, not just rehearse, so many, many striking moments in the technical rehearsal. Just to name a few: Malvolio's exit in the house, Shakespeare in the gay bar, Olivia holding a cigarette holder in her "Hollywood mansion," and so on.

—Serban telling the company in notes to "take the benefit" of being in this extraordinary play and to re-create it fresh every night.

A few days after I return home, Romanian dictator Ceausescu is toppled, sparking instant rumors that Serban will be invited to head The Romanian National Theatre. Whatever the future holds for this "Dangerous Gypsy," I am certain that he will bring to it a record of genuine achievement and unrelenting intensity unparalleled in the work of contemporary directors.

Notes

1. Cherry Jones, personal interview, 18 February 1990.
2. Howell Binkley, personal interview, 11 December 1989.
3. Cherry Jones did indeed have trouble with loving such an apparently shallow and conceited Duke. When she asked Serban about this in rehearsal, he responded jokingly "That's your problem!" to which she answered "It sure the hell is!" Jones and Kario Salem (Duke Orsino) continued to work throughout the run of the show to find more tender and believable moments that would support the love between them. Nevertheless, it remained a difficult attraction for the audience to accept believably in the play. Serban apparently sometimes decides on a character's negative qualities before rehearsal thereby forcing the actor into a difficult situation in truthfully developing character relationships in the play.
4. Paul Walker, personal interview, 14 December 1989.
5. Robert Scanlan, personal interview, 13 December 1989.
6. Bonnie Raphael, personal interview, 15 December 1989.
7. Scanlan.
8. Jones.
9. Andrei Serban, "Andrei Serban Leads a Journey into *Twelfth Night*," recorded by A.R.T. Institute dramaturg Chris Baker at the first rehearsal, 10 October 1989, *A.R.T. News* X, No. 1 November, 1989: 3.
10. Robb Baker, "Andrei Serban: Genius or Charlatan?", *After Dark* June 1977: 31.
11. Raphael.
12. Scanlan.
13. Raphael.
14. Serban, "The Life in a Sound," *The Drama Review* 20.4 (1976): 25–26.
15. Robert Brustein, personal interview, 12 December 1989.
16. Brustein, *Making Scenes: A Personal History of the Turbulent Years at Yale 1966–1979* (New York: Limelight Editions, 1981) 252.
17. Brustein, personal interview.
18. Jones.
19. Tommy Derrah, personal interview, 14 December 1989.

20. Scanlan.
21. In a series of articles for *Back Stage*, actress Catherine Burns, who played Marcelline, offered a "behind-the-scenes" look at the rehearsal process of *Marriage of Figaro*. In a children's theatre improvisation, Serban divided the cast into two teams. Burns describes how her team lead by Robert Dorfman (Figaro), at a loss of what to improvise, crawled through the house of the Guthrie theatre in order to spy on the first team and steal their ideas. As a self-proclaimed conservative actor, a "learn your lines and don't bump into the furniture type," Burns admitted she was "not ready for Andrei Serban." Catherine Burns, "Performer on the Road: *Marriage* at The Guthrie," *Back Stage* 2 July 1982: 35, 37.
22. Jones.
23. Rodney Hudson, personal interview, 15 December 1989.
24. Brustein, personal interview.
25. Jeremy Geidt, personal interview, 15 December 1989.
26. Derrah.
27. Hudson.
28. Jones.
29. Raphael.
30. Derrah.
31. "Playfully demanding" may perhaps be a term to describe Serban's relationship with some actors in rehearsal. Mark Linn-Baker recalled one moment in rehearsal for the original production of *Sganarelle: An Evening of Molière Farces* at the Yale Repertory Theatre in which Serban told actor William Roberts to cross the stage without touching the floor. Mark Linn-Baker, personal interview, 27 April 1979.
32. Raphael.
33. Hudson. See Chapter One for a discussion of this incident in context of the rehearsal of *Agamemnon*.
34. Jones.
35. When I proposed this idea of Serban deliberately creating a chaotic atmosphere for actors in rehearsal to Ellen Stewart and Priscilla Smith, they were both extremely dubious.
36. Raphael.
37. Jones.
38. Jacques le Sourd, "Santo Loquasto to Center Stage," *Sunday Magazine* 12 June 1977: G13–14.
39. Laurence Shyer, "In Collaboration: Michael Yeargan and Andrei Serban," *Theater Crafts* May 1982: 23, 60–64.
40. Derek McLane, personal interview, 11 December 1989.
41. Michael Yeargan, personal interview, 16 February 1990.
42. McLane.
43. McLane.
44. Catherine Zuber, personal interview, 15 December 1989.

45. Binkley.
46. Binkley.
47. Kevin Kelly, "Serban's *Night* Dark and Stirring," rev. of *Twelfth Night*, *The Boston Globe* 15 December 1989: 65, 73.
48. Mel Gussow, "Romanian Directors' Views on Shakespeare and Ionesco," rev. of *Twelfth Night*, *The New York Times*: 20 December 1989: C20.

5

In Place of a Conclusion:
Serban in the 90s

THERE really can be no definitive conclusion to this study as Andrei Serban is still very much alive and creating theatre. As of this writing (Winter, '94), Serban is fifty years old, presumably far from the end of his professional career. It is possible that his greatest work may still be ahead of him. Nonetheless, the purpose of these final remarks is to update briefly Serban's activities in the 90s. Since *Twelfth Night* at A.R.T. in 1989, Serban has really been leading three professional lives simultaneously: his ever-expanding international career in opera, his directorship of the Romanian National Theatre from 1990–93, and his appointment in 1992 as Director of The Oscar Hammerstein II Center for Theatre Studies and Head of the M.F.A. Acting Program at Columbia University.

Twelfth Night had been a huge success at A.R.T. Serban confided to Michael Yeargan that it was one of the best things he'd ever done. Still, apparently Serban and Robert Brustein decided that they needed a break from each other and for the first time in a decade, Serban did not direct a play at A.R.T. in 1990 or in the following seasons. *Twelfth Night* remains his last production there. Despite Brustein's open invitation to Serban to direct any project of his choosing,[1] for whatever reasons, Serban has yet to return to A.R.T. But that didn't stop Serban from beginning the 90s at a furious pace.

Since 1980, Serban has been increasingly directing operas, most of them in Europe. He has staged few plays since 1989 outside of Romania. In 1990, he assumed a temporary residence at the theatre department of the University of California at San Diego to direct students in a production of *Our Country's Good*, Timberlake Wertenbaker's drama of Australian settlers producing Farquhar's *The Recruiting Officer*. In London at the Almeida Theatre in May, he directed another new script, *Desire,* by British playwright David Lan and returned to that theatre in 1992, continuing his lifelong interest in Greek tragedy with a staging of Euripides' rarely produced *Hippolytos*. But these have been exceptions. More and more, Serban's professional directing work has been in opera rather than theatre.

In 1978, The Welsh National Opera had invited him by telegram to direct Verdi's *La Traviata*. Thinking it was a joke, Serban never answered. He later admitted he'd never heard of The Welsh National Opera.[2] But manager Brian McMasters was persistent and personally flew to New York a year later to corner Serban who was rehearsing *The Umbrellas of Cherbourg* at The Public Theatre. This time he invited Serban to stage Tchaikovsky's *Eugene Onegin*. Serban replied, "I would go to the end of the world to do *Onegin*. It's my favorite love story in the world."[3] And a new career was born.

Actually, Serban's gradual crossover into opera was not atypical among noted international theatre directors. Peter Brook, Robert Wilson, Peter Sellars, and Richard Foreman, just to name a few, were all part of the new breed of opera directors in the 1980s who were consciously attempting to change the ironclad traditions of the genre's staging with their own more personal and conceptual visions. Perhaps in no other performing art has convention been so instilled than in opera where a production might remain unchanged—sets, costumes, and staging—in a company's repertory for more than a decade. For directors like Brook and Serban, such convention is antithetical to the ephemeral and vital nature of living theatre. Yet despite the specter of such traditions and the production and critical battles a director invites when challenging them, Serban was keenly attracted to opera because of its possibilities of total theatre, i.e., a fusion of music, text, performer, and myth, as Wagner might have defined it. As a student at the Institute in Bucharest, Serban recalled giggling at the ridiculousness of the form. Now he noted, "... (it's) the most exciting field to work in, the place where everything can be done—more than theatre. If one goes deep enough into the work, it can be the most powerful, magnetizing form."[4]

In 1980, Serban's *Onegin*, with bold, impressionistic designs by Michael Yeargan that placed the first scene in in a vast wheat field, was a huge success in Wales. Through 1985, Serban directed a production at The Welsh National Opera each year, including Handel's *Rodelinda*, (1981), Bellini's *I Puritani*, (1982), and *Norma* (1985). Serban has always been grateful to the company in Cardiff for giving him his start: "It used to be the best place to work in opera: long rehearsals, singers interested in acting, and freedom to explore opera as theatre with music."[5] Numerous productions followed at some of the most prestigious opera houses in Europe, including Mozart's *The Magic Flute* (1983) at The Nancy Opéra and later re-staged at Paris Opéra, Strauss' *Elektra* (1986) at Geneva Opera, one of his biggest successes that would later be repeated in San Francisco and Houston, and Verdi's *Don Carlo* (1988) at Bologna Opera, and also Verdi's *Otello*, (1993) produced at the ancient outdoor Roman theatre in Orange, France, with an international cast of leading singers and several French choruses for a company that totaled over 200 performers and seen by up to 10,000 spectators at any given performance.[6]

Serban made his American opera debut in 1981 with *La Traviata* with the students of the Juilliard American Opera Center, but his debut with a professional company in the United States came with Handel's *Alcina* at New York City Opera in 1983. While critical reaction to these productions was decidedly mixed, one of his most significant forays in American opera was the world premiere of *The Juniper Tree* at A.R.T. in 1985, based on a Brothers Grimm fairy tale with music by Philip Glass and Robert Moran and libretto by Arthur Yorinks. Serban's lyrical and restrained staging of this tale of transformation and regeneration, combined with Michael Yeargan's pristine setting, well-complemented the minimalist score of Glass and Moran, resulting in a unique and hauntingly beautiful work. Serban has also directed for such

American opera companies as Houston Grand Opera, San Francisco Opera, and The Lyric Opera in Chicago.

Two of Serban's greatest triumphs in the field were Puccini's *Turandot* (1984) for The Royal Opera at Covent Garden, London, originally produced for the Los Angeles Olympic Arts Festival, and *The Tales of Hoffman* (1993) at The Vienna State Opera. The former was part of Serban's "year of Gozzi," as described in Chapter Three. Starring Placido Domingo and Gwyneth Jones, and designed by Sally Jacobs, *Turandot* combined the striking visual techniques of New Fabulism, i.e., commedia dell'arte, Asian Theatre, and fairy tale, that Serban would use in his staging of Gozzi's plays *The King Stag* and *The Serpent Woman*. In the latter opera in Vienna, reunited with Domingo after almost ten years, Serban scored one of the biggest critical successes ever in his professional career. He and British designer Richard Hudson fashioned a surrealist and fantastic world for the poet-composer Hoffman sung by Domingo that took the normally staid Vienna Opera community by storm. On opening night, the production received a 48 minute ovation and Serban was chosen by public popular vote as the best opera director of the current Vienna season.[7]

But there have been "scandalous failures" as well as triumphs. (Sometimes it seems that few productions in the opera community seem to fall between these two extremes!) Serban himself cheerfully acknowledges his production of Beethoven's *Fidelio* (1986) as "... a big flop! I worked twice at Covent Garden: *Turandot*—one of their biggest hits, and *Fidelio*—a noble failure. If you asked me which one would I see again, it would certainly be *Fidelio*, because of its spiritual aspect that overshadowed the political."[8] Still, *Fidelio* seemed to be the exception rather than the rule. As of this writing, The Royal Opera maintains *Turandot* in its repertory, even if it shuns *Fidelio*.

In many ways, opera would seem to be the perfect form for Serban's fertile imagination and his by now well-known ability to create breathtaking visual images. And although he is not a formally trained musician, he has a strong sense of communicating emotion directly through music. Since beginning his opera career, he has learned to read music and and has developed an understanding of what can only be expressed by singing and why it cannot be spoken.[9] His strongest theatre work, from *Fragments of a Greek Trilogy* to *Twelfth Night*, has always pushed the efforts of his musical collaborators such as Liz Swados and Mel Marvin to the forefront of his productions. And while Serban enjoys the greater production possibilities that come with the larger budgets for opera as opposed to most regional theatres, he considers the form simply another type of theatre. In 1994, almost four years since his last non-opera production in the United States, he offered these thoughts:

> Opera *is* theatre to me. It's like a play—with music. It's still about relationships. It tells a story ... Opera can be total theatre in a way that theatre can never be. In the theatre, as in a Shakespeare play, there is music in the text, but an actor rarely brings it to life. In an opera, the

music is there. If one is sensitive to it, one can really do something: extend music into visual and life experience. Because of the music, there are possibilities in opera that don't exist in the theatre.[10]

Yet it is evident that Serban misses doing plays, especially when his singers are not sensitive to acting. But he did have an outlet in the 90s for directing plays—his Romanian homeland.

Two months after Romanian dictator Ceausescu was overthrown in December of 1989, Serban was invited to head the Romanian National Theatre and the State Opera House, both in Bucharest. The exile who had left his country in 1969 was now invited to return and help lead a true cultural revolution in the highest artistic posts in the land. Actually, since 1975, Serban had been returning to Romania almost every year to visit family and friends. In 1982, while attempting to deliver a package for a friend, he discovered he was not even allowed to enter the stage door of The National Theatre to view a rehearsal. When Serban protested and explained who he was and that he knew everyone at the theatre, he was told that since he was now an American citizen, he wasn't allowed inside because rehearsals were considered "state secrets."[11] Serban accepted the offer of General Director of The National Theatre, but his response was guarded: "For 20 years I've been trying to work there and I wasn't even allowed to cross the door of the theatre. Now, I'm offered the highest positions anyone could get."[12]

Despite reservations, Serban couldn't resist the opportunity and his own deep personal need to return to his homeland and create theatre in his original language. "It's always been important for me to go back to my roots for my attempt to clarify what I am and who I am," he stated.[13] Too, Serban hoped to help end the artistic isolation of his country by producing not only his own work, but by bringing in other theatre artists from Europe and the United States to introduce a new repertory.

Serban never intended to live in Romania full-time. For the next three years, he returned in the spring and stayed for the summer, directing plays and administrating the theatre while he was there and advising on the repertory when he was back in the States or elsewhere in Europe. His situation in Romania was complicated and delicate. In one sense, he enjoyed the return of "a conquering hero" as one of Romania's most famous citizens, let alone his artistic achievements. On the other hand, some Romanians, especially a few of the long-time actors and other employees at The National Theatre, viewed Serban as an American defector. In addition to this complex emotional situation, because of the extremely precarious economic and social circumstances in Romania, daily working conditions at the theatre and in Romania itself were difficult and often in a state of disarray. Due to a lack of staff and managerial leadership, Serban found himself doing his own publicity. Lighting instruments were old and needed repair. The air conditioning of the building was often broken. Funding for new productions was practically non-existent. Even with the little money he had, obtaining materials such as wood for scenery and fabric for costumes was almost impossible.

Moreover, Serban had inherited mostly a company of state subsidized, older actors who had been at the theatre for years and were not always up to the extreme physical and vocal demands of *Fragments of a Greek Trilogy*, the production Serban had chosen to inaugurate his return. Serban reflected that if he had chosen to stage *Romeo and Juliet*, his youngest actress for Juliet would have been 42 years old—"surely a very experimental production."[14] Priscilla Smith accompanied him to Bucharest that summer to help him teach *The Trilogy* to the Romanian actors and she helped him audition many new performers. In all, Serban hired twenty-five younger actors to join the existing company at The National. Naturally, this created some tension between the older and younger members of the company, although some of the senior actors welcomed Serban's more experimental methods as an opportunity to break away from the realistic traditions of performance that had always been the officially accepted form in Romania. The eventual popular and critical acclaim accorded to *The Trilogy* and Serban's successive productions at The National also undoubtedly helped ease some of the conflict. Serban summarized his feelings regarding the chaotic conditions in directing the company:

> From inside, The National Theatre is a big elephant, as are all national theatres around the world. It is also a great bureaucratic body that cannot be changed. This is a big Kafkaesque institution with very heavy and unnecessary administration: too many departments, too many technicians ...[15] There are also too many actors whom I didn't choose and didn't train. They imagine they have the right of a landlord without a birthright. I thought, "if I cannot make this elephant dance, I shall not stay long."[16]

At the same time, Serban felt deeply for his fellow artists who had suffered far more than he under the Communist regime and he recognized the very painful change for them in creating theatre that was so different than what had been done for forty years. Hence, he chose to add to the company, rather than replacing anyone.

The Trilogy proved to be a powerful event for both the Romanian performers and audiences. Although he'd been requested to revive some of the old plays from The National's repertory, Serban refused to do any of the plays that were produced during Ceausescu's regime. "They were written with false situations and false characters," he replied.[17] Because the Romanian theatre had essentially missed the experimentation of the West in the 1960s and 1970s, and because he still considered it a "career signature piece," Serban had chosen *The Trilogy* for the initial production of his directorship. But in both rehearsal and performance *The Trilogy* proved to be far more than a period piece of experimentation. In June of 1990, thousands of miners from the Valley of Jiu were transported to Bucharest in special trains. Although the Romanian government denied it, the violent tactics of the miners were used to intimidate the student demonstrators and others in Bucharest who were accusing the government of continuing the policies of Ceausescu. (There were many "hardline" former Communists still in power.) There was rioting in University Square, the location of The National Theatre. At one point, the miners stormed into the theatre while searching for a printing press in the basement and interrupted a rehearsal of *The Trilogy*. They accosted Priscilla Smith and a Romanian actor and forced Smith to show her passport. The miners viewed with with suspicion Smith's script, the text of the ancient Greek, believing it to be a secret code. When they took away some of the pages, she grabbed them back and demanded "Don't touch that Greek!" Serban recalled "Somehow that really commanded respect ... the miners just looked at her and said, 'well, here's a crazy woman,' and went away. It was an amazing thing. She really transmitted something."[18]

The contemporary political resonance of *The Trilogy*, especially *The Trojan Women*, helped to make it a popular and critical sensation when it opened later that summer. The chaotic energy of a forbidden city had helped to create the original production of *The Trojan Women* in Sao Paulo, Brazil, in 1974. And while the audience in New York had subliminally recognized their own violent city as they participated in the play's wild action in surrounding the performers, the audience in Bucharest experienced an electric shock in participating in the depiction of a city under attack when right outside the theatre in University Square the miners had destroyed buildings, burned books, and assaulted people a scant few weeks earlier. "The experience for the actors became the experience of life. And for the audience, because of what they had been going through for forty years, *The Trilogy* became a realistic, naturalistic experience," Serban commented.[19]

Serban presented three plays that first season at The National Theatre—*The Trilogy*, *Our Country's Good,* and *Auditia*, a cabaret production based upon the actors' audition material—all of which were received with great critical and popular acclaim. Undoubtedly, many Romanians were thrilled to view finally the works of one of their most famous citizens. But it was *The Trilogy*, in particular, that the Romanian audience wanted to see as Serban, as usual, reworked much of the play, even staging a scene in the house seats that had been formerly occupied by Ceausescu.[20]

Later that year, Serban prepared the company to tour throughout Romania and locations in Europe and South America. Over 20 years after the original *Medea* had premiered at La Mama, *The Trilogy* was still touring internationally and vitally communicating ancient tragedy to audiences who could not understand a syllable of ancient Greek. Over the next two years, The National Theatre of Romania's touring production of *The Trilogy* was hailed in Paris, Milan, Edinburgh, Salzburg (where they were played at the special invitation of director

Peter Stein), and won first prize at The Bienniale in Sao Paulo, Brazil, where the first production of *The Trojan Women* had been attempted so long ago.

Still, despite this huge success and others, including a controversial 1990 production of Caryl Churchill's *Mad Forest*, a script based directly on the events of the Romanian revolution, and a re-creation of Serban's *The Cherry Orchard* which was invited to play at The Moscow Art Theatre in 1993, Serban grew increasingly disenchanted with the political climate in Romania and its frustrating consequences in directing The National Theatre. The nation's political leaders had failed to make a clean break with their communist past. He explained: "The same corrupt people were in power. Now they could get rich fast, not having to hide their dirty deals anymore. ... in the arts, censorship was the common enemy. But to resist that, one had to gather force and an aim. Today there is a confusion that acts like a disease—a moral and artistic one."[21]

Serban longed for the opportunity to completely restructure the huge size of The National Theatre which had 500 employees. But without this possibility, unable to pay guest directors or even himself, and with neo-communism so healthy in Romania, Serban resigned his position as General Director of The National Theatre in December, 1993, although he did not rule out returning to Romania from time to time to direct. It is clear that Romania still wants him back at anytime. While he'd accomplished some of his goals in his tenure there, all of his productions had been recreations of his most important American theatre pieces. One goal that remains is a lifelong dream to create a new theatre piece based upon Romanian folk tales and legends. But with his opera commitments and later his work at Columbia, he was not able to initiate this project.[22]

The financial situation of the theatre in Romania had not allowed him to reside there permanently and he had kept his house in Cambridge where his two sons had entered school. Serban had returned briefly to the University of California at San Diego in the Fall of 1991 and Joseph Papp had tentatively planned to have Serban direct all three *Henry VI* plays in the Fall of 1992 as part of the complete Shakespeare canon for The New York Shakespeare Festival at The Public Theatre,[23] but, with Papp's death on October 31, 1991, this project was never realized. Instead, another opportunity arose to return to New York and which ultimately contributed to his decision to resign from his position in Romania: the chance to make his mark in educational theatre at one of America's top universities.

In April of 1992, Columbia University announced that beginning that Fall, Serban would join the faculty as Professor of Theatre Arts and Director of the Oscar Hammerstein II Center for Theatre Studies. Serban's appointment was the culmination of a comprehensive plan at Columbia to re-structure the School of the Arts in general and the Theatre Program in particular. Since Peter Smith had been named Dean of the School of the Arts in 1988, there had been several appointments of leading theatre professionals in an attempt to rejuvenate a program that had fallen into serious disrepair in the 1970s and 80s.[24] These included Arnold Aronson to chair the Graduate Theatre Division, Ann Bogart to teach directing, and Romulus Linney to teach playwriting.

Serban came to the academic world with significant previous experience in higher education. He'd taught previously at the Yale Drama School in 1977–78 and at the Institute for Advanced Theatre Training at Harvard in association with A.R.T. from 1981–89. In addition, he'd held numerous teaching residencies around the world including those at University of California-San Diego, *La Conservatoire de Paris*, and the Stockholm Dramatic School. But now at Columbia, for the first time, Serban would have a chance to lead a program that would reflect his personal vision of theatre training. He stated: "My first leading role in an educational setting brings me back to a city I loved in my youth because it gave me so much energy. An opportunity to create a distinctive training program for actors at Columbia University, building on the strengths of New York and its potential, is irresistible."[25]

One of Serban's major priorities at Columbia was to institute a new M.F.A. Acting Program. Although he began teaching acting and directing classes and administrative duties at the Hammerstein Center in the Fall of 92, he didn't assemble the new degree program immediately, preferring instead to "get his feet wet" at Columbia and taking his time auditioning M.F.A. candidates for the following year. In the Fall of 93, Serban began working with 16 brand new M.F.A. acting students.

In February of 1994, I had the opportunity to observe Serban working with his students over a period of a week. Virtually without exception, the students were delighted to work with him. Although he was often away because of his opera commitments, when he was at Columbia he seemed to be working triple overtime, teaching classes almost everyday and meeting with students in individual conferences outside of class. Serban enjoys being in the classroom. He jokes with the students often, sharing amusing theatre anecdotes from a lifetime in the theatre. At the same time, he is extremely demanding with his expectations of them as artists-in-training and is absolutely uncompromising in his criticism of their work. He also listens respectfully to his students as human beings. He conducts classroom discussions in a circle on the floor and always withholds his comments completely until after every student has give her/his opinion. He often holds even more intimate discussions in smaller groups in his office where he encourages the students to share personally what the process of theatre means to each of them. Serban repeatedly challenges them to ask themselves why they are interested in theatre at all, why they came to this program at Columbia, and, in general, encourages them to take personal risks as human beings as well as artists. He tells them, "Ingmar Bergman said that he felt most alive as an artist when he sensed a mad cat moving in his belly."[26]

Serban has arranged a unique program in graduate actor training. Declaring a radical and experimental approach, and consciously avoiding the psychological overtures so long associated with Method-based American actor training, Serban enlisted the talents of many of his longtime associates, including Priscilla Smith who also joined the faculty at Columbia. The students take classes in acting, voice and movement, mask work, clowning, and Kathakali. There are no formal syllabi or reading lists, but Serban has organized the first year of study around the core of Greek texts. In the Fall, in combination with some of the graduate directors and playwriting students, the acting students were assigned in groups to a Greek tragedy. Each ensemble had a director and a dramaturg and/or playwright to create a new adaptation or translation of the text and minimal props, costumes, and furniture to present their "research" in performance in a tiny black box theatre after an investigation period of about a full semester.[27] In the Spring term, they repeated the same process with Greek and Roman comedy, culminating the year's investigation with a three hour performance of twenty Greek plays interspersed with thirteen fables from Aesop. Projects for the next two years may consist of medieval mystery plays, Spanish classical drama, Shakespeare, and finally, plays from the 19th and 20th centuries, including Samuel Beckett and David Mamet.[28] In the first year of training, there was absolutely no element or technique, whether it be in voice or movement, that the students were not encouraged to put into immediate practice—a true "learning by doing" situation. Ironically, to some observers, Serban's methods seemed so simple that, rather than being radically different, they were almost conservative.[29]

If much of this self-questioning and experimentation in the philosophy of theatre seems reminiscent of Serban's own period of study with Peter Brook in 1970–71, this is even truer of the practical exercises Serban conducts in his classes, especially the famous bamboo pole exercises which he'd adapted over the years from Brook. While the students call it "stick work," for Serban, they are "like garden tools, concrete objects to help the voice and body grow. They could also be magic wands for the imagination."[30] Exercises with the sticks range from the performer attempting to connect with emotions of humility and power by holding the stick motionless in front of her/him and moving the body up and down in front of it, to devising their own personal exercises in body, voice, and imagination, i.e., using the sticks in a variety of patterns and rhythms in combination with voice and movement.

The students seem to be aware of the extraordinary opportunity they have in studying with Serban. One morning, *New York Times* critic Mel Gussow observed a class, then asked a single question: "Why are you here?" The student actors responded enthusiastically: "To create a new technique ... we're looking for a different kind of attitude that is disciplined and spiritual ... a fresh approach to theatre ... training that would develop me as an individual ... the key word is passion ... we're starting from scratch ... a brand new approach to American acting ... we've been awakened."[31]

As for Serban himself, it is impossible to predict what the end result of his work at Columbia might be. Perhaps he might eventually assemble graduates of the Columbia program into his long hoped for company. For now, he's committed to the academic world and transmitting his theatre experiences to a younger generation in order to "make them aware of my own questions and confusions in the process."[32] He adds, "I needed to clarify for myself all those journeys I took, from the La MaMa basement to Covent Garden."[33] Once again, Serban has become a Manhattan resident, moving his family to Morningside Heights where his two sons now attend school. Although the family usually continues to summer in Europe, Serban uses the New York base at Columbia while he continues his opera work, and up until his 1993 resignation, his work in Romania.

A Classical Director in a Modern Context

In 1989, I asked Robert Brustein to characterize Serban's greatest contribution as a director and to place him in the context of directing in theatre history. Brustein paused lengthily before answering that as an alternative to the tradition of Stanislavsky, and, in the non-realistic tradition of Meyerhold, Serban emerged as "one of the most impressive theatre directors of the post-war period. I think he emerged as essentially a *classical* director ... in a *modern* context."[34] (italics mine)

Although in many ways Serban's eclecticism has been a strength, (he truly is a flexible director in his choice of material), this book has generally supported Brustein's conclusion. Certainly in his work with Greek tragedy and Chekhov, Serban's work has helped to forge new ways of of viewing these texts, i.e., a "classical director in a modern context." And with his experiments in The New Fabulism, Serban has not only revived Carlo Gozzi, he's worked with Molière and Brecht. Finally, this study concludes with an analysis of *Twelfth Night*, only the second Shakespeare play Serban has ever directed in the United States, but if reaction from his fellow artists are any indication, it will most likely not be his last. Perhaps he had stayed away from Shakespeare earlier because he wasn't totally confident of his own English. Even in his production of *As You Like It* in France in 1976, he made many cuts and had, in a way, somewhat sacrificed the language for the effect of outdoor environmental setting and pastoral pageantry. In 1989, Serban was much more concerned with doing justice to fully exploring Shakespeare's text. *Twelfth Night* eventually took on the look of the usual Serban visual feast in a very eclectic and postmodern fashion, but, again, one is reminded of A.R.T. Literary Director Robert Scanlan's remark: "It still gave us Shakespeare on a silver platter."[35] And, as also noted in Chapter Four, A.R.T. Vocal Coach Bonnie Raphael observed that the production was a big departure for Serban—the strongest she had seen his work in terms of text.[36] And when Serban had the opportunity to inaugurate the new Romanian National Theatre, it is significant that he chose to re-stage *The Trilogy*, not just because it was a re-working of one of his greatest personal successes, but because the material of Greek tragedy still held great appeal for him. Surely Serban *is* a classical director in a modern context.

It seems fitting that this particular study of Serban's life in the American theatre should end with the play that catapulted him to fame in the States. The startling imagery, the mysterious and beautiful sounds of *The Trilogy*, the extraordinary commitment from the actors, the attempt at a spiritual connection with the audience, and, above all, the disturbing and compelling poetry of the senses that create "the magic behind the curtain" are all still very much at the heart of what Serban wishes to achieve in making theatre. Only the element of fully exploring the possibilities of the written text would I add to the above list of how Serban has fundamentally changed as a director from those early days. Above all, it seems that he would benefit most from working with his own company in a less institutionalized atmosphere having to churn out productions on regular schedule, an atmosphere where he could return to the long periods of research and experimentation as he did so successfully in the beginning years at La MaMa. Serban himself corroborated this notion when he told Arthur Bartow:

> I've attempted my Greek Investigation. I've attempted the major plays of Chekhov, and then I've done the commedia dell'arte, and I've tried five years of directing opera, from Covent Garden to Los Angeles. I did Ronald Ribman's new play, *Sweet Table at the Richelieu*. So I'm trying to escape the identity box, a certain perception that my repertoire is limited. I even did a musical, *The Umbrellas of Cherbourg*, to prove the impossible to myself ... I've really covered a great deal of territory in different ways, and now I'd like to bring it together and truly create a theatre of my own, concentrate on working with a group of ten to fifteen actors instead of going all over the globe as a kind of salesman director. I'm ready to a develop an expression which is not superficially my own, but *truly* my own.[37]

Again, perhaps the opportunity to develop that "expression" will eventually be possible for him at Columbia.

In the meantime, the only thing one can count on with this "dangerous director" is his commitment to "unsafe theatre." Serban's controversial reputation for both audiences and his fellow theatre artists stems from his uncompromising desire for the element of surprise in the theatre in order "to keep the theatre event alive ... if there is no surprise, there is no life. The surprise must be a shock to make us feel alive, not just a gimmick for shallowness ... This is what I wish I could do in my work."[38] Further elaborating upon the role of the audience, Serban notes "It's all a very delicate communication like between lovers. The success of the dialogue depends on the rhythm shared by both partners: performers and audience."[39]

In our last interview, I asked Serban to characterize personally the meaning of the theatre event, as he himself asks his students to do so often:

> Life in the theatre is a search—the search for living. Because, like life, the theatre is also for living. If living in peace may be one's aim in life, for the theatre, peace is "undramatic material." What is dramatic? What we experience as contradiction, as paradox. Shakespeare's last play, where we assume he found peace, is called *The Tempest*. Maybe in this word—tempest—there is a clue for us to understand creativity.[40]

Nonetheless, the experience of the theatre itself remains both vital and mysterious for Serban, after so many years of experimentation in so many different venues:

> What is this experience that theatre gives? It is ephemeral. It disappears. On the last night of a play, the set is destroyed. There is nothing that remains ... except the possibility to live life more fully, less fragmented, and more harmoniously. Why does a child play with toys or puppets? Because he is trying to clarify for himself why he is alive. That's how he learns about the world. When we go to the theatre, the child in us is still full of the expectation of discovering the secret of what is behind the curtain. In the subconscious, we are also trying to verify something about our lives, to find some answers. There are no answers, only the joy of living in that mystery. Our mission, if there is one, is to actively address the present-day spiritual impasse of the theatre.[41]

After a lifetime in the theatre, Andrei Serban continues to search for the essence in order to discover "the magic world behind the curtain."

Notes

1. Margaret Croyden, "A Director Revolts," *TheaterWeek* 21 February 1994: 22–23.
2. Will Crutchfield, "Bellini's *Norma* Gets a Touch of The Avant-Garde," *The New York Times* 4 August 1985: Sec. II, p.20.
3. Croyden, 23.
4. Crutchfield, 20.
5. Andrei Serban, letter to author, 13 June 1994.
6. Rebecca Holderness, "Orange Journal," unpublished journal, Columbia University, 1993. At the opening night performance of *Otello*, Serban, perhaps stealing a page from the book of Alfred Hitchcock whom he has long admired, appeared costumed onstage in the opera with his two sons in Desdemona's funeral procession. He commissioned a huge oil painting to commemorate the event which hangs in his office at Columbia.
7. Hammerstein Center News, Columbia University, February, 1994.

8. Serban, 13 June 1994.
9. Croyden 23.
10. Andrei Serban, personal interview, 5 February, 1994.
11. Serban, 5 February 1994.
12. Susan Heller Anderson, "Now Romania Wants Serban Back," *The New York Times* 17 February 1990: Chronicle: 32.
13. Serban, 5 February 1994.
14. Julius Tyszka, *Ars Nova* (Poznan, Poland: Widowiska Nowojorskie, 1994) 61–71.
15. Tyszka 67.
16. Serban, 13 June 1994.
17. James Leverett, "Serban in the Mad Forest," *Performing Arts*, program for Berkeley Repertory Theatre, Fall, 1992: P-1.
18. Leverett, P-6.
19. Leverett, P-2.
20. Priscilla Smith, personal interview, 6 March 1991.
21. Serban, 13 June 1994.
22. From our last interview, it is clear that Serban still very much wants to create this piece, but, for him, it would require living in Romania for a great length of time which he doesn't currently see as a realistic possibility. Andrei Serban, personal interview, 5 February, 1994.
23. During our interview, approximately one and one-half years before his death, Papp spoke with obvious pleasure of his plan to bring Serban back to The New York Shakespeare Festival.
24. John Istel, "Educating Prosperos," *American Theatre*, January, 1994: 27.
25. Serban, 13 June 1994.
26. Serban, Acting & Directing class, 2–3 February 1994, Columbia University, New York.
27. I witnessed some of these final projects in Greek tragedy during my visit and was struck by how much they were reminiscent of Serban's own early investigations in Greek tragedy at La MaMa in the early 1970s—the experimentation in voice, movement, and even in the fashion of how the audience was repeatedly invited to enter the playing space in a ritual procession. Yet in my talks with the students, all of them admitted to being too young to have ever seen *Fragments of Greek Trilogy*!
28. Mel Gussow, "Drama Teacher's Drill: Re-invent the Classics," *The New York Times* 7 June 1994: C17.
29. Istel 27.
30. Serban, 13 June 1994.
31. Students of Andrei Serban's Acting class, 7 February 1994, Columbia University, New York.
32. Serban, 13 June 1994.
33. Gussow.
34. Robert Brustein, personal interview, 12 December 1989.

35. Robert Scanlan, personal interview, 13 December 1989.
36. Bonnie Raphael, personal interview, 15 December 1989.
37. Arthur Bartow, *The Director's Voice: Twenty-one Interviews* (New York: Theatre Communications Group, 1988) 299.
38. Serban, 5 February 1994.
39. Serban, 5 February 1994.
40. Serban, 5 February 1994.
41. Serban, 5 February 1994.

Appendix

PRODUCTION HISTORY
ANDREI SERBAN, THEATRE DIRECTOR

PLAYS

1961–69
At The Theatre & Film Institute, Bucharest, Romania
1. *The Man Who Changed Into a Dog* by Osvaldo Dragun
2. *Ubu Roi* by Alfred Jarry
3. *The Chief of the Sector Souls* by Al. Mirodan
4. *I Am Not the Eiffel Tower* by Ecaterina Oproiu
5. *Arden of Faversham* (Anonymous)
6. *Jonah* by Marin Soreseu
7. *Nocturne* (An evening of original poetry and pantomime)

At The Bulandra Theatre, Bucharest, Romania and Piatra Neamtz
8. *Julius Caesar* by William Shakespeare
9. *The Good Woman of Setzuan* by Bertolt Brecht
10. *She Stoops to Conquer* by Oliver Goldsmith

1969–70
11. *Ubu Roi* by Alfred Jarry & *Arden of Faversham*
La MaMa E.T.C.
Costumes: C.J. Strawn
Lights: John Dodd
Music: Lamar Alford
With Billy Crystal, Lou Zeldis, Michelle Collison

12. *She Stoops to Conquer* by Oliver Goldsmith
Nassau Community College Theatre
Sets: Hobart Hays
Music: Michelle Collison

1971
Assistant Director to Peter Brook
CIRT
Orghast by Ted Hughes
Persepolis, Iran

1972
13. *Medea* based on texts by Euripides and Seneca
La MaMa E.T.C., New York

Sets: Charles Terryl
Lights: Laura Rambaldi
Music: Liz Swados
With Priscilla Smith, Jamil Zakkai, Valois Mickens.

14. *Romeo and Juliet* by William Shakespeare
Nassau Community College Theatre
Sets & Lights: Keith Michael
Costumes: Allen Munch
Music: Liz Swados

1973
15. *Electra* by Sophocles
La MaMa E.T.C., Bordeaux, France
Music: Catherine Mueller & Liz Swados
With Priscilla Smith

1974
16. *The Trojan Women* by Euripides
La MaMa E.T.C., New York
Music: Liz Swados
With Priscilla Smith

17. *Fragments of a Greek Trilogy* (*Medea, Electra, & The Trojan Women*)
La MaMa E.T.C., New York
Sets: Jun Maeda
Costumes: Sandra Muir
Lights: Laura Rambaldi
Music: Liz Swados
With Priscilla Smith, Stuart Baker-Bergen, Natalie Gray
*This production toured throughout Europe and the Middle East from 1975–79.

1975
18. *The Good Woman of Setzuan* by Bertolt Brecht
La MaMa E.T.C., New York
Sets: Jun Maeda
Lights: Larry Steckman
Music: Liz Swados
With Priscilla Smith, William Duff-Griffin, Peter John De Vries
*This production was revived in New York and also toured Europe in 1976 and 1978.

19. *The Threepenny Opera* by Bertolt Brecht and Kurt Weill
American Conservatory Theatre, San Francisco

Sets and Costumes: Robert Blackman
Lights: F. Mitchell Dana
With Anthony Teague, Ray Reinhardt, Randall Duk Kim

1976
20. *As You Like It* by William Shakespeare
La MaMa E.T.C. La Rochelle and Paris, France; Shiraz Festival, Persepolis, Iran
Sets: Jun Maeda
Costumes: Radu & Miruna Boruzescu
Music: Liz Swados
With Priscilla Smith, William Duff-Griffin, Charles Hayward
* This production also toured Europe and the Middle East in 1977.

1977
21. *The Cherry Orchard* by Anton Chekhov
New York Shakespeare Festival at The Vivian Beaumont Theatre at Lincoln Center
Sets and Costumes: Santo Loquasto
Lights: Jennifer Tipton
Music: Liz Swados
With Irene Worth, Raul Julia, Meryl Streep, Priscilla Smith

22. *Agamemnon* by Aeschylus
New York Shakespeare Festival at The Vivian Beaumont Theatre at Lincoln Center & Delacorte Theatre, Central Park
Sets: Douglas Schmidt
Costumes: Santo Loquasto
Lights: Jennifer Tipton
Music: Liz Swados
With Priscilla Smith, (later replaced by Gloria Foster), Jamil Zakkai

23. *The Ghost Sonata* by August Strindberg
Yale Repertory Theatre, New Haven
Sets: Michael Yeargan
Costumes: Dunya Ramicova
Lights: Thomas Skelton
Music: Liz Swados
With Priscilla Smith, Max Wright, Stephen Rowe

1978
24. *Sganarelle: An Evening of Molière Farces*; based on *The Flying Doctor, The Forced Marriage, Sganarelle*, and *The Doctor in Spite of Himself* by Molière
Yale Repertory Theatre, New Haven

Sets: Michael Yeargan
Costumes: Dunya Ramicova
Lights: James Gage
With Mark Linn-Baker, Michael Gross, Eugene Troobnick

25. *Mad Dog Blues* by Sam Shepard
Yale Drama School, presented on the beach of Fort Nathan Hale Park, East Haven, CT
Designed by Adrianne Lobel
With the third year acting students of the Yale Drama School

26. *The Master and the Margarita* adapted by Serban from the novel by Mikhail Bulgakov
New York Shakespeare Festival at The Public Theater, New York
Sets: Andrei Serban
Costumes: Dunya Ramicova
Lights: Victor En Yu Tan
With Jan Triska, F. Murray Abraham, Wallace Shawn

1979
27. *The Umbrellas of Cherbourg* by Jacques Demy & Michel Legrand
New York Shakespeare Festival at The Public Theater, New York
Sets: Michael Yeargan
Costumes: Jane Greenwood
Lights: Ian Calderon
With Stefanianne Christopherson, Dean Pitchford

28. *Happy Days* by Samuel Beckett
New York Shakespeare Festival at The Public Theater, New York
Sets: Michael Yeargan & Lawrence King
Costumes: Jane Greenwood
Lights: Jennifer Tipton
With Irene Worth

29. *The Cherry Orchard* by Anton Chekhov
The Shiki Theatre, Tokyo

1980
30. *As You Like It* by William Shakespeare
La MaMa E.T.C., New York
Sets: Jun Maeda
Costumes: Gabriel Berry & Miruna Boruzescu
Lights: Beverly Emmons
Music: Liz Swados

With Priscilla Smith, Don Scardino, William Duff-Griffin

   31. *The Seagull* by Anton Chekhov
The Shiki Theatre, Tokyo
Designed by Kaoru Kanamuri
With Retsuke Sugamote, Kazuyo Mita

   32. *The Seagull* by Anton Chekhov
New York Shakespeare Festival at The Public Theater, New York
Sets: Michael Yeargan
Costumes: Jane Greenwood
Lights: Jennifer Tipton
Music: Liz Swados
With: Rosemary Harris, Christopher Walken, F. Murray Abraham

1981
   33. *Sganarelle: An Evening of Molière Farces*
American Repertory Theatre, Cambridge, MA
Sets: Michael Yeargan
Costumes: Dunya Ramicova
Lights: James Ingalls
With Cherry Jones, Thomas Derrah, Jeremy Geidt

1982
   34. *Zastrozzi* by George Walker
New York Shakespeare Festival at The Public Theater, New York
Sets and Costumes: Manuel Lutgenhorst
Lights: Jennifer Tipton
With Jan Triska, Frances Conroy, Judith Roberts

   35. *The Marriage of Figaro* by Beaumarchais
The Guthrie Theatre, Minneapolis
Sets and Costumes: Beni Montresor
Lights: Duane Schuler
Music: Richard Peaslee
With David Warrilow, Robert Dorfman, Caitlin Clarke

   36. *Three Sisters* by Anton Chekhov
American Repertory Theatre, Cambridge, MA
Designed by Beni Montresor
Music: Richard Peaslee
With Cherry Jones, Cheryl Giannini, Marianne Owen

1983
37. *The Master and the Marguerite* adapted by Jean-Claude Carrière, Jean-Claude van Itallie, and Serban from Bulgakov's novel
Théâtre de la Ville, Paris
Sets & Costumes: Miruna Boruzescu and Sturmer
With Fanny Cottencon, Andrzej Seweryn, Priscilla Smith

38. *Uncle Vanya* by Anton Chekhov
La MaMa E.T.C., New York
Sets and Costumes: Santo Loquasto
Lights: Jennifer Tipton
With Joseph Chaikin, F. Murray Abraham, Frances Conroy

1984
39. *The King Stag* by Carlo Gozzi
American Repertory Theatre, Cambridge, MA
Sets: Michael Yeargan
Costumes, Masks, & Puppetry: Julie Taymor
Lights: Jennifer Tipton
Music: Elliot Goldenthal
With Thomas Derrah, Priscilla Smith, Diane D'Aquila

1985
40. *The Marriage of Figaro* by Beaumarchais
Circle in the Square, New York
Designed by Beni Montresor
Music: Richard Peaslee
With Christopher Reeve, Mary Elizabeth Mastrantonio, Dana Ivey, Anthony Heald, Caitlin Clarke

1986
41. *Sweet Table at the Richelieu* by Ronald Ribman
American Repertory Theatre, Cambridge, MA
Sets and Costumes: John Conklin
Lights: Howell Binkley
With Ken Howard, Lucinda Childs, Elizabeth Franz

42. *Fragments of a Greek Trilogy*
La MaMa E.T.C., New York (25th Anniversary of La MaMa)
Sets: Jun Maeda
Costumes: Sharon Lynch (based on the original designs by Sandra Muir)
Lights: Carol Mullins
Music: Liz Swados
With Priscilla Smith, Valois, Onni Johnson, Dan Nutu

1987
43. *The Good Woman of Setzuan* by Bertolt Brecht
American Repertory Theatre, Cambridge, MA
Sets: Jeff Muskovin
Costumes: Catherine Zuber
Lights: Howell Binkley
Music: Liz Swados
With Priscilla Smith, Thomas Derrah, Harry Murphy, Alvin Epstein, James Andreassi

1988
44. *The Serpent Woman* by Carlo Gozzi
American Repertory Theatre, Cambridge, MA
Sets, Costumes, and Puppets: Setsu Asakura
Lights: Victor En Yu Tan
Music: Elliot Goldenthal
With Cherry Jones, Derek Smith, Thomas Derrah, Jeremy Geidt

1989
45. *The Miser* by Molière
American Repertory Theatre, Cambridge, MA
Sets: Derek McLane
Costumes: Judith Dolan
Lights: Howell Binkley
With Alvin Epstein, Cherry Jones, Derek Smith, Harry Murphy

46. *Twelfth Night* by William Shakespeare
American Repertory Theatre, Cambridge, MA
Sets: Derek McLane
Costumes: Catherine Zuber
Lights: Howell Binkley
Music: Mel Marvin
With Cherry Jones, Kario Salem, Diane Lane, Robert Stanton

1990
47. *Our Country's Good* by Timberlake Wertenbaker
Student Production at the University of California at San Diego

48. *Desire* by David Lan
Almeida Theatre, London
Sets & Costumes: Richard Hudson
Lights: Gerry Jenkinson
With: Vicky Licorish, Cyril Nri, Marcia Myrie

49. *Fragments of a Greek Trilogy*
Romanian National Theatre, Bucharest

50. *Our Country's Good* by Timberlake Wertenbaker
Romanian National Theatre, Bucharest
Sets & Costumes: Andrei Both

51. *Auditia* (A Cabaret b/o Audition Material of the Performers)

1991
52. *Hippolytos* by Euripides
Almeida Theatre, London
Sets: Richard Hudson
Costumes: Sue Blane
Lights: Simon Corder
With: Janet Suzman, Duncan Bell, Ian McDiarmid

1992–93
53. *The Cherry Orchard* by Anton Chekhov
Romanian National Theatre, Bucharest

OPERAS

1980
1. *Eugene Onegin* by Tchaikvosky
Welsh National Opera
Conductor: Mark Ermler
Sets & Costumes: Michael Yeargan
Lights: Robert Bryan
With Thomas Allen, Josephine Barstow, Anthony Rolfe Johnson

2. *The Magic Flute* by Mozart
Nancy Opéra, France
Conductor: Jerome Kaltenbach
Sets: Michael Yeargan
Costumes: Daniel Chompres
With Anthony Rolfe Johnson, Nan Christie, Stephen Dickson

1981
3. *Rodelinda* by Handel
Welsh National Opera
Conductor: Julian Smith
Sets & Costumes: Michael Yeargan

Lights: Robert Bryan
With Suzanne Murphy, Robin Martin-Oliver, Richard Morton

4. *La Traviata* by Verdi
Juilliard American Opera Center
Conductor: Christian Badea
Sets: Adrianne Lobel
Costumes: Dunya Ramicova
Lights: F. Mitchell Dana
With Roseann Del George, Kathryn Cowdrick, Michael Austin

1982
5. *I Puritani* by Bellini
Welsh National Opera
Conductor: Julian Smith
Sets & Costumes: Michael Yeargan
Lights: Robert Bryan

1983
6. *The Drama of Aïda* adapted from Verdi by Serban, Richard Armstrong, & Daryl Runswick
Welsh National Opera
Conductor: Richard Armstrong
Sets & Costumes: Michael Yeargan
Lights: John Waterhouse
With Anne Williams-King, Beverly Mills, Donald Stephenson

7. *Il Trovatore* by Verdi
Opera North, Leeds
Conductor: Yan Pascal Tortelier
Sets & Costumes: Michael Yeargan
Lights: Andrew Cunningham
With Natalia Rom, Cynthia Buchan, James Dietsch

8. *The Magic Flute* by Mozart
Théâtre Musical de Paris at the Chatelet
Conductor: Gyorgy Fischer
Sets: Michael Yeargan
Costumes: Daniel Chompres
With Stephen Dickson, Veronique Dietschy, Robin Leggate

9. *Alcina* by Handel
New York City Opera
Conductor: Raymond Leppard

Designed by Beni Montresor
With Carol Vaness, D'Anna Fortunato, Harry Dworchak

1984
10. *The Merry Widow* by Lehar
Welsh National Opera
Conductor: Julian Smith
Sets: Michael Yeargan
Costumes: Jacques Schmidt
Lights: Jennifer Tipton
With Thomas Allen, Suzanne Mercy

11. *I Puritani* by Bellini
Netherlands Opera
Conductor: Kees Bakals
Sets & Costumes: Michael Yeargan
Lights: Robert Bryan
With Cristina Deutekom, David Pittman-Jennings, Van den Berg

12. *The Love of Three Oranges* by Prokofiev
Geneva Opera
Conductor: Horst Stein
Designed by Beni Montresor
With Joseph Evans, Ricardo Cassinelli, Jules Bastin

13. *Turandot* by Puccini
The Royal Opera at Covent Garden (originally produced at The Los Angeles Olympic Arts Festival)
Conductor: Colin Davis
Sets and Costumes: Sally Jacobs
Lights: F. Mitchell Dana
With Placido Domingo, Gwyneth Jones, Yoko Watanabe

1985
14. *Norma* by Bellini
Welsh National Opera
Conductor: Julian Smith
Sets and Costumes: Michael Yeargan
Lights: Robert Bryan
With Kathryn Harries, Frederick Donaldson, Suzanne Murphy

15. *The Juniper Tree* by Philip Glass and Robert Moran
American Repertory Theatre
Conductor: Richard Pittman

Sets and Costumes: Michael Yeargan
Lights: Jennifer Tipton
With Jayne West, Sanford Sylvan, Lynn Torgove, Ruby Hinds

16. *Norma* by Bellini
New York City Opera
Conductor: Richard Bonynge
Sets and Costumes: Michael Yeargan
Lights: Mark Stanley
With Olivia Stapp, Robert Grayson, Judith Forst

1986
17. *Fidelio* by Beethoven
The Royal Opera at Covent Garden
Conductor: Colin Davis
Sets & Costumes: Sally Jacobs
Lights: William Ould
With Hartmu Welker, Elizabeth Connell, Klaus Konig

18. *Elektra* by Richard Strauss
Geneva Opera
Conductor: Friedemann Layer
Sets & Costumes: Yannis Kokkos
With Gwyneth Jones, Helga Dernesch, Alfred Muff

1987
19. *The Fiery Angel* by Prokofiev
Paris Opéra
Conductor: Lawrence Foster
Sets & Costumes: Robert Israel
With Marilyn Zschau

20. *The Fiery Angel* by Prokofiev
Los Angeles Center Opera
Conductor: Lawrence Foster
Sets & Costumes: Robert Israel
Lights: Marie Barrett
With Marilyn Zschau, Roger Roloff, Ken Remo

21. *I Puritani* by Bellini
Paris Opéra

1988
22. *Don Carlo* by Verdi
Geneva Opera
Conductor: Richard Armstrong
Sets & Costumes: Yannis Kokkos
With Samuel Rammey, Keith Langan, Neil Schicoff

23. *The Fiery Angel* by Prokofiev
Bologna Opera
Sets & Costumes: Robert Israel

24. *Don Carlo* by Verdi
Bologna Opera
Conductor: Richard Armstrong
Sets: Yannis Kokkos
With Samuel Rammey, Keith Langan, Neil Schicoff

1990
25. *Prince Igor* by Borodin
Royal Opera at Covent Garden
Conductor: Bernard Haitink
Sets: Liviu Ciulei
Costumes: Deidre Clancy
With Sergei Leiferkus, Khan Konchak, Elena Zaremba

26. *Lucia Di Lammermoor* by Donizetti
Lyric Opera of Chicago
Conductor: Donato Renzetti
Sets: William Dudley
Costumes: Anna Watkins
Lights: Duane Schuler
With June Anderson, Alfredo Kraus

1991
27. *Elektra* by Strauss
San Francisco Opera
Conductor: Christian Thielemann
Sets & Costumes: Yannis Kokkos
Lights: Thomas J. Munn
With Gwyneth Jones, Helga Dernesch, Nadine Secunde, Monte Peterson

28. *Eugene Onegin* by Tchaikovsky
Opera La Fenice, Venice
Conductor: J. Sutej

Sets: Chloe Oboelenski

1992
29. *Rigoletto* by Verdi
Opera La Fenice, Venice
Conductor: J. Sutej
Sets: Johnny Quaranta

1993
30. *Lucia Di Lammermoor* by Donizetti
Los Angeles Center Opera
Conductor: Richard Buckley
Sets & Costumes: William Dudley
Lights: Duane Schuler
With June Anderson, Craig Sirianni, Dimitri Kharitonov

31. *Otello* by Verdi
Choregies D'Orange, France
Conductor: Alain Guingal
Sets: Guy Claude Francois
Costumes: Daniela Kamiliotis
Lights: Claude Tissier
With Vladimir Atantov, Alain Fondary, Martine Olmeda

32. *Elektra* by Strauss
Houston Grand Opera
Conductor: Christoph Eschenbach
Sets & Costumes: Yannis Kokkos
Lights: Noel Stollmack
With Hildegard Behrens, Josephine Barstow, Leonie Rysanek

33. *Tales of Hoffman* by Offenbach
Vienna State Opera
Conductor: Christian Badea
Sets & Costumes: Richard Hudson
With Placido Domingo

1994
34. *Adrianna Lecouvreur* by Cilea
Zurich Opera
Conductor: Lomberto Gardelly
Sets: Chloe Oboelenski
Costumes: Claudine Gastin

Bibliography

I Writings by Andrei Serban.

Serban, Andrei. "Andrei Serban on *The Miser*." Theatre Program. *The Miser*. American Repertory Theatre, 1989, n. pag.

_____. "Director's Statement." Theatre Program. *The Threepenny Opera*. American Conservatory Theatre, 1975, n. pag.

_____. "Gozzi's Theatre: A Provocation For Awakening." Theatre Program. *The Serpent Woman*. American Repertory Theatre, 1988, n. pag.

_____. Letters to author. 7, 10, and 13 June 1994.

_____. "Serban Defends His *Cherry Orchard*." Letter, Theatre Mailbag. *The New York Times* 13 March 1977: D4.

_____. "Taking the Imaginary Seriously." Theatre Program. *The King Stag*.American Repertory Theatre, 1984, n. pag.

_____. "The Life in a Sound." Trans Eileen Blumenthal. *The Drama Review* 20.3 (1976): 25–26.

II. Interviews with Serban.

_____. Personal interview. 11 December 1989.

_____. Personal interview. 5 February 1994.

_____. Interviewed by Arthur Bartow. *The Director's Voice: Twenty-one Interviews*. New York: Theatre Communications Group, 1988. 290–299.

_____. Interviewed by Eileen Blumenthal. *Yale/Theater* 8 (1977): 66–77.

_____. Interviewed by Dean Drury. *Keynote* July 1977: 4–13.

_____. Interviewed by Arthur Holmberg. *A.R.T. News* IX No. 1 November 1988: 1, 4.

_____. Interviewed by Dan Isaac. "A Non-verbal Approach to Chekhov." *New York Theatre Critics' Review* Spring/Summer (1977): 11.

_____. Interviewed by James Leverett. "Serban in the Mad Forest," *Performing Arts*, program for Berkeley Repertory Theatre, Fall, 1992: P-1–P-6.

_____. Interviewed by Joel Schechter and Colette Brooks. "Andrei Serban on Artaud." *Theater* 9.3 (1978): 25–29.

_____. Interviewed by Laurence Shyer. "Andrei Serban Directs Chekhov: *The Seagull* in New York and Japan." *Theater* 13.1 (1981): 56–66.

_____. Interviewed by Juliusz Tyszka. *Ars Nova.* Poznan, Poland: Widowiska Nowojorski, 1994. 61–71.

III. Interviews with Theatre Collaborators

Binkley, Howell. Personal interview. 11 December 1989.

Brustein, Robert. Personal interview. 12 December 1989.

Derrah, Thomas. Personal interview. 14 December 1989.

Finlay, William. Personal interview. 6 December 1989.

Geidt, Jeremy. Personal interview. 15 December 1989.

Hudson, Rodney. Personal interview. 15 December 1989.

Jones, Cherry. Personal interview. 18 February 1990.

Koppleman, Mona. Personal interview. 3 February 1994.

Linn-Baker, Mark. Personal interview. 27 April 1979.

McLane, Derek. Personal interview. 11 December 1989.

Nutu, Dan. Personal interview. 12 December 1989.

Papp, Joseph. Telephone interview. 13 April 1990.

Raphael, Bonnie. Personal interview. 15 December 1989.

Scanlan, Robert. Personal interview. 13 December 1989.

Smith, Priscilla. Personal interview. 13 February 1990.

_____. Personal interview. 7 March 1991.

_____. Personal interview. 2 June 1991.

Stewart, Ellen. Personal interview. 12 February 1990.

Walker, Paul. Personal interview. 14 December 1989.

Yeargan, Michael. Personal interview. 16 February 1990.

IV. Performances and Videotapes.

Serban, Andrei, dir. *Fragments of a Greek Trilogy*. Based on *Medea*, and *The Trojan Women* by Euripides and *Electra* by Sophocles. With Priscilla Smith. La Mama E.T.C. La MaMa Annex, New York. April 1979.

_____. *Happy Days*. By Beckett. With Irene Worth. The New York Shakespeare Festival Public Theater. Newman Theatre, New York. June 1979.

_____. *Sganarelle: An Evening of Molière Farces*. *The Flying Doctor*, *The Forced Marriage*, *Sganarelle*, and *A Dumb Show*, based on *The Doctor in Spite of Himself* by Molière. Trans. Albert Bermel. With Mark Linn Baker and Michael Gross. The Yale Repertory Theatre, New Haven. January 1979.

_____. *Sweet Table at the Richelieu*. By Ribman. American Repertory Theatre. Loeb Drama Center, Cambridge. Video recording. 1987.

_____. *The Ghost Sonata*. By Strindberg. Trans. Evert Sprinchorn. With Priscilla Smith and Max Wright. The Yale Repertory Theatre, New Haven. October 1978.

_____. *The Good Woman of Setzuan*. By Brecht. Trans. Eric Bentley. American Repertory Theatre. With Priscilla Smith. Loeb Drama Center, Cambridge. Video recording. 1987.

_____. *The Juniper Tree.* Based on a fairy tale by the Brothers Grimm. Music by Glass and Moran. Libretto by Yorinks. American Repertory Theatre. Loeb Drama Center, Cambridge. Video recording. 1986.

_____. *The King Stag.* By Gozzi. English version by Albert Bermel. American Repertory Theatre. Loeb Drama Center, Cambridge. Video Recording. 1984.

_____. *The Miser.* By Molière. Trans. Albert Bermel. With Alvin Epstein and Cherry Jones. The American Repertory Theatre. The Power Center, Ann Arbor. 7 July 1989.

_____. *The Seagull.* By Chekhov. New version by Jean-Claude van Itallie. With Rosemary Harris, F. Murray Abraham, and Christopher Walken. The New York Shakespeare Festival. The Public Theater, New York. Video recording. 1981.

_____. *The Serpent Woman.* By Gozzi. English version by Albert Bermel and Ted Emery. With Cherry Jones. American Repertory Theatre. Loeb Drama Center, Cambridge. 28 December 1988.

_____. *The Umbrellas of Cherbourg.* Book by Demy. Music by Legrand. Trans. Sheldon Harnick. The New York Shakespeare Festival Public Theater. Theater Cabaret in Martinson Hall, New York. February 1979.

_____. *Twelfth Night or What You Will.* By Shakespeare. With Cherry Jones and Diane Lane. American Repertory Theatre. Loeb Drama Center, Cambridge. Technical rehearsals, preview performances, opening and post-opening performances. 5–16 December 1989.

V. Notes, Theatre Programs, and Theatre Newsletter Essays.

Serban, Andrei. Notes and Discussion with Graduate Acting and Directing Classes. Columbia University. 2–8 February 1994.

_____. Notes to actors after first preview performance of *Twelfth Night.* American Repertory Theatre. 9 December 1989.

_____. Notes to actors on rehearsal of opening night of *Twelfth Night.* American Repertory Theatre. 13 December 1989.

_____. Notes to actors on first rehearsal of *Twelfth Night*. Recorded by Chris Baker. American Repertory Theatre. 10 October 1989. Printed in *A.R.T. News* X No. 1 Nov. 1989: 3.

_____. Notes to actors on first rehearsal of *The Miser*. 4 April 1989. American Repertory Theatre. Printed in *A.R.T. News* IX No. 3 April 1989: 3.

Arden of Faversham. La MaMa Repertory Theatre. New York, February 1970.

As You Like It. Eleventh Festival of Arts. Shiraz/Persepolis, Iran. 17–26 August 1977. Includes brief biography and description of methods of rehearsal.

_____. La MaMa E.T.C. New York, 18 January–12 February 1980.

Fragments of a Greek Trilogy. La MaMa E.T.C. New York, 18 October 1974. With performance notes on all three plays.

_____. La MaMa E.T.C. New York, April 1979.

_____. La MaMa E.T.C. presents The Great Jones Repertory Company. New York, 28 December 1986–15 March 1987.

I Am Not the Eiffel Tower. The Bucharest Drama Students' Group. Romania, 1966. Includes a brief essay on Serban.

Romeo and Juliet. Nassau Community College Department of Theatre and Dance. 1–5 and 8–12 March 1972. Includes a brief essay on Serban.

Sganarelle: An Evening of Molière Farces. Yale Repertory Theatre. New Haven, Spring 1978. With an essay on rehearsal methods of the piece.

_____. American Repertory Theatre. Cambridge, December 1981–March 1982. With an essay on re-creating the piece from the original production at Yale four years later.

She Stoops to Conquer. Nassau Community College Department of Speech-Theatre. 22–25 April and 29 April–May 2 1970. Includes a brief essay on Serban.

The Ghost Sonata. Yale Repertory Theatre. New Haven, Fall 1977. Includes essay on methods of rehearsal by dramaturg Colette Brooks.

The Good Woman of Setzuan. La MaMa E.T.C presents The Great Jones Repertory Project. New York, 1976.

The Good Woman of Setzuan. American Repertory Theatre. Cambridge, May–July 1987.

The Juniper Tree. American Repertory Theatre. Cambridge, December 1985–February 1986.

The King Stag. American Repertory Theatre. Cambridge, November 1984–January 1985. Includes "Taking the Imaginary Seriously" by Serban.

The Marriage of Figaro. The Guthrie Theatre. Minneapolis, July–August 1982.

The Master and Margarita. The New York Shakespeare Festival at The Public Theater. November, 1978.

The Miser. American Repertory Theatre. Cambridge, May–June 1989. Includes "Andrei Serban on *The Miser*."

_____. American Repertory Theatre. Ann Arbor Summer Festival 89. 7 July 1989.

The Serpent Woman. American Repertory Theatre. Cambridge, November 1988--February 1989. Includes "Gozzi's Theatre: A Provocation for Awakening" by Serban.

The Threepenny Opera. American Conservatory Theatre. San Francisco, April–May, 1975. Includes director's statement.

The Umbrellas of Cherbourg. New York Shakespeare Festival at The Public Theater. February–March, 1979.

Sweet Table at the Richelieu. American Repertory Theatre. Cambridge, February–March 1987.

Three Sisters. American Repertory Theatre. Cambridge, December 1982–February 1983.

Twelfth Night. American Repertory Theatre. Cambridge, December 1989–March 1990.

Uncle Vanya. La MaMa E.T.C. New York, September, 1983.

VI. Articles and Books Regarding Serban's Work.

Anderson, Susan Heller. "Now Romania Wants Serban Back." *The New York Times* 17 February 1990: Chronicle, 32.

Baker, Robb. "Andrei Serban: Genius or Charlatan?" *After Dark* June 1977: 28–30.

_____. "Andrei Serban: The Intelligence of Emotion." *The Soho Weekly News* 17 October 1974: 18–20.

_____. "Summer With Serban: Fragments of a Work in Limbo." *The Soho Weekly News* 6 January 1977: 13–15, 26.

Bartow, Arthur. *The Director's Voice: Twenty-one Interviews.* New York: Theatre Communications Group, 1988. 286–290, 376–378.

Bentsen, Cheryl. "Swados in Wonderland." *New York* 29 December 1980: 38–42.

Bermel, Albert. "Afterword." *Five Tales for the Theatre.* By Gozzi. Trans. and ed. by Bermel and Ted Emery. Chicago: University of Chicago Press, 1989. 309.

Blumenthal, Eileen. "Andrei Serban Makes Dead Languages Live Again." *The Village Voice* 26 January 1976: 107–108.

Brustein, Robert. "Defending Serban's Vision of Aeschylus." Letter, Theatre Mailbag, *The New York Times* 12 June 1977: 3, 9.

_____. *Making Scenes: A Personal History of the Turbulent Years at Yale 1966–1979.* New York: Limelight Editions, 1984.

_____. "Re-working the Classics: Homage or Ego Trip?" *The New York Times* 6 November 1988: Sec. 2, 5, 16.

_____. "Serban Under Siege." *Who Needs Theatre?: Dramatic Opinions.* New York: Atlantic Monthly Press, 1987. 115–119.

Cartwright, Diane. "Priscilla Smith of The Great Jones Repertory Project." *The Drama Review* 20.3 (1976): 75–83.

Cole, Gloria. "Elizabeth Swados Defies Musical Cliches." *Tempo* Fall 1977.

Croyden, Margaret. "A Director Revolts." *TheaterWeek* 21 February 1994: 22–26.

———. "Seeking the Emotions that Stirred the Ancient Greeks." *The New York Times* 8 May 1977: D1, D14.

Crutchfield, Will. "Bellini's *Norma* Gets a Dash of the Avant-Garde." *The New York Times* 4 August 1985: Sec. 2, 1, 20.

"Serban, Andrei." *Current Biography*. 1978 ed. 376–380.

Eder, Richard. "A Fiery Stage Troupe Moving to Paris." *The New York Times* 24 March 1976: 28.

———. "Andrei Serban's Theatre of Terror and Beauty." *The New York Times Magazine* 13 February 1977: 42–46, 50–54.

Eddy, Bill. "*The Trojan Women* at La MaMa." *The Drama Review* 18.4 (1974): 112–113.

Eichelbaum, Stanley. "Staging an Upside-Down Opera." *The San Francisco Examiner* 8 April 1975: 27.

Fanger, Iris. "Japan's Asakura is Hot Commodity in World of Theater." *The Boston Herald* 2 December 1988: S22.

Fox, Terry Curtis. "Andrei Serban is a Hip Hal Prince." *The Village Voice* 23 February 1976: 125.

Frankel, Haskel. "A Cultural Explorer in New Haven." *The New York Times* 5 February 1978: Sec. 23, 14.

Gilman, Richard. "How the New Theatrical Directors Are Upstaging the Playwright." *The New York Times* 31 July 1977: Sec. 2, 1, 18.

Goldenthal, Elliot. "Elliot Goldenthal Composes for Gozzi: Big Music for Big Mythic Themes." Interviewed by Christopher Baker. *A.R.T. News* IX No.1 November 1988: 9.

Green, Amy S. "American Directors Reinvent the Classics." *On-Stage Studies* 16 (1993): 23–39.

Gussow, Mel. "Drama Teacher's Drill: Re-invent the Classics." *The New York Times* 7 June 1994: C17, C22.

Bibliography

_____. "Serban: His Vanya and His Career." *The New York Times* 6 September 1983: C11.

_____. "Troy is Falling Again Off Off Broadway." *The New York Times* 31 December 1976: C1, C12.

"The View From Vienna." *Hammerstein Center News*, Columbia University. February 1994.

Higgins, John. "Serban's Ever-Broadening Horizons." *The Times* 14 February 1980: 13.

Hodenfield, Jan. "Romania's Gift to the Theater Raises His Repertory Sights." *The New York Post* 31 January 1976: 8.

Holderness, Rebecca. "Orange Journal." Journal. Columbia University. 1993.

Holmberg, Arthur. "Greek Tragedy in a New Mask Speaks to Today's Audiences." *The New York Times* 1 March 1987: Sec. 2, 1, 28.

Istel, John. "Educating Prosperos." *American Theatre* January 1994: 27, 80–82.

Karmali, Hafiz. "Andrei Serban and the Meaning of *The Serpent Woman*." *A.R.T. News* IX No. 1 November 1988: 1, 4.

Knubel, Fred. Publicity release. Office of Public Information, Columbia University. 1992.

Kott, Jan. "Where are *Ajax* and *Philoctetes* Now That We Need Them?" Interviewed by Joel Schechter. *Theater* 11 (1980): 18–22.

le Sourd, Jacques. "Santo Loquasto to Center Stage." *Sunday Magazine* 12 June 1977: G13–14.

Lubianitsky, Leonid. "The Serban Takeover." *Vogue* August 1977: 152–153.

Marks, Jonathan. "Andrei Serban's *Three Sisters*." *Winter Symposium, Literary Managers and Dramaturgs of America*. New York: Columbia University. 9 February 1987.

_____. "Born Again *Sganarelle*." Theatre program, *Sganarelle: An Evening of Molière Farces*. American Repertory Theatre 1981, n. pag.

Narti, Ana Maria. "*Medea*: Andrei Serban's Work on the Tragic Acting." Thesis. Institute of Theatre and Film, Stockholm University, 1974.

Nelsen, Don. "A Smith Forges Her Mettle in Theater." *The Daily News* 15 1977: 8.

Novick, Julius. "Releasing the Cosmic Intensity of the Classics." *The New York Times* 18 January 1976: D5.

Popkin, Henry. "Another Romanian Theatrical Master Gets a Showing." *The New York Times* 2 July 1978: Sec. 2, 3, 12.

Robertson, Allan. "Andrei Serban: Theater Magician." *Minneapolis-St. Paul* July 1982: 23.

Shyer, Laurence. "In Collaboration: Michael Yeargan and Andrei Serban." *Theater Crafts* May 1982: 23, 60–64.

Stasio, Marilyn. "Unwrapping Serban's Turban." *Cue* March 5 1977: 25.

Steele, Mike. "The Romanian Connection." *American Theatre* August 1985: 4–11.

Swados, Elizabeth. "Music for a New Theater." Interviewed by Peter Zummo. *The Soho Weekly News* 5 February 1976: 16.

Taylor, Markland. "Serban: Love Him or Leave Him." *The New Haven Register* 25 September 1977: D4.

Wallach, Alan. "*Romeo and Juliet* Reaches New Heights." *Newsday* 16 February 1972.

Weymouth, Lally. "'In Order to Achieve Real Wings in Chekhov, You Just Live It." *The New York Times* 6 March 1977: Sec. 2, 5, 24.

Wetzsteon, Ross. "The Theater's New Stars: The Directors." *New York* 23 February 1981: 24–30.

Witchel, Alexandra. "Bad Boy Director in Wonderland." *Elle* December 1985: 42.

Zuber, Catherine. "Dressing *Twelfth Night*: A Talk with Cathy Zuber." *A.R.T. News* X No. 1 November 1989: 3, 5.

VII. Reviews of Selected Serban Productions

A. *Agamemnon.*

Baker, Robb. rev. of *Agamemnon*, by Aeschylus. *The Soho Weekly News* 30 May 1977.

Barnes, Clive. "Aeschylus Alive." *The New York Times* 19 May 1977: Sec. 3, 26.

Beaufort, John. "An *Agamemnon* of Uneven Effects." *The Christian Science Monitor* 23 May 1977. Reprinted in *New York Theatre Critics' Review* 1977: 237.

Gottfried, Martin. "*Agamemnon* Off the Wall." *New York Post* 19 May 1977. Reprinted in *New York Theatre Critics' Review* 1977: 235–236.

Gussow, Mel. rev. of *Agamemnon*, by Aeschylus. *The New York Times* 18 August 1977: Sec. 3, 18.

Kalem, T.E. "Vandal Sacks Atreus." *Time* 30 May 1977: 76.

Kerr, Walter. "Andrei Serban's *Agamemnon*: Why? Why? Why? Why?" *The New York Times* 29 May 1977: Sec. 2, 3.

Kissel, Howard. rev. of *Agamemnon*, by Aeschylus. *Women's Wear Daily* 19 May 1977. Reprinted in *New York Theatre Critics' Review* 1977: 237.

Knox, Bernard. rev. of *Agamemnon*, by Aeschylus. *New York Review of Books* 14 July 1977. Reprinted in *Word and Action: Essays on the Ancient Theater*. By Knox. Baltimore: John Hopkins Press, 1979: 78.

Kroll, Jack. "Greek Fury." *Newsweek* 30 May 1977: 89.

Munk, Erika. "Flashes of Astonishment." *The Village Voice* 30 May 1977: 87.

Wallach, Alan. rev. of *Agamemnon*, by Aeschylus. *Newsday* 18 August 1977: Sec. 3, 18.

Watt, Douglas. "De Mille Would've Loved It." *The Daily News* 19 May 1977. Reprinted in *New York Theatre Critics' Review* 1977: 235.

Wilson, Edwin. "Misdirection of a Great Greek Play." *The Wall Street Journal* 19 May 1977. Reprinted in *New York Theatre Critics' Review* 1977: 236.

B. *Arden of Faversham.*

Barnes, Clive. "Double-Bill at La MaMa." *The New York Times* 17 February 1970: 33.

Peter, John. "Theatre of Gesture." *The Sunday Times* 24 May 1970: 33.

C. *Fragments of a Greek Trilogy.*

Baker, Robb. "Catoptromanica." *The Soho Weekly News* 3 July 1974.

———. "Off Off and Away." *After Dark* August 1974.

Barnes, Clive. "Serban's *Trilogy* is an Event." *The New York Times* 20 October 1974: 64.

———. "Superb *Medea*." *The New York Times* 25 January 1972: 26.

Clurman, Harold. rev. of *Fragments*. *The Nation* 18 January 1975: 58–60.

Copeland, Roger. "Avant-Garde Stage: From Primal Dreams to Split Images." *The New York Times* 11 January 1987: H4, 14.

Feingold, Michael. "Toward a Pure Theatre." *The Village Voice* 20 January 1987: 85.

Gold, Sylviane. "Catharsis in a Modern Key." *The Wall Street Journal* 20 February 1987: 19.

Gussow, Mel. rev. of *Fragments*. *The New York Times* 25 June 1974: 27.

———. "*Greek Trilogy* Returns to La MaMa." *The New York Times* 6 January 1987: C16.

———. "Two Classics in One." *The New York Times* 31 December 1975: 17.

Hewes, Henry. "Subterranean Sounds Surfacing." *Saturday Review* 3 March 1972: 12–13.

Kauffman, Stanley. rev. of *Fragments*. 23 November 1974. Reprinted in *Persons of the Drama: Theater Criticism and Comment*. New York: Harper and Row, 1976: 108–111.

Kerr, Walter. "Of Poetry Heard and Seen." *The New York Times* 25 January 1976: Sec. 2, 5.

Novick, Julius. "La MaMa Rekindles an Ancient Fire." *The New York Times* 17 November 1974: Sec. 2, 5, 7.

Rabkin, Gerald. "Rediscovered Mysteries." *The Soho Weekly News* 8 January 1976: 28.

Sainer, Arthur. "A Night at Blockbusters Anonymous." *The Village Voice* 24 October 1974: 87.

Simon, John. "All Greek to Them." *New York* 3 February 1987: 64.

Wardle, Irving. "Edinburgh Festival: Prison Themes." *The Times* 26 August 1976: 15.

Watt, Douglas. "La MaMa Gives Birth to a Bouncing Baby." *The Daily News* 20 October 1974: 120.

D. *Sganarelle: An Evening of Molière Farces*.

Angermann, Chris. "Farce without Stuffing." *New Haven Advocate* 1 February 1978: S9.

Barnes, Clive. "Farcing It Up at The Public." *The New York Post* 8 June 1978. Reprinted in *New York Theatre Critics' Review* 1978: 183.

Christiansen, Richard. "Serban Directs Fitful Evening of Laughs." *Chicago Tribune* 4 June 1982: Sec. 3, 7.

Clay, Carolyn. "Revival of the Fittest." *The Boston Phoenix* December 1981.

Gussow, Mel. "Molière Farce Staged by Serban." *The New York Times* 8 June 1978: 113.

Johnson, Malcolm. "Serban's *Sganarelle*: Strong, But Overlong." *The Hartford Courant* 29 January 1979.

Kerr, Walter. "Serban Puts Molière Through the Hoops at Yale." *The New York Times* 5 February 1978: Sec. 2, 3.

Kroll, Jack. "Tours de Farce." *Newsweek* 13 February 1978: 34.

Novick, Julius. "Serban, *Sganarelle*, Show-Biz, and the Shatapupu." *The Village Voice* 13 February 1978: 71.

Norton, Elliot. "Mad Molière Skits." *The Boston Herald* 2 December 1981.

Roberts, John. "Molière's *Sganarelle*." *The New Haven Register* 25 January 1978: S2.

Simon, John. "French Without Tears." *New York* 10 July 1978: 66.

E. *The Cherry Orchard.*

Barnes, Clive. "A *Cherry Orchard* that Celebrates Genius." *The New York Times* 18 February 1977: C3.

Beaufort, John. "An 'Opened -Up' *Cherry Orchard*: Less Light." *The Christian Science Monitor* 23 February 1977. Reprinted in *New York Theatre Critics' Review* 1977: 339.

Clurman, Harold. rev. of *Cherry Orchard*. *The Nation* 12 March 1977: 313–314.

Eder, Richard. "Two Versions." *The New York Times* 10 March 1977: 46.

_____, Hewes, Henry; Kalem, T.E.; and Simon, John. "Critics' Roundtable." *New York Theatre Critics' Review* Spring/Summer 1977: 5–10.

Feingold, Michael. "Chekhov's Ant Farm." *The Village Voice* 14 March 1977: 97, 99.

Gottfried, Martin. "A Beautiful *Cherry Orchard* Blooms." *The New York Post* 18 February 1977. Reprinted in *New York Theatre Critics' Review* 1977: 337.

Higgins, John. "New York Theatre." *The Times* 10 February 1977: 13.

Kauffman, Stanley. rev. of *Cherry Orchard*. *The New Republic*. 26 March 1977: 28, 41–42.

Kerr, Walter. "A Daring, Perverse, and Deeply Original *Cherry Orchard.*" *The New York Times* 27 February 1977: Sec. 2, 1, 5.

Kissel. Howard. rev. of *Cherry Orchard*. *Women's Wear Daily* 22 February 1977. Reprinted in *New York Theatre Critics' Review* 1977: 339–340.

Kroll, Jack. "Chekhov Without Tears." *Newsweek* 28 February 1977: 78–79.

le Sourd, Jacques. *Cherry Orchard* in Landmark Production." *Tarrytown News* 18 February 1977.

Novick, Julius. "One and a Half Cheers for Serban." *The Village Voice* 7 March 1977: 65.

Porterfield, Christopher. "Magnified Gestures." *Time* 28 February 1977. Reprinted in *New York Theatre Critics' Review* 1977: 337.

Watt, Douglas. "Sad *Cherry Orchard.*" *The Daily News* 18 February 1 1977. Reprinted in *New York Theatre Critics' Review* 1977: 338.

Wilson, Edwin. "Chekhov and Shaw Back on Broadway." *The Wall Street Journal* 1 March 1977. Reprinted in *New York Theatre Critics' Review* 1977: 340

F. *The Good Woman of Setzuan.*

Barnes, Clive. "La MaMa's Prolific Virtues Crown *Good Woman.*" *The New York Times* 4 February 1975: 24.

Clay, Carolyn. "*Setzuan* Smorgasbord: Why can't the A.R.T. Give Us a Brecht?" *The Boston Phoenix* 29 May 1987: 8, 15.

Friedman, Arthur. "*Good Woman* Has Faults." *The Boston Herald* 26 May 1987: 35.

Gold, Sylviane. "*Setzuan* Retains Brecht Message." *The New York Post* 27 January 1976: 18.

Gussow, Mel. "A Fresh Brecht." *The New York Times* 27 January 1976: 28.

Marranca, Bonnie. rev. of *Good Woman*. *Changes* April 1975: 30.

Wetzsteon, Ross. "Who Ever Heard of a Cute Brecht?" *The Village Voice* 2 February 1976: 107.

G. *The King Stag.*

Blumenthal, Eileen. "Beauty's Orient." *The Village Voice* 8 January 1985: 71.

Gussow, Mel. "Once Upon a Time." *The New York Times* 19 December 1984: C19.

Kelly, Kevin. "*The King Stag* Casts a Brilliant Spell." *The Boston Globe* 29 November 1984.

Kroll, Jack. "In the Kingdom of Serendippo." *Newsweek* 17 December 1984: 79.

McNiff, Brian. "Repertory Company Presents a Pair of Fables." *The Worcester Telegram* 3 December 1984.

H. *The Seagull.*

Asahina, Robert. "Theatre Chronicle." *The Hudson Review* 34 (1981): 99–100.

Barnes, Clive. "Serban's *Seagull* Soars." *The New York Post* 12 November 1980. Reprinted in *New York Theatre Critics' Review* 1980: 103–104.

Feingold, Michael. "Vodka and Apple Pie." *The Village Voice* 12 November 1980: 91.

Kalem, T.E. "Quartet." *Time* 24 November 1980: 64–65.

Kerr, Walter. "*Seagull* Gone Astray." *The New York Times* 23 November 1980: D3, 9.

Kissel, Howard. rev. of *Seagull*. *Women's Wear Daily* 12 November 1980. Reprinted in *New York Theatre Critics' Review* 1980: 104.

Kroll, Jack. "Chekhov in Daylight." *Newsweek* 24 November 1980: 131.

Rich, Frank. "Serban Directs *The Seagull*." *The New York Times* 12 November 1980: C25.

Shewey, Don. "The Chekhov List." *The Soho Weekly News* 12 November 1980: 45.

Simon, John. "Gulling the Audience." *New York* 24 November 1980: 55–57.

Wallach, Alan. "Chekhov's *Seagull* a la Serban." *Newsday* 12 November 1980.

Watt, Douglas. "*The Seagull* Soars at Public." *The Daily News* 12 November 1980. Reprinted in *New York Theatre Critics' Review* 1980: 103.

I. *The Serpent Woman.*

Clay, Carolyn. "Hiss and Tell: Is *The Serpent Woman* Snakebit?" *The Boston Phoenix* 9 December 1988: 7–8.

Gussow, Mel. "Fabulist *Serpent Woman.*" *The New York Times* 30 December 1988: C3.

Kelly, Kevin. "A.R.T. Season Off to Excessive Start." *The Boston Globe* 5 December 1988: 12–13.

Lehman, Jon. "A.R.T.'s *The Serpent Woman.*" *The Patriot Ledger* 6 December 1988: 13.

J. *Three Sisters.*

Clay, Carolyn. "Chekhov's Dinner With Andrei: *Three Sisters* a la Serban." *The Boston Phoenix* 14 December 1982: Sec. 3.

Holmberg, Arthur. rev. of *Three Sisters*. *Performing Arts Journal* 7 (1983): 71–72.

Jenkins, Ron. rev. of *Three Sisters*. *Theatre Journal* June (1983): 243–244.

Kelly, Kevin. "A.R.T.'s Wrongheaded *Three Sisters.*" *The Boston Globe* 3 December 1982: 25.

Kroll, Jack. "A Pair of *Three Sisters.*" *Newsweek* 10 January 1983: 70.

Pfeifer, Ellen. "*Three Sisters* Uneven." *The Boston Herald* 2 December 1982: B11.

Weigland, David. "Sorority Party" A.R.T. Plays Chekhov for Laughs in *Three Sisters*." *Cambridge (Mass.) Chronicle* December 1982.

K. *Twelfth Night.*

De Vries, Hilary. " Shakespeare and Ionesco at A.R.T." *The Wall Street Journal* 20 December 1989: A12.

Friedman, Arthur. "Sparkling Shakespeare." *The Boston Herald* 15 December 1989: S17–18.

Gussow, Mel. "Romanian Directors' Views on Shakespeare and Ionesco." *The New York Times* 20 December 1989: C20.

Kelly, Kevin. "Serban's Night Dark and Stirring." *The Boston Globe* 15 December 1989: 65, 73.

L. *Uncle Vanya.*

Beaufort, John. "Poor Direction Can't Wreck *Uncle Vanya*." *The Christian Science Monitor* 28 September 1983. Reprinted in *New York Theatre Critics' Review* 1983: 159–160.

Kalson, Albert. rev. of *Uncle Vanya. Theatre Journal* 36 (1984): 107–108.

Kissel, Howard. rev. of *Uncle Vanya. Women's Wear Daily* 12 September 1983. Reprinted in *New York Theatre Critics' Review* 1983: 158–159.

Kroll, Jack. "*Uncle Vanya* on the Boards." *Newsweek* 26 September 1983: 93.

Nightingale, Benedict. "Would Chekhov Have Embraced This *Vanya*?" *The New York Times* 18 September 1983: Sec. 2, 1, 4.

Novick, Julius. "Avanya Garde." *The Village Voice* 20 September 1983: 97.

O'Haire, Patricia. "A New Interpretation of *Uncle Vanya*." *The Daily News* 13 September 1983. Reprinted in *New York Theatre Critics' Review* 1983:158.

Oliver, Edith. "The Theatre." *The New Yorker* 26 September 1983: 126–127.

Rich, Frank. "New Serban *Uncle Vanya*." *The New York Times* 15 September 1983: C27.

Schechner, Richard. "*Vanya* at La MaMa: We Do Chekhov Right." *The Village Voice* 4 October 1983: 121.

Simon, John. "Overdirected, Underachieved." *New York* 26 September 1983: 101–102.

Stasio, Marilyn. "*Vanya*: Bold and Beautiful." *The New York Post* 16 September 1983.

Wallach, Alan. "Serban's New Version of *Uncle Vanya*." *Newsday* 12 September 1983.

VIII. General Sources on Contemporary and Classical theatre, and Other Related Fields.

Artaud, Antonin. *The Theater and its Double*. Trans. Mary Richards. New York: Grove Press, 1958.

Beckett, Samuel. *Waiting For Godot*. Trans. by the author. New York: Grove Press, 1954.

Berry, Cicely. *The Actor and His Text*. New York: Charles Scribner's Sons, 1987.

Braun, Edward. *The Director and the Stage: From Naturalism to Stanislavsky*. London: Metheun, 1982.

Brecht, Bertolt. *Brecht on Theatre*. Trans. and ed. John Willett. New York: Hill and Wang, 1964.

Brook, Peter. *The Empty Space*. New York: Atheneum, 1968.

_____. *The Shifting Point*. New York: Harper and Row, 1987.

Brustein, Robert. *The Theater of Revolt: An Approach to the Modern Drama*. Boston: Little, Brown, and Company, 1962.

Chekhov, Anton. *The Major Plays*. Trans. Ann Dunnigan. New York: New American Library, 1964.

Croyden, Margaret. "Peter Brook Learns to Speak Orghast." *The New York Times* 3 October 1971: Sec. 2, 1, 3, 5.

Emery, Ted. "Carlo Gozzi in Context." Introduction. *Five Tales for the Theatre*. By Carlo Gozzi. Ed. and Trans. Albert Bermel and Emery. Chicago: University of Chicago Press, 1989. 1–19.

Epstein, Helen. "The N.Y. Shakespeare Festival—Does Biggest Mean Best?" *The New York Times* 27 February 1977: Sec. 2, 1, 26.

Euripides. *The Trojan Women* in *Greek Tragedies Volume Two*. Ed. and trans. David Grene and Richard Lattimore. Chicago: University of Chicago Press, 1960.

——. *Medea*. Trans. E.P. Coleridge. *Seven Famous Greek Plays*. Ed. Whitney J. Oates and Eugene O'Neill, Jr. New York, Vintage, 1950.

Fowler, Keith. "On the Excesses of Directors." Letter, Theatre Mailbag. *The New York Times* 14 August 1977: D5.

Gozzi, Carlo. *Five Tales for the Theatre*. Ed. and trans. Albert Bermel and Ted Emery. Chicago: University of Chicago Press, 1989.

Herrington, John. *Aeschylus*. New Haven: Yale University Press, 1986.

Jones, David Richard. *Great Directors at Work: Stanislavsky, Brecht, Kazan, Brook*. Berkeley: University of California Press, 1986.

Kissel, Howard. "New York Repertory Follies." *Horizon* December 1980: 41–46.

Leach, Robert. *Vsevolod Meyerhold*. Cambridge: Cambridge University Press, 1989.

Lester, Elenore. "Mama Makes Wanton Soup." *The New York Times* 5 April 1970: D5.

Meyerhold, Vsevolod. *Meyerhold on Theatre*. Ed. and trans. Edward Braun. New York: Hill and Wang, 1969.

Patterson, Michael. *Peter Stein: Germany's Leading Theatre Director*. Cambridge: Cambridge University Press, 1981.

Popkin, Henry. "The Brilliance, Dazzle and Despair of the East European Stage." *The New York Times* 31 July 1977: D4, D18.

Rogers, Priscilla. "Greek Tragedy in the New York Theatre: A Historic Interpretation." Ph.D. diss., University of Michigan, 1986.

Russell, John. "The Arts in the '70s: New Tastes on Stage." *The New York Times* 23 January 1977: Sec. 2, 1, 20.

Shakespeare, William. *Twelfth Night*. The Pelican Shakespeare. Ed. Charles Prouty. New York: Penguin, 1972.

Simmons, Ernest. *Chekhov: A Biography*. Chicago: University of Chicago Press, 1962.

Sophocles. *Electra* in *The Complete Plays of Sophocles*. Ed. and trans. Moses Hadas. New York: Bantam, 1971.

Stanislavsky, Constantin. *My Life In Art*. Trans. J.J. Robbins. New York: Theater Arts Books, 1952.

Swados, Elizabeth. "Stretching Boundaries: The Merlin of La MaMa." *The New York Times* 26 October 1986: Sec. 2, 16.

Winfrey, Carey. "Papp Quits Lincoln Center; Citing Artistic-Fiscal Trap." *The New York Times* 10 June 1977: A1, C17.

Index

Abraham, F. Murray, 5, 66, 70, 164-66
Adrianna Lecouvreur (Zurich Opera), 173
Aeschylus, 8, 9, 34, 37, 38, 39. See *Agamemnon, The Persians*
Aesop, 155
Agamemnon (NYSF), 13, 15, 32-41, 46, 73, 81-82 (Fig. 3-4), 99,128, 139,140, 163
Akalaitis, JoAnne, 40, 73, 97
Alcina (N.Y. City Opera), 148, 169-70
Alford, Lamar, 161
Alice in Wonderland, 27
Allen, Thomas, 168, 170
Almeida Theatre, 40, 147, 167-68
American *avant-garde* theatre, 13, 28-31,33
American Conservatory Theatre, 64, 90, 162
American National Theatre, 73
American Repertory Theatre, 38, 45, 64-65, 93, 96-97, 99-101, 147-48, 165-67, 170-71; Institute for advanced Training, 97, 101, 154; rehearsal of *Twelfth Night*, See Chapter Four
American Theatre (magazine), 3
Anderson, June, 172-73
Andreassi, James, 167
"Andrei Serban Directs Chekhov," (Laurence Shyer), 54. See Chapter Two
Arden of Faversham (Theatre and Film Institute, Bucharest), 4; (Cafe La MaMa), 6-7, 161
Arena Theatre, 73
Armstrong, Richard, 169, 172
Aronson, Arnold, 154
Artaud, Antonin, 6, 13, 26, 28, 31-32, 39, 61, 89, 123; *The Cenci*, 21
Asakura, Setsu, 101-02, 167

Asahina, Robert, 63
Asari, Keita, 54
As You Like It (La MaMa E.T.C.), 9, 14, 15, 32, 70, 127, 131-32, 156, 163, 164
Atanton, Vladimir, 173
Auditia (Romanian National Theatre), 152, 168
Austin, Michael, 169

Bacchae, The, 13
Back, Maribeth, 113, 143
Badea, Christian, 169, 173
Bakals, Kees, 170
Baker-Bergen, Stuart, 18, 19, 37, 162
Bakker, Jim, 114, 128
Bald Soprano, The (A.R.T.), 131
Barnes, Clive, 7, 20, 25, 52, 92
Barrault, Jean-Louis, 21
Barrett, Marie, 171
Barstow, Josephine, 168, 173
Bartow, Arthur, 50, 51, 157
Bastin, Jules, 170
Beaumarchais, 4, 165-66. See *Marriage of Figaro*
Beaumont Theatre, Vivian, 32, 34-38, 46, 38-49, 69, 81 (Fig. 3), 163
Beck, Julian, 29
Beckett, Samuel, 64, 67-68, 70-71, 111, 155, 164. See *Happy Days, Waiting for Godot*
Beethoven, Ludwig van, *(Fidelio)*, 149, 171
Behrens, Hildegard, 173
Bell, Duncan, 168
Bellini, Vincenzo, *(I Puritani, Norma)*, 71, 148, 169-171
Berg, Van den, 170
Bergman, Ingmar, 154
Bermel, Albert, 95, 99, 101
Berry, Cicely, 122, 132
Berry, Gabriel, 164
Binkley, Howell, 109, 110, 131, 140-42, 166-67
Bitef Festival, 26
Blackman, Robert, 163
Blane, Sue, 168
Bogart, Ann, 97, 130, 154
Bologna, Opera, 148, 172

Bonynge, Richard, 171
Borodin, Aleksandr, *(Prince Igor)*, 172
Boruzescu, Miruna, 163-64, 166
Boston Globe, The, 100, 103, 143
Boston Herald, The, 93
Boston Phoenix, The, 103
Both, Andrei, 168
Bouffes du Nord, 53
Bread and Puppet Theatre, The, 89
Brecht, Bertolt, 4,5, 67, 72, 73, 89, 90-94, 156, 161-162, 167. See *Good Woman of Setzuan, Threepenny Opera*
Broadway Bound, 27
Brook, Peter, 7, 21, 23, 33, 37, 40, 45, 50, 56, 89, 90, 96, 122, 124-25, 133, 148; production of *Orghast,* 7-10, 13, 26, 29, 41, 161; creation of CIRT, 7-8; influence on Serban, 8-10, 13, 16, 17, 29, 131, 155; author of *The Empty Space,* 27, 31, 89; production of *The Cherry Orchard,* 53, 59
Brothers Grimm, 148
Brustein, Robert, 38, 40, 47, 55, 63, 64, 70, 71, 72, 94-97, 101, 103, 107, 111,113, 117, 121, 127, 134, 136-37, 140, 147, 156
Bryan, Robert, 168-70
Buchan, Cynthia, 169
Buckley, Richard, 173
Bunraku, 89, 100, 103
Bulandra Theatre, 1, 3-4, 161
Bulgakov, Mikhail, 93, 94-95, 164, 166
Bullins, Ed, 5
Burke, Patrick, 7, 18, 21

Cabal of Hypocrites, A, 94-95
Cafe La MaMa, 2, 5-6 39. *See La MaMa E.T.C.*
Cahill, James, 70
Calderon, Ian, 164
Carnegie-Mellon Institute, 22
Carrie, 115
Carrière, Jean-Claude, 166
Cassinelli, Ricardo, 170

Cazale, John, 37
Ceausescu, Nicolae, 4, 10, 144, 150-52
Cenci, The, 21
Chaikin, Joe, 6, 29, 47, 69, 70-72, 166
Chairs, The (A.R.T.), 131
Chausow, Lynn, 108
Chekhov, Anton, 4, 37, 122, 124-26, 133-35, 156-57, 163-6, 168. See Chapter Two, *The Cherry Orchard, Uncle Vanya, The Seagull, Three Sisters, Ivanov,* and *Platonov*
Cherry Orchard, The (NYSF), 4, 14-15, 27, 32, 35, 37, 39, 45, 55-56, 59-60, 62, 68-73, 83 (Fig. 5), 96, 99, 132, 135, 140, 163; creation of, 46-52; critical reaction to, 46, 52-53, 63; influence of Meyerhold, 45, 47-48; re-staging of, 53; rehearsal of, 51-52; (Shiki Theatre), 54,164; (Arena Theatre), 73; (Romanian National Theatre), 153, 168
Chief of the Sector Souls, The (Theatre and Film Institute, Bucharest), 2, 161
Childs, Lucinda, 166
Chompres, Daniel, 168-69
Chong, Ping, 6
Choregies D'Orange, 173
Christie, Nan, 168
Churchill, Caryl, *(Mad Forest),* 153
Christopherson, Stefanianne, 164
Cilea, Francesco, *(Adrianna Lecouvreuer),* 173
Circle in the Square, 72, 166
CIRT (International Centre for Theatre Research), 7-8, 161
Ciulei, Livui, 1, 3-4, 172
CIVIL warS (A.R.T.), 118
Clancy, Deidre, 172
Clarke, Caitlin, 165-66
Clarke, Martha, 89
Classic Stage Company, 64
Clay, Carolyn, 103

Clurman, Harold, 26, 31
Collison, Michelle, 7, 161
Columbia University, 17, 126, 147, 153-57
Commedia dell'arte, 89, 92, 94, 98, 100-04, 115, 149
Conference of the Birds (CIRT), 33
Conklin, John, 166
Connell, Elizabeth, 171
Conroy, Frances, 70, 72, 165-66
Conservatoire de Paris, La, 154
Constant Prince, The (Polish Lab Theatre), 2, 71
Conway, Kevin, 5
Corder, Simon, 168
Cottencon, Fanny, 166
Covent Garden. *See Royal Opera*
Cowdrick, Kathryn, 169
Craig, Gordon, 7, 61
Cristofer, Michael. 51
Croyden, Margaret, 9
Crucible, The, 9
Crystal, Billy, 5, 7, 161
Cunliffe, Jerry, 37
Cunningham, Andrew, 169
Cunningham, Merce, 6

Damon, Cathryn, 49
Dana, F. Mitchell, 163, 169-70
Daniels, Ron, 47
D'Aquila, Diane, 85 (Fig. 7), 100, 166
D'Avignon Festival, 97
Davis, Colin, 170-71
Delacorte Theatre, 38, 46. 163
Del George, Roseann, 169
Demy, Jaques, *(Umbrellas of Cherbourg)*, 142, 147, 157, 164
De Palma, Brian, 115
Dernesch, Helga, 171-72
Derrah, Thomas, 64, 99-101, 110, 131, 135, 137-38, 165-167
Desire (Almeida Theatre), 147, 167
Dessau, Paul, 91
Deutekom, Cristina, 170
De Vries, Peter John, 22, 37, 47, 91, 162
Dickson, Stephen, 168-69

Dietsch, James, 169
Dietschy, Verinoque, 169
Dionysus in '69 (The Performance Group), 13
Dishy, Bob, 95-96
Doctor in Spite of Himself, The. See Sganarelle: An Evening of Molière Farces
Dodd, John, 161
Dolan, Judith, 167
Domingo, Placido, 149, 170, 173
Donaldson, Frederick, 170
Don Carlo (Bologna Opera), 148, 171-72
Donizetti, Gaetano, *(Lucia Di Lammermoor)*, 172-73
Dorfman, Robert, 165
Dostoyevsky, Fyodor, 101
Dragun, Osvaldo, *(The Man Who Changed into a Dog)*, 2, 161
Drama Desk Award, 21
Drama of Aïda (WNO), 169
Dream Play, A, 94
Dudley, William, 172-73
Duff-Griffin, William, 7, 21, 47, 162-63, 165
Dukakis, Michael, 109
Dumb Show, A. See Sganarelle: An Evening of Molière Farces
Durang, Christopher, *(A History of the American Film)*, 107
Dworchak, Harry, 170

Eder, Richard, 6-7, 55
Electra (La MaMa E.T.C.), 8, 21-23, 27, 31, 80 (Fig. 2), 162. *See Fragments of a Greek Trilogy*
Elektra (Geneva Opera), 148, 171-73
Emery, Ted, 101
Emmons, Beverly, 164
Empty Space, The, 27, 31, 89. *See Peter Brook*
Epstein, Alvin, 47, 167
Ermler, Mark, 168
Eschenbach, Cristoph, 173
Esrig, David, 3
Eugene Onegin (WNO), 147-48, 168, 172

Euripides, 8, 14, 18, 20, 39-40, 134, 147, 161-62, 168. See *Medea, The Trojan Women, Fragments of a Greek Trilogy, The Bacchae, Hippolytos*
Evans, Joseph, 170

Farquhar, George, *(The Recruiting Officer)*, 147
Federal Theatre Project, The, 13
Feingold, Michael, 13, 28
Feldman, Richard, 84-88 (Fig. 6-10)
Fidelio (Royal Opera), 149, 171
Fierstein, Harvey, 5
Fiery Angel, The (Los Angeles Center Opera), 171-72
Finlay, Bill, 111, 115-117
Fischer, Gyorgy, 169
Flying Doctor, The. See *Sganarelle: An Evening of Molière Farces*
Fondary, Alain, 173
Forced Marriage, The. See *Sganarelle: An Evening of Moliere Farces*
Ford, John, *('Tis Pity She's a Whore)*, 94
Foreman, Richard, 32-33, 35, 39, 148
Forst, Judith, 171
Fortunato, D'Anna, 170
Foster, Gloria, 37-38, 163
Foster, Lawrence, 171
Foster, Paul, 5
Fragments of a Greek Trilogy (La MaMa E.T.C.), 1, 8-9, 13, 32, 73, 79-80 (Fig. 1-2), 89-90, 93, 97, 103, 113, 123, 127, 132, 134-135, 149; creation of, 14-26, critical reaction to, 25-28; differences from *Agamemnon*, 33, 38-39; La MaMa 25th anniversary revival of, 18, 27-28, 34, 166; significance of Serban's work in Greek tragedy, 13-14, 28, 32, 39-41; tours of, 26-27; as work-in-progress, 23; *Medea*, 14-21; *Electra*, 21-22; *Trojan Women, The*, 22-25; (at Romanian National Theatre), 28, 151-53, 156-57, 168

Franz, Elizabeth, 166
Friedman, Arthur, 93

Gabor, Nancy, 18
Gage, James, 164
Gardelly, Lomberto, 173
Gastin, Claudine, 173
Geidt, Jeremy, 47, 64, 67, 97, 101, 108, 119, 131, 137, 143, 165, 167
Geneva Opera, 98, 148, 170-72
Ghosts, 94
Ghost Sonata, The (Yale Repertory Theatre), 14-15, 38, 94, 123, 135, 142, 163
Giannini, Cheryl, 84 (Fig. 6), 165
Glass Menagerie, The, 30
Glass, Philip, 6, 148, 170. See *The Juniper Tree*
Godspell (La MaMa E.T.C.), 6
Gogol, Nikolai, 61
Gold, Sylviane, 28
Goldenthal, Elliot, 99, 101, 103, 166-67
Goldoni, Carlo, 98, 124. See *The Servant of Two Masters*
Goldsmith, Oliver, *(She Stoops to Conquer)*, 4, 21, 161
Goodman Theatre, The, 73, 97
Good Woman of Setzuan, The (Piatra Neamtz), 4-5, 161; (La MaMa E.T.C.), 14-15, 32, 90-94, 96, 162; (A.R.T.), 93, 131, 141, 167
Gozzi, Carlo, 89, 95, 97-104, 124, 134, 149, 156, 166-67. See *The Green Bird, The King Stag, The Serpent Woman, Turandot*
Gray, Natalie, 18, 21, 37, 162
Grayson, Robert, 171
Great Jones Repertory Company, The, 32, 47, 90-92
Green Bird, The (A.R.T.), 103
Greenwood, Jane, 164-65
Gross, Michael, 95, 164
Grotowski, Jerzy, 2, 7, 29, 31, 33, 71, 89
Guingal, Alain, 173
Grusin, Richard, 85 (Fig. 7)

Index

Gussow, Mel, 23, 27, 38, 89, 92, 96, 100, 103, 143, 155
Guthrie Theatre, The, 3-5, 27, 65, 72, 109, 118, 135, 165

Haitink, Bernard, 172
Hall, George, 61
Hamilton, Edith, 34, 38
Handel, George F., *(Alcina, Rodelinda)*, 148, 168-69
Happy Days (NYSF), 164
Harries, Kathryn, 170
Harris, Rosemary, 60-61, 165
Harvard University, 64, 96-97, 154
Hays, Hobart, 161
Hayward, Charles, 22, 37, 163
Heald, Anthony, 166
Heikin, Nancy, 18
Henry VI (NYSF), 153
Hercules, 14
Hewes, Henry, 7, 20
Hinds, Ruby, 171
Hippolytos (Almeida Theatre), 40, 147, 168
History of the American Film, A, 107
Holmberg, Arthur, 64, 101
Houston Grand Opera, 148-49, 173
Howard, Ken, 166
Hudson Review, The, 63
Hudson, Richard, 149, 167-68, 173
Hudson, Rodney, 37, 99-100, 109, 128, 131, 136-139
Hughes, Ted, 8, 161
Hurt, Mary Beth, 46

I Am Not the Eiffel Tower (Theatre and Film Institute, Bucharest), 2, 161
Ibsen, Henrik, 89, 94. See *Ghosts* and *The Wild Duck*
Idol, Billy, 114
Ik, The, (CIRT), 33
Il Trovatore (Opera North), 98, 169
Imaginary Invalid, The , 94-95
Ingalls, Jim, 165
Ionesco, Eugene, *(The Bald Soprano* and *The Chairs)*, 131

I Puritani (WNO), 71, 98, 148, 169-71
Israel, Robert, 171-72
Ivanov (Yale Repertory Theatre), 47
Ivey, Dana, 166

Jackson, Glenda, 7
Jacobs, Sally, 7, 149, 170-71
Jarry, Alfred, *(Ubu Roi)*, 2, 6-7, 161
Jenkins, Ron, 64, 66, 68
Jenkinson, Gerry, 167
Jensby, Wesley J., 21
Johnson, Anthony Rolfe, 168
Johnson, Onni, 37, 166
Jonah (Theatre and Film Institute, Bucharest), 161
Jones, Cherry, 64, 68-69, 84 (Fig. 6), 86-87 (Fig. 8-9), 102, 108-109, 113, 116, 118, 131, 135-39, 165, 167
Jones, Walt, *(The 1940s Radio Hour)*, 96
Joseph, George, 81-83 (Fig. 3-5)
Juan Darien: A Carnival Mass, 103
Julia, Raul, 46, 49, 53, 163
Julius Caesar (Bulandra Theatre) 3-4, 161
Juilliard Center for the Arts, 97, 148, 169

Kabuki Theatre, 3-4, 17, 58, 89, 100, 102-03
Kahn, Michael, 127
Kalem, T. E., 37, 62
Kaltenbach, Jerome, 168
Kamiliotis, Daniela, 173
Kanamuri, Kaoru, 55, 165
Kaprow, Alan, 29
Kathakali, 17, 20, 155
Kaufmann, Stanley, 25
Kelly, Kevin, 103, 143
Kennedy Center, 62
Kerr, Walter, 38, 50, 62
Kharitonov, Dimitri, 173
Kim, Randall Duk, 163
King, Annie, 119, 143
King Lear, 7, 50, 69

King Stag, The (A.R.T.), 15, 85 (Fig. 7), 89, 98-101, 103, 127, 131, 149, 166
Knox, Bernard, 40
Kohrman, Ellen, 102
Kokkos, Yannis, 171-73
Konchak, Khan, 172
Konig, Klaus, 171
Kraus, Alfredo, 172
Kroll, Jack, 62, 64, 100
Krutch, Joseph Wood, 41
Kyte, Mary, *(Tintypes)*, 107

Lally, Jim, 108, 112, 127
La MaMa E.T.C., 2, 6, 28, 32, 45-47, 69-70, 90, 93, 133, 143, 152, 156, 161-163, 166; Annex, 23, 70-73; tours, 7, 9, 21, 26, 28; training and discipline of company, 14, 16-17, 30-31, 91; 25th anniversary, 13, 27, 80 (Fig. 2), 93, 166. See Cafe La MaMa, Ellen Stewart, Great Jones Repertory Project
Lan, David, *(Desire)*, 147, 167
Lane, Diane, 18, 24, 36-37, 49, 79 (Fig. 1), 113, 115, 167
Langan, Keith, 172
La Traviata (Juilliard), 97, 147-48, 169
Layer, Friedemann, 171
Leach, Wilford, 6
Leggate, Robin, 169
Legrand, Michel, *(The Umbrellas of Cherbourg)*, 142, 147, 157, 164
Lehar, Franz, *(The Merry Widow)*, 98, 170
Leiberson, Dennis, 18
Leiferkus, Sergei, 172
Leppard, Raymond, 169
Les Miserables, 27
Levin, Chuck, 95
Licorish, Vicky, 167
Lincoln Center, 27, 32, 37-40, 45-46, 48, 54, 163. See New York Shakespeare Festival
Linn-Baker, Mark, 95-96, 164
Linney, Romulus, 154

Littlewood, Joan, 7
Living Theatre, The, 29-30, 33
Lobel, Adrianne, 164, 169
Loquasto, Santo, 35, 45, 47-48, 53, 70-71, 140, 163, 166
Loeb Drama Center, 100, 107
Los Angeles Center Opera, 171, 173
Love of Three Oranges, The (Geneva Opera), 98, 103, 170
Lucia Di Lammermoor (Lyric Opera), 172-73
Lupu, Michael, 3
Lutgenhorst, Manuel, 165
Lynch, Sharon, 166
Lyric Opera, 149, 172
Lyubimov, Yuri, 93

Mabou Mines, 6
Mad Dog Blues (Yale Drama School), 164
Mad Forest (Romanian National Theatre), 153
Maeda, Jun, 23, 47, 70, 91, 93, 140, 162-164, 166
Maeterlinck, Maurice, 48, 55
Maggio, Michael, 73
Magic Flute, The (Nancy Opera), 148, 168-69
Making Scenes: A Personal History of the Turbulent Years at Yale 1966 - 1979 (Robert Brustein), 94-96
Malina, Judith, 29
Mamet, David, 155
Man Who Changed Into a Dog, The (Theatre and Film Institute, Bucharest), 2, 161
Marat/Sade (CIRT), 7
Marfield, Dwight, 49
Marks, Jonathan, 45, 64-65, 99
Marriage of Figaro, The (Guthrie Theatre), 4, 27, 65, 109, 118, 135, 165; (Circle in the Square), 28, 72, 166
Martin-Oliver, Robin, 169
Mason, Marshall, 6
Marvin, Mel, 107-09, 143, 149, 167

Master and the Margarita, The (A.R.T.), 93; (NYSF), 94, 164; (*Théâtre de la Ville*), 166
Mastrantonio, Mary Elizabeth, 166
McLane, Derek, 131, 140-42, 167
McDiarmid, Ian, 168
McMasters, Brian, 147
Measure For Measure, 14
Medea: Andrei Serban's Work on the Tragic Acting, (Ana Maria Narti), 14
Medea (La MaMa E.T.C.), 8, 14-23, 26-28, 30-31, 79 (Fig. 1), 152, 161-62
Melfi, Leonard, 5
Mercy, Suzanne, 170
Merry Widow, The (WNO), 98, 170
Method acting, 14, 19, 30, 68, 154
Meyerhold, Vsevolod, 4, 45, 47-52, 55-60, 62, 64-65, 69, 73, 98-99, 124
Michael, Keith, 162
Midler, Bette, 5
Midsummer Night's Dream, A, 7, 17
Mikhalkov, Nikita, (*An Unfinished Piece for Player Piano*), 68. See Platonov
Miller, Arthur, *(The Crucible)*, 30
Miller, Jonathan, 115
Mills, Beverly, 169
Mirodan, Al., *(Chief of the Sector Souls)*, 2, 161
Miser, The (A.R.T.), 113, 140-142, 167
Molière, 125, 137, 156, 167. See The Imaginary Invalid, The Miser, Sganarelle: An Evening of Molière Farces
Mita, Kazuyo, 165
Mnouchkine, Ariane, 89, 121
Montresor, Beni, 65-66, 165-66, 170
Moran, Robert, *(The Juniper Tree)*, 148, 170
Morton, Richard, 169
Moscow Art Theatre, 46, 48, 55, 65, 153
Mozart, Wolfgang Amadeus, *(The Magic Flute)*, 148, 168-69

Mueller, Catherine, 21, 162
Muff, Alfred, 171
Muir, Sandra, 162, 166
Mullins, Carol, 166
Munch, Allen, 162
Munn, Thomas J., 172
Murphy, Harry S., 100-01, 167
Murphy, Suzanne, 169-70
Muskovin, Jeff, 167
My Life in Art, (Konstantin Stanislavsky), 65
Myrie, Marcia, 167

Nancy Opera, 148, 168
Narti, Ana Maria, 14, 17
Nassau Community College, 21, 161-62
Nation, The, 26
"Naturalistic Theatre and the Theatre of Mood," (Leo Tolstoi), 65
Netherlands Opera, 98, 170
New Leader, The, 52
Newman Theatre, 73
New Republic, The, 25
Newsday, 38
Newsweek, 64, 100
New York City Opera, 148, 169, 171
New York Daily News, The, 25
New York Shakespeare Festival, 32-33, 45-46, 54, 94, 153, 163-65
New York Times, The, 6-7, 9, 20, 23, 25, 27, 38, 46, 52, 55, 63, 72, 89, 92, 100, 103, 112, 130, 143, 155
Nightingale, Benedict, 72
1940s Radio Hour, The (Yale Repertory Theatre), 96
Nocturne (Theatre and Film Institute, Bucharest), 161
Noh Theatre, 17, 58, 137
"No More Masterpieces," (Antonin Artaud), 32
Norma (New York City Opera), 148, 170-71
Nri, Cyril, 167
Nutu, Dan, 2, 80 (Fig. 2), 112, 166

Obie award, 26

Oboelenski, Chloe, 172-73
Offenbach, Jacques, *(Tales of Hoffman)*, 149, 173
O'Horgan, Tom, 6
Oida, Katsurhiro, 17
Old Vic, The, 50
Olmeda, Martine, 173
O'Neal, Ron, 38
Open Theatre, The, 6, 29, 33, 47, 70
Opera la Fenice, 172-73
Opera North, 98, 169
Oproiu, Ecaterina, *(I Am Not the Eiffel Tower)*, 2, 161
Orghast (CIRT), 7-10, 13-14, 20, 26, 29, 40, 161
Otello (Choregies D'Orange), 148, 173
Otte, Charles, 93
Ould, William, 171
Our Country's Good (University of California - San Diego and Romanian National Theatre), 147, 152, 167-68
Ovanessian, Arby, 98
Owen, Marianne, 66, 84 (Fig. 6), 165

Palais-Royal Theatre, 94
Papp, Joseph, 27, 32-35, 46, 49, 52-55, 153
Paris Opera, 148, 171
Payton-Wright, Pamela, 60-61
Peaslee, Richard, 165
Peled, Joana, 24
Penciulescu, Radu, 2
Performing Garage, The, 23
Performing Group, The, 13, 23, 29, 33
Perloff, Carey, 64
Persians, The, 9
Peterson, Monte, 172
Phillips, Jack, 65
Pintilie, Lucian, 3, 47, 73
Pitchford, Dean, 164
Pittman, Richard, 170
Pittman-Jennings, David, 170
Platonov, 68. See *An Unfinished Piece for Player Piano*
Polish Lab Theatre, 29, 31, 71

Posin, Kathryn, 49
Prince Igor (Royal Opera), 172
Prokofiev, Sergei, *(The Fiery Angel, The Love of Three Oranges)*, 170-72
Public Theatre, The, 45-46, 54, 70, 73, 147, 153, 164-65. See New York Shakespeare Festival
Puccini, Giacomo, *(Turandot)*, 93, 98, 149, 170

Quaranta, Johnny, 173
Quiroga, Horacio, *(Juan Darien: A Carnival Mass)*, 104

Rambaldi, Laura, 16, 162
Ramicova, Dunya, 96, 163-65, 169
Rammey, Samuel, 172
Ramos, Richard Russell, 61
Raphael, Bonnie, 131-33, 138-39, 156
Rashid, Justin, 37
Recruiting Officer, The, 147
Reeve, Christopher, 166
Reinhardt, Ray, 163
Remo, Ken, 171
Renzetti, Donato, 172
Ribman, Ronald, *(Sweet Table at the Richelieu)*, 125, 157, 166
Rich, Frank, 63, 112
Rigoletto (Opera a Fenice), 173
Roberts, Judith, 165
Rodelinda (WNO), 148, 168-69
Rojo, Jerry, 23
Roloff, Roger, 171
Romanian National Theatre, 144, 147, 150-53, 156, 168
Romanian theatre, 3-4, 151
Romeo and Juliet (Nassau Community College), 21, 162
Rom, Natalia, 169
Rosenblum, David, 18
Rowe, Stephen, 163
Royal Opera, The, 93, 98, 149, 170-72
Royal Shakespeare Company, The, 50, 122
Runswick, Daryl, 169

Index 205

Rysanek, Leonie, 173

Salem, Kario, 108, 127, 167
San Francisco Opera, 148-49, 172
Saturday Night Live, 7
Saturday Review, The, 7, 20
Sao Paulo Festival, 22, 152
Scanlan, Robert, 111, 117-18, 127, 131-33, 135, 139, 156
Scardino, Don, 165
Scofield, Paul, 7
Schechner, Richard, 23, 29, 70, 72
Schicoff, Neil, 172
Schmidt, Douglas, 35, 81 (Fig. 3), 163
Schmidt, Jaques, 170
Schuler, Duane, 165, 172-73
Seagull, The, 72, (NYSF), 15, 45, 57-63, 68-69, 73, 99, 165; acting of, 60-62, critical reaction to, 58, 63; Japanese influence, 58; rehearsal, 60-61; (Shiki Theatre), 54-57, 69, 165; (aka *A Seagull at Kennedy center*), 62; (Washington Square Players), 45
Second City, 95
Secunde, Nadine, 172
Sellars, Peter, 40, 62, 73, 97, 148
Seneca, *(Medea* and *Hercules)*, 14, 20, 161
Serban, Andrei, American directorial debut, 6-7; and The New Fabulism, 149, 156, *See Chapter Three*; approach to acting, 2, 14, 19, 30-31, 40, 51-52, 56-57, 60-62, 64, 71-72, 91, 95-96, 100, 104, 108, 118-19, 121-123, 126-30, 134-139, 144, 154-55; as Romanian exile, 10, 45, 150-51; awards, 2, 21, 26, 53, 149; childhood, 1; cinematic techniques of directing, 45, 57, 62, 64, 66-67, 69-71; collaboration with Liz Swados, 14-18, 21-23, 27, 33-34, 36, 90-91, 96, 149; collaboration with Michael Yeargan, 57-58, 99-100, 140-41; collaboration with Priscilla Smith, 14-15, 18-19, 30-31, 61-62, 92-93, 151-52, 154-55; at Columbia University, 147, 153-57; at Romanian National Theatre, 147, 150-53, 156; classical director in a modern context, 127, 156-58; coming to USA, 5-6; and Greek Tragedy, 8, 10, 133-34, 147-48, 155-57, *See Chapter One, Fragments of Greek Trilogy, and Agamemnon*; interviewed by author, 120-27, 158; marriage and children, 97, 109, 115, 120, 143, 153, 156; on emotion, 20, 39-40, 57; on language, 10, 29-30, 32, 34, 57, 112-13, 121, 123, 132-33; on modern theatre, 101-126, 129-30, 157-58; on opera, 98-99, 147-50, 157; on "world behind the curtain," 1, 12, 125, 159; rehearsal methods, 6, 16-19, 37, 51-52, 56-57, 60-61, 64, 68-69, 92-96, 101, 103, *See Chapter Four*; training at Theatre and Film Institute, Bucharest, 1-3, 148; use of space, 1,4, 15, 19-27, 30-31, 34-36, 38, 45, 48-49, 58-58, 62, 65-66, 70-71, 73, 102, 114-15, 152; use of stick exercises, 17, 155; visual techniques of staging, 1, 4, 6-7, 13, 20, 22-26, 35-40, 49, 54-55, 57-59, 63, 65-68, 70-73, 89, 91, 99-100, 102, 108, 110-115, 117-18, 123-24, 140-44, 152; work with text, 13, 16-19, 29, 31, 33-34, 36-41, 46, 50-51, 55, 57, 60, 62, 73-74, 94-95, 98, 110-14, 119, 121-23, 127-28, 131-34, 156
Serpent, The, 47
Serpent Woman, The, (A.R.T.), 86 (Fig. 8), 89, 100-03, 109, 149
Servant of Two Masters, The, 98
Seweryn, Andrej, 166
Sganarelle: An Evening of Molière Farces, (A.R.T. and Yale

Repertory Theatre), 14, 38, 94-97, 113, 134-35, 141, 163-64
Shakespeare, William, 37, 89, 121, 153, 156, 158, 161-164, 167; See Twelfth Night (Chapter Four), As You Like It, Romeo and Juliet, Measure For Measure, Henry VI, King Lear, A Midsummer Night's Dream, The Tempest
Shawn, Wallace, 164
Shepard, Sam, *(Mad Dog Blues)*, 5, 164
She Stoops to Conquer, (Bulandra Theatre and Nassau Community College), 4, 21, 161
Shifting Point, The, (Peter Brook), 53
Shiki Theatre, The, 53-57, 164-65
Shiraz Festival of the Arts, 26, 163
Short Organum to the Theatre, A, (Bertolt Brecht), 91
Shyer, Laurence, 54, 57, 59
Simon, John, 52, 63, 96
Simon, Neil, *(Broadway Bound)*, 27
Sirianni, Craig, 173
Skelton, Thomas, 142, 163
Skybell, Stephen, 109, 116
Smith, Derek, 102, 167
Smith, Julian, 168-70
Smith, Peter, 153
Smith, Priscilla, 15-16, 18-22, 24, 26-27, 30-31, 33, 35-37, 47, 53, 61, 79-80 (Fig. 1-2), 90-93, 99, 113, 146, 151-52, 154, 162-63, 165-67
Soho Weekly News, The, 23
Sophocles, 8, 39, 162. See Electra
Soreseu, Marin, *(Jonah)*, 161
Spiner, Brent, 61
Stanislavsky, Konstantin, 19, 45-48, 51, 55-56, 59-60, 64-65, 68-69, 98-99, 124
Stanislavsky system, The, 19, 56, 63, 68
Stanley, Mark, 171
Stanton, Robert, 108, 110, 143, 167
Stapp, Olivia, 171

Star Trek: The Next Generation, 61
Starlight Express, 27
State Opera House of Bucharest, 150
Steckman, Larry, 162
Steele, Mike, 3
Stein, Horst, 170
Stein, Peter, 40, 153
Stephenson, Donald, 169
Stewart, Ellen, 2, 5-6, 14-15, 20, 22, 27, 32, 93, 130
Stockholm Dramatic School, 154
Stollmack, Noel, 173
Strauss, Richard, *(Elektra)*, 148, 171-73
Strawn, C.J., 161
Streep, Meryl, 47, 49, 163
Strindberg, August, *(A Dream Play and The Ghost Sonata)*, 38, 94, 163
Sugamote, Resuke, 165
Sutej, J., 172-73
Suzman, Janet, 168
Swados, Liz, 6, 14-15, 17-18, 21, 22-23, 27-28, 30, 33-34, 36, 47, 90-91, 96, 149, 162-67
Sweet Table at the Richelieu (A.R.T.), 125, 131, 141, 157, 166
Sylvan, Sanford, 171

Tales of Hoffman (Vienna State Opera), 149, 173
Talking Band, The, 89
Tan, Victor En Yu, 164, 167
Taymor, Julie, 85 (Fig. 7), 89, 99-101, 103, 140, 166
Tchaikovsky, Peter, *(Eugene Onegin)*, 147, 168, 172
Teague, Anthony, 163
Tebelak, John-Michael, *(Godspell)*, 6
Tempest, The, 157
Terry, Megan, *(Viet Rock)*, 6
Terryl, Charles, 162
Théâtre Musical de Paris, 169
Theater (magazine), 54
Theatre and Film Institute, Bucharest, 1-3, 148, 161
Théâtre du Soleil, 121

Théâtre des Nations, 2
Thielemann, Christian, 172
Threepenny Opera, The (NYSF), 32, 35; (American Conservatory Theatre), 90, 162-63
Three Sisters (A.R.T.), 45, 59, 63-69, 71, 73, 84 (Fig. 6), 113, 127, 138, 165-66; as evidence of connection between Chekhov and Beckett, 64, 67-68; critical reaction to 64, 66-67; influence of Meyerhold, 64-65; rehearsal of, 68-69
Three Stooges, The, 114, 128
Time, 37
Tintypes, 107
Tipton, Jennifer, 35, 47-48, 53, 58, 70, 99, 163-66, 170-71
'Tis Pity She's a Whore, 94
Tissier, Claude, 173
Tolstoi, Leo, 65
Tony Awards, 53
Torgove, Lynn, 171
Tortelier, Yan Pascal, 169
"Tragic Fallacy, The," (Joseph Wood Krutch), 41
Trinity College, 64
Trinity Repertory, 130
Triska, Jan, 164-65
Trojan Incident, The, 13
Trojan Women, The, (La MaMa E.T.C.), 8, 13, 21-25, 29, 31, 41, 152, 162
Troobnick, Eugene, 95, 164
Turandot (Royal Opera), 93, 98, 149, 170
Twelfth Night (A.R.T.), 1, 64, 66, 87 (Fig. 9), 103, 147, 149, 156; critical reaction to, 130, 143; opening night, 127-31; preview performances, 117-20, 127; technical rehearsals, 107-117; (Théâtre du Soleil), 121

Ubu Roi, 2, (Cafe La MaMa), 6-7, 161
Umbrellas of Cherbourg, The (NYSF), 142, 147, 157, 164

Uncle Vanya (La MaMa E.T.C.), 28, 45, 69-73, 140, 166; critical reaction to, 72, use of cinematic techniques, 69-71; (Goodman Theatre), 73
Unfinished Piece for Player Piano, An, 68. See Platonov
University of California - San Diego, 147, 153-54, 167

Valois, 18, 21-22, 24, 27, 37, 162, 166
Vaness, Carol, 170
Van Itallie, Jean-Claude, 45, 47, 71, 166
Van Patten Joyce, 60
Venora, Diane, 70, 72
Verdi, Giuseppe, *(Don Carlo, Drama of Aïda, Il Trovatore, La Traviata, Otello, Rigoletto)*, 97, 148, 169, 171-73
Vienna Festival, 26
Vienna State Opera, 149, 173
Viet Rock (Cafe La MaMa), 6
Village Voice, The, 28
Vogue, 34
Voskovec, George, 34, 46, 49, 83 (Fig. 5)

Wagner, Richard, 148
Waiting For Godot, 68, 111
Walken, Christopher, 60-61, 165
Walker, George, *(Zastrozzi)*, 99, 165
Walker, Paul, 114, 119, 131, 133
Wallach, Alan, 38
Wall Street Journal, The, 28
Warrilow, David, 165
Washington Square Players, 45
Watanabe, Yoko, 170
Waterhouse, John, 169
Watkins, Anna, 172
Watt, Douglas, 25
Weill, Kurt, 15, 162
Welsh National Opera, 71, 98, 147-48, 168-70
Weiss, Peter *(Marat/Sade)*, 7
Welker, Hartmu, 171
Welk, Lawrence, 108

Wertenbaker, Timberlake, *(Our Country's Good)*, 147, 152, 167-68
West, Jayne, 171
Wiest, Dianne, 37
Wild Duck, The, 94
Williams, Tennessee, *(The Glass Menagerie)*, 30
Williams-King, Anne, 169
Wilson, Lanford, 5
Wilson, Robert, 33, 39, 73, 89, 97, 136, 142, 148
Wolcz, Nikolaus, 101
Wooster Group, The, 33
Worth, Irene, 46, 49-53, 83 (Fig. 5), 163-64
Wright, Max, 49, 163

Yale Drama School, 38, 95, 154, 164
Yale Repertory Theatre, 38, 47, 55, 94, 96, 163-64
Yeargan, Michael, 47, 55, 57-58, 63, 96, 99-100, 140, 142, 147-48, 163-66, 168-71
Yeats, William Butler, 58, 89
Yentl, 107
Yorinks, Arthur, *(The Juniper Tree)*, 148, 171

Zakkai, Jamil, 18, 35-37, 79 (Fig. 1), 82 (Fig. 4), 162-63
Zaremba, Elena, 172
Zastrozzi (NYSF), 99, 165
Zeldis, Lou, 7, 161
Zschau, Marilyn, 171
Zuber, Cathy, 131, 140-41, 167
Zurich Opera, 173